Praise for *Breaking the Habit of Being Yourself*

"Dr Joe Dispenza wants to empower you to let go of negative beliefs and embrace the positive. This intelligent, informative, practical book will help you be your best, freest self so that, as Dr Joe puts it, you can 'step toward your own destiny.'"

— **Judith Orloff, M.D.**, author of *Emotional Freedom*

*"In **Breaking the Habit of Being Yourself**, Dr Joe Dispenza explores the energetic aspects of reality with sound science and provides the reader with the necessary tools to make important positive changes in their life. Anyone who reads this book and applies the steps will benefit from their efforts. Its cutting-edge content is explained in a simple language that is accessible to anyone, and provides a user-friendly guide for sustained change from the inside out."*

— **Rollin McCraty, Ph.D.**, Director of Research,
HeartMath Research Center

"Dr Joe Dispenza's entertaining and highly accessible manual for rewiring your mental and emotional circuitry carries a simple but potent message: what you think today determines how you live tomorrow."

— **Lynne McTaggart**, best-selling author of *The Field,*
The Intention Experiment, and *The Bond*

*"**Breaking the Habit of Being Yourself** is a powerful blend of leading-edge science and real-life applications woven into the perfect formula for everyday living.*

"The hierarchy of scientific knowledge tells us that when new discoveries change what we know about the atom, what we know of ourselves and our brains must change as well. Through the 14 concise chapters of this book, Dr Joe Dispenza draws upon a lifetime of experience to describe how subtle shifts in the way we use our brains are the quantum key to life-affirming changes in our bodies, our lives, and our relationships. In a responsible, well-researched, and practical manual that you'll want at your fingertips for your personal practice, Dr Joe's easy-to-use, step-by-step techniques give everyone the opportunity to experiment with their own quantum field to discover for themselves what works best.

"From the powerful exercises highlighting the thinking that keeps us stuck in old beliefs, to the simple practices that catapult us beyond our limiting beliefs, this book is the owners' manual to a successful life we wish we'd been given in first grade. If you've always known that there's more to you than you learned in Biology 101, but find yourself intimidated by the technical language of science, this is the beautiful book you've been waiting for!"

— **Gregg Braden**, *New York Times* best-selling author
of *Deep Truth* and *The Divine Matrix*

Breaking the Habit of Being Yourself

ALSO BY DR JOE DISPENZA

EVOLVE YOUR BRAIN: The Science of Changing Your Mind

Please visit:

Hay House UK: **www.hayhouse.co.uk**
Hay House USA: **www.hayhouse.com**®
Hay House Australia: **www.hayhouse.com.au**
Hay House South Africa: **www.hayhouse.co.za**
Hay House India: **www.hayhouse.co.in**

Breaking the Habit of Being Yourself

*How to Lose Your Mind and
Create a New One*

Dr Joe Dispenza

HAY HOUSE

Australia • Canada • Hong Kong • India
South Africa • United Kingdom • United States

First published and distributed in the United Kingdom by:
Hay House UK Ltd, 292B Kensal Rd, London W10 5BE. Tel.: (44) 20 8962 1230;
Fax: (44) 20 8962 1239. www.hayhouse.co.uk

Published and distributed in the United States of America by:
Hay House, Inc., PO Box 5100, Carlsbad, CA 92018-5100. Tel.: (1) 760 431 7695 or
(800) 654 5126; Fax: (1) 760 431 6948 or (800) 650 5115. www.hayhouse.com

Published and distributed in Australia by:
Hay House Australia Ltd, 18/36 Ralph St, Alexandria NSW 2015. Tel.: (61) 2 9669 4299;
Fax: (61) 2 9669 4144. www.hayhouse.com.au

Published and distributed in the Republic of South Africa by:
Hay House SA (Pty), Ltd, PO Box 990, Witkoppen 2068. Tel./Fax: (27) 11 467 8904.
www.hayhouse.co.za

Published and distributed in India by:
Hay House Publishers India, Muskaan Complex, Plot No.3, B-2, Vasant Kunj, New Delhi
– 110 070. Tel.: (91) 11 4176 1620; Fax: (91) 11 4176 1630. www.hayhouse.co.in

Distributed in Canada by:
Raincoast, 9050 Shaughnessy St, Vancouver, BC V6P 6E5. Tel.: (1) 604 323 7100;
Fax: (1) 604 323 2600

Copyright © 2012 by Joe Dispenza

Interior design: Nick C. Welch • *Interior illustrations:* Laura S. Craig • *Indexer:* Jay Kreider

The following illustrations incorporate copyrighted images used with permission: *Figure 1E, 3C, 7C:* People figures, © Izabela Zvirinska - Fotolia.com • *Figure 3B:* Man silhouette, © styleuneed - Fotolia.com • *Figures 3B, 5B, 5C, 6A:* Human brain, © Alila - Fotolia.com • *Figure 5B:* Neurons and nucleus, © ktsdesign - Fotolia.com • *Figure 6A:* Human brain, © Pavel Eltsov - Fotolia.com • *Figures 7A, 7B, 7D, 7E:* Hands, © lom123 - Fotolia.com • *Figure 8D:* Retro laser gun, © LHF Graphics - Fotolia.com • *Figure 8D:* Sketchy bulb, © get4net - Fotolia.com • *Figure 8K:* Brain, © Oguz Aral

The moral rights of the author have been asserted.

The author of this book does not dispense medical advice or prescribe the use of any technique as a form of treatment for physical or medical problems without the advice of a physician, either directly or indirectly. The intent of the author is only to offer information of a general nature to help you in your quest for emotional and spiritual wellbeing. In the event you use any of the information in this book for yourself, which is your constitutional right, the author and the publisher assume no responsibility for your actions.

A catalogue record for this book is available from the British Library.

ISBN 978-1-84850-856-9

Printed and bound in Great Britain by CPI Group (UK), Ltd, Croydon, CR0 4YY.

For Robi

CONTENTS

FOREWORD

Your brain is involved in everything you do, including how you think, how you feel, how you act, and how well you get along with other people. It's the organ of personality, character, intelligence, and every decision you make. From my brain-imaging work with tens of thousands of patients worldwide over the past 20 years, it is very clear to me that when your brain works right, *you* work right, and when your brain is troubled, you are much more likely to have trouble in your life.

With a healthier brain, you are happier, physically healthier, wealthier, wiser, and just make better decisions, which helps you be more successful and live longer. When the brain is not healthy for whatever reason—such as a head injury or past emotional trauma—people are sadder, sicker, poorer, less wise, and less successful.

It is easy to understand how trauma can hurt the brain, but researchers have also seen how negative thinking and bad programming from our past can also affect it.

For example, I grew up with an older brother who was intent on shoving me around. The constant tension and fear I felt then led to a higher level of anxiety, anxious thinking patterns, and always being on guard, never knowing when something bad was about to happen. This fear caused long-term overactivity in my brain's fear centers, until I was able to work through it later on in life.

In *Breaking the Habit of Being Yourself*, my colleague Dr. Joe Dispenza is your guide to optimize both the hardware and software of your brain to help you reach a new state of mind. His new book is based on solid science, and he continues to speak with kindness and wisdom, as he did in the award-winning film *What the BLEEP Do We Know!?* and in his first book, *Evolve Your Brain.*

Even though I think of the brain like a computer, with both hardware and software, the hardware (the actual physical functioning of the brain) is not separate from the software or the constant programming and reshaping that occurs throughout our lives. They have a dramatic impact on each other.

Most of us have had trauma of some kind in our lives and live with the day-to-day scars that have resulted. Cleaning out those experiences that have become part of the brain's structure can be incredibly healing. Of course, engaging in brain-healthy habits, such as a proper diet and exercise and certain brain nutrients, is critical to the brain working right. But in addition, your moment-by-moment thoughts exert a powerful healing effect on the brain . . . or they can work to your detriment. The same is true for past experiences that can become wired in the brain.

The study we do at the Amen Clinics is called "brain SPECT imaging." SPECT (single-photon emission computed tomography) is a nuclear-medicine study that looks at blood flow and activity patterns. It is different from CT scans or MRI, which examine the brain's anatomy, because SPECT looks at how the brain functions. Our SPECT work, now over 70,000 scans, has taught us so many important life lessons about the brain, such as:

- Brain injuries can ruin people's lives;

- Alcohol is not a health food and often shows significant damage on SPECT scans;

- A number of the medications people routinely take, such as some common anti-anxiety medications, are not good for the brain; and

- Diseases like Alzheimer's actually start in the brain decades before people have any symptoms.

SPECT scans have also taught us that as a society, we need to have much more love and respect for the brain, and that allowing children to play contact sports, like football and hockey, is not a smart idea.

One of the most exciting lessons I have learned is that people can literally change their brains and change their lives by engaging in regular brain-healthy habits, such as correcting negative beliefs and using meditative processes such as those discussed by Dr. Dispenza.

In one series of studies we published, the practice of meditation, such as what Dr. Dispenza recommends, boosted blood flow to the prefrontal cortex, the most thoughtful part of the human brain. After eight weeks of daily meditation, the prefrontal cortex at rest was stronger, and the memories of our subjects were better, too. There are so many ways to heal and optimize the brain.

My hope is that, like me, you will develop "brain envy" and want a better-functioning brain. The brain-imaging work we do has changed everything in my own life. Shortly after I started ordering SPECT scans in 1991, I decided to look at my own brain. I was 37 years old. When I saw the toxic, bumpy appearance, I knew it was not healthy. All of my life I have been someone who rarely drank alcohol, never smoked, and never used an illegal drug. Then why did my brain look so bad? Before I really understood about brain health, I'd had many *bad* brain habits. I ate lots of fast food, drank diet soda like she was my best friend, often slept only four to five hours at night, and carried unexamined hurts from the past. I didn't exercise, felt chronically stressed, and carried an extra 30 pounds. What I didn't know was hurting me . . . and not just a little.

My last scan looks healthier and *much* younger than it did 20 years earlier. My brain has literally aged backward—that's how changeable your brain is, too, when you make up your mind to take care of it properly. After seeing my original scan, I wanted my brain to be better. This book will help yours be better, too.

I hope you enjoy reading it as much as I did.

— **Daniel G. Amen, M.D.**,
author of *Change Your Brain, Change Your Life*

INTRODUCTION

The Greatest Habit You Can Ever Break Is the Habit of Being Yourself

When I think about all the books on creating the life we desire, I realize that many of us are still looking for approaches that are grounded in sound scientific evidence—methods that truly work. But already new research into the brain and body, the mind, and consciousness—and a quantum leap in our understanding of physics—is suggesting expanded possibilities on how to move toward what we innately know is our real potential.

As a practicing chiropractor who runs a busy integrated-health clinic and as an educator in the fields of neuroscience, brain function, biology, and brain chemistry, I have been privileged to be at the forefront of some of this research—not just by studying the fields mentioned above, but also by observing the effects of this new science, once applied by common people like you and me. That's the moment when the possibilities of this new science become reality.

As a consequence, I have witnessed some remarkable changes in individuals' health and quality of life when they truly change their minds. Over the last several years, I have had the opportunity to interview a host of people who overcame significant health conditions that were considered either terminal or permanent. Per the contemporary model of medicine, these recoveries were labeled "spontaneous remissions."

However, upon my extensive examination of their inner journeys, it became apparent to me that there was a strong element of mind involved . . . and their physical changes weren't so spontaneous after all. This discovery furthered my postgraduate studies in brain imaging, neuroplasticity, epigenetics, and psychoneuroimmunology. I simply figured that something had to be happening in the brain and body that could be zeroed in on and then replicated. In this book, I want to share some of what I learned along the way and show you, by exploring how mind and matter are interrelated, how you can apply these principles not only to your body, but to any aspect of your life.

Go Beyond Knowing . . . to Knowing How

Many readers of my first book, *Evolve Your Brain: The Science of Changing Your Mind,* voiced the same honest and heartfelt request (along with a fair amount of positive feedback), such as the person who wrote: "I really liked your book; I read it twice. It had lots of science and was very thorough and inspiring, but can you tell me *how* to do it? *How* do I evolve my brain?"

In response, I began teaching a workshop series on the practical steps anyone can take to make changes at the level of mind and body that will lead to lasting results. Consequently, I have seen people experience unexplainable healings, release old mental and emotional wounds, resolve so-called impossible difficulties, create new opportunities, and experience wonderful wealth, just to name a few. (You will meet some of those people in these pages.)

It's not necessary that you read my first book to digest the material in this one. But if you *have* been exposed to my work, I wrote *Breaking the Habit of Being Yourself* to serve as a practical, how-to companion to *Evolve Your Brain.* It is my earnest objective to make this new book simple and easy to understand. There will be times, though, that I will have to give you bits of knowledge to act as the forerunner to a concept I want to develop. The purpose is to build a realistic working model of personal transformation that will help you understand how we can change.

Breaking the Habit of Being Yourself is a product of one of my passions—a sincere effort to demystify the mystical so that every person understands that we have, within our reach, all we need to make significant changes in our lives. This is a time when not only do we want to "know," but we want to "know how." *How* do we apply and personalize both emerging scientific concepts and age-old wisdom to succeed at living a more enriched life? When you and I can connect the dots of what science is discovering about the nature of reality, and when we give ourselves permission to apply those principles in our day-to-day existence, then each of us becomes both a mystic and a scientist in our own life.

So I invite you to experiment with everything that you learn in this book, and to objectively observe the results. What I mean is that if you make the effort to change your inner world of thoughts and feelings, your external environment should begin to give you feedback to show you that your mind has had an effect on your "outer" world. Why else would you do it?

If you take intellectual information that you learn as a *philosophy*, and then *initiate* that knowledge into your life by applying it enough times until you *master* it, you will ultimately move from being a philosopher to an initiate to a master. Stay tuned . . . there is sound scientific evidence that this is possible.

I do ask you up front to keep an open mind so that we can build, step-by-step, the concepts I outline in this book. All of this information is for you to do something with—otherwise it's just good dinner conversation, isn't it? Once you can open your mind to the way things really are, and let go of your conditioned beliefs with which you are accustomed to framing reality, you should see the fruits of your efforts. That is my wish for you.

The information in these pages is there to inspire you to prove to yourself that you are a divine creator.

We should never wait for science to give us permission to do the uncommon; if we do, then we are turning science into another religion. We should be brave enough to contemplate our lives, do what we thought was "outside the box," and do it repeatedly. When we do that, we are on our way to a greater level of personal power.

True empowerment comes when we start to look deeply at our beliefs. We may find their roots in the conditioning of religion, culture, society, education, family, the media, and even our genes (the latter being imprinted by the sensory experiences of our current lives, as well as untold generations). Then we weigh those old ideas against some new paradigms that may serve us better.

Times are changing. As individuals awaken to a greater reality, we are part of a much larger sea change. Our current systems and models of reality are breaking down, and it is time for something new to emerge. Across the board, our models for politics, economics, religion, science, education, medicine, and our relationship with the environment are all showing a different landscape than just ten years ago.

Letting go of the outmoded and embracing the new sounds easy. But as I pointed out in *Evolve Your Brain,* much of what we have learned and experienced has been incorporated into our biological "self," and we wear it like a garment. But we also know that what is true today might not be true tomorrow. Just as we have come to question our perception of atoms as solid pieces of matter, reality and our interaction with it is a progression of ideas and beliefs.

We also know that to leave the familiar life that we have grown accustomed to and waltz into something new is like a salmon swimming upstream: it takes effort—and, frankly, it's uncomfortable. And to top it off, ridicule, marginalization, opposition, and denigration from those who cling to what they think they know greet us along the way.

Who, with such an unconventional bent, is willing to meet such adversity in the name of some concept they cannot embrace with their senses, yet which is alive in their minds? How many times in history have individuals who were considered heretics and fools, and thus took the abuse of the unexceptional, emerged as geniuses, saints, or masters?

Will *you* dare to be an original?

Change as a Choice, Instead of a Reaction

It seems that human nature is such that we balk at changing until things get really bad and we're so uncomfortable that we can no longer go on with business as usual. This is as true for an individual as it is for a society. We wait for crisis, trauma, loss, disease, and tragedy before we get down to looking at who we are, what we are doing, how we are living, what we are feeling, and what we believe or know, in order to embrace true change. Often it takes a worst-case scenario for us to begin making changes that support our health, relationships, career, family, and future. My message is: *Why wait?*

We can learn and change in a state of pain and suffering, or we can evolve in a state of joy and inspiration. Most embrace the former. To go with the latter, we just have to make up our minds that change will probably entail a bit of discomfort, some inconvenience, a break from a predictable routine, and a period of not knowing.

Most of us are already familiar with the temporary discomfort of not knowing. We stumbled through our early efforts to read until this skill became second nature. When we first practiced the violin or the drums, our parents wished they could send us to a soundproofed room. Pity the hapless patient who has his blood drawn by a medical student who has the requisite knowledge but still lacks the finesse that she will only gain through practice.

Absorbing knowledge (*knowing*) and then gaining practical experience by applying what you learned until a particular skill became ingrained in you (*knowing how*) is probably how you acquired most of the abilities that now feel like a part of your being (*knowingness*). In much the same way, learning how to change your life involves knowledge and the application of that knowledge. That is why this book is divided into three overarching sections.

Throughout Parts I and II, I will build ideas in sequence, forming a bigger and broader model of understanding for you to personalize. If some ideas seem repetitive, they are there to "re-mind" you about something that I don't want you to forget. Repetition reinforces the circuits in your brain and forms more neural connections so that in your weakest hour, you don't talk yourself out of greatness. When you ease into Part III of the book with a sound knowledge base, you can experience for yourself the "truth" of what you learned earlier.

Part I: The Science of You

Our exploration will start with an overview of philosophical and scientific paradigms related to the latest research about the nature of reality, who you are, why change has been so difficult for so many, and what is possible for you as a human being. Part I will be an easy read, I promise.

— **Chapter 1: The Quantum You** introduces you to a bit of quantum physics, but don't be alarmed. I start there because it is important that you begin to embrace the concept that your (subjective) mind has an effect on your (objective) world. The observer effect in quantum physics states that where you direct your attention is where you place your energy. As a consequence, *you* affect the material world (which, by the way, is made mostly of energy). If you entertain that idea even for a moment, you might start focusing on what you want instead of what you don't want. And you might even find yourself thinking: *If an atom is 99.99999 percent energy and .00001 percent physical substance,[1] then I'm actually more nothing than something! So why do I keep my attention on that small percentage of the physical world when I am so much more? Is defining my present reality by what I perceive with my senses the biggest limitation I have?*

In Chapters 2 through 4, we will look at what it means to change—to become greater than the environment, the body, and time.

— You've probably entertained the idea that your thoughts create your life. But in **Chapter 2: Overcoming the Environment,** I discuss how if you allow the outer world to control how you think and feel, your external environment is patterning circuits in your brain to make you think "equal to" everything familiar to you. The result is that you create more of the same; you hardwire your brain to reflect the problems, personal conditions, and circumstances in your life. So to change, you must be *greater than* all things physical in your life.

— **Chapter 3: Overcoming the Body** continues to look at how we unconsciously live by a set of memorized behaviors, thoughts, and emotional reactions, all running like computer programs behind the scenes of our conscious awareness. That's why it is not enough to "think positive," because most of who we are might reside subconsciously as negativity in the body. By the end of this book, you will know how to enter into the operating system of the subconscious mind and make permanent changes where those programs exist.

— **Chapter 4: Overcoming Time** examines how we either live in the anticipation of future events or repeatedly revisit past memories (or both) until the body begins to believe it is living in a time other than the present moment. The latest research supports the notion that we have a natural ability to change the brain and body by thought alone, so that it looks biologically like some future event has already happened. Because you can make thought more real than anything else, you can change who you are from brain cell to gene, given the right understanding. When you learn how to use your attention and access the present, you will enter through the door to the quantum field, where all potentials exist.

— **Chapter 5: Survival vs. Creation** illustrates the distinction between living in survival and living in creation. Living in survival entails living in stress and functioning as a materialist, believing that the outer world is more real than the inner world. When you are under the gun of the fight-or-flight nervous system, being run by its cocktail of intoxicating chemicals, you are programmed to be concerned only about your body, the things or people in your environment, and your obsession with time. Your brain and body are out of balance. You are living a predictable life. However, when you are truly in the elegant state of creation, you are no body, no thing, no time—you forget about yourself. You become pure consciousness, free from the chains of the identity that needs the outer reality to remember who it thinks it is.

Part II: Your Brain and Meditation

— In **Chapter 6: Three Brains: Thinking to Doing to Being,** you will embrace the concept that you have three "brains" that allow you to move from thinking to doing to being. Even better, when you focus your attention to the exclusion of your environment, your body, and time, you can easily move from thinking to being without having to *do* anything. In that state of mind, your brain does not distinguish between what is happening in the outer world of reality and what is happening in the inner world of your mind. Thus, if you can mentally rehearse a desired experience via thought alone, you will experience the emotions of that event before it has physically manifested. Now you are moving into a new state of being, because your mind and body are working as one. When you begin to feel like some potential future reality is happening to you in the moment that you are focusing on it, you are rewriting your automatic habits, attitudes, and other unwanted subconscious programs.

— **Chapter 7: The Gap** explores how to break free from the emotions that you've memorized—which have become your personality—and how to close the gap between who you really are in your inner, private world and how you appear in the outer, social world. We all reach a certain point when we stop learning and realize that nothing external can take away those feelings from our past. If you can predict the feeling of every experience in your life, there is no room for anything new to occur, because you are viewing your life from the past instead of the future. This is the juncture point where the soul either breaks free or falls into oblivion. You will learn to liberate your energy in the form of emotions, and thus narrow the gap between how you appear and who you are. Ultimately, you will create transparency. When how you appear is who you are, you are truly free.

— Part II concludes with **Chapter 8: Meditation, Demystifying the Mystical, and Waves of Your Future**, in which my purpose is to demystify meditation so that you know what you are doing and why. Discussing brain-wave technology, made simple, I show you how your brain changes electromagnetically when you are focused versus when you are in an aroused state due to stressors in your life. You will learn that the true purpose of meditation is to get beyond the analytical mind and enter into the subconscious mind so you can make real and permanent changes. If you get up from meditation as the same person who sat down, nothing has happened to you on any level. When you meditate and connect to something greater, you can create and then memorize such coherence between your thoughts and feelings that nothing in your outer reality—no thing, no person, no condition at any place or time—could move you from that level of energy. Now you are mastering your environment, your body, and time.

Part III: Stepping Toward Your New Destiny

All of the information in Parts I and II is provided in order to equip you with the necessary knowledge so that when you demonstrate (apply) this information in Part III, which supplies the "how-to," you will have a direct experience of what you've been taught. Part III is all about applying yourself in an actual discipline—a mindful exercise to use in your daily life. It's a step-by-step meditation process, created so you can actually do something with the theories given to you.

By the way, did your mind balk when I mentioned that multistep process? If so, it's not what you think. Yes, you will learn a *sequence* of actions, but soon you will experience them as one or two simple steps. After all, you probably perform multiple actions every time you prepare to drive your car (for example, you adjust the seat, put on your seat belt, check the mirrors, start the car, turn on the headlights, look around, use a turn signal, apply the brake, put the car in drive or reverse, apply pressure to the gas pedal, and so on). Ever since you learned to drive, you have executed this procedure easily and automatically. I assure you, the same will be true once you learn each step in Part III.

You may be asking yourself, *Why do I need to read Parts I and II? I'll just jump to Part III.* I know, I'd probably be thinking the same. I decided to offer the relevant knowledge in the first two Parts of the text so that when you get to the third section, nothing will be left to conjecture, dogma, or speculation. When you begin the steps of the meditation, you'll know exactly what you're doing and why. When you comprehend the *what* and the *why,* the more you will *know* and thus the more you will *know how* when the time comes. Therefore, you will have more power and intention behind the practical experience of truly changing your mind.

By using the steps in Part III, you may be more prone to accept your innate ability to change so-called impossible situations in your life. You might even give yourself permission to entertain potential realities that you never considered prior to your exposure to these new concepts—*you might just begin to do the uncommon!* That is my aim for you by the time you finish this book.

So if you can resist the temptation to jump ahead to Part III, I promise that when you get there, you'll be quite empowered by what you learn. I've seen this approach work throughout the world in the series of three workshops I lead. When people gain the right knowledge, in such a way that they understand it completely, and then have the opportunity for effective instruction to apply what they comprehend . . . then like magic, they can see the fruits of their efforts in the form of changes that serve as feedback in their lives.

Part III will give you the meditative skills to change something within your mind and body and to produce an effect outside of you. Once you can notice what you did inside of you that produced an outcome outside of you, you'll do it again. When a new experience manifests in your life, you'll embrace the energy you feel in the form of an elevated emotion such as empowerment, awe, or immense gratitude; and that energy will drive you to do it again and again. Now you are on the path to true evolution.

Each meditation step delineated in Part III is associated with a piece of meaningful information presented earlier in the book. Because you'll have cultivated the meaning behind exactly what you're doing, there should be no ambiguity that might cause you to lose your vision.

Like many skills you've learned, in the beginning it may take all of your conscious effort to stay focused as you learn how to meditate to evolve your brain. In the process, you must restrain yourself from your typical behaviors and maintain your thoughts on what you are doing, without wandering to extraneous stimuli, so your actions are aligned with your intention.

Just as you might have experienced when you first learned to cook Thai food, play golf, dance the salsa, or drive a stick shift, the newness of the endeavor will require you to practice this ability continually, training both mind and body to memorize each step.

Remember, most types of instruction are formatted in bite-size chunks so that the mind and body can begin to work together. Once you "get it," all the individual steps you kept reviewing merge into one smooth process. The methodical, linear approach seamlessly flows into a holistic, effortless, unified demonstration. This is the point of personal ownership. At times, the effort this takes can be tedious. But if you persist with a certain amount of will and energy, in time you'll enjoy the results.

When you *know* that you know "how" to do something, you're on your way to mastering it. I am overjoyed to say that many people around the world are already using the knowledge in this book to make demonstrable changes in their lives. It is my sincere passion that you, too, break the habit of being yourself and create the new life you desire.

Let's get started. . . .

PART I

THE
SCIENCE
OF YOU

CHAPTER ONE

THE QUANTUM YOU

Early physicists divided the world into matter and thought, and later, matter and energy. Each member of those pairs was considered to be entirely separate from the other . . . but they're not! Nevertheless, this mind/matter duality shaped our early worldview—that reality was essentially predetermined and that people could do little to change things through their own actions, let alone their thoughts.

Fast-forward to our current understanding—that we are part of a vast, invisible field of energy, which contains all possible realities and responds to our thoughts and our feelings. Just as today's scientists are exploring the relationship between thought and matter, we are eager to do the same in our own lives. And so we ask ourselves, *Can I use my mind to create my reality?* If so, is that a skill that we can learn and use to become who we want to be, and create the life we want to experience?

Let's face it—none of us is perfect. Whether we'd like to make some change to our physical self, emotional self, or spiritual self, we all have the same desire: we want to live life as an idealized version of who we think and believe we can be. When we stand in front of the mirror and look at our love handles, we don't just see that slightly too-pudgy vision reflected in the glass. We also see, depending on our mood that day, a slimmer, fitter version of ourselves or a heavier, chunkier version. Which of our images is real?

When we lie in bed at night reviewing our day and our efforts to be a more tolerant, less reactive person, we don't just see the parent who lashed out at our child for failing to quietly and quickly submit to a simple request. We envision either an angelic self whose patience was stretched like an innocent victim on the rack or a hideous ogre laying waste to a child's self-esteem. Which of *those* images is real?

The answer is: *all of them are real*—and not just those extremes, but an infinite spectrum of images ranging from positive to negative. How can that be? For you to better understand why none of those versions of self is more or less real than the others, I'm going to have to shatter the outmoded understanding about the fundamental nature of reality and replace it with a new one.

That sounds like a major undertaking, and in some ways it is, but I also know this: The most likely reason why you were drawn to this book is that your past efforts to make any lasting change in your life—physical, emotional, or spiritual—have fallen short of the ideal of yourself that you imagined. And why those efforts failed has more to do with your beliefs about why your life is the way it is than with anything else, including a perceived lack of will, time, courage, or imagination.

Always, in order to change, we have to come to a new understanding of self and the world so that we can embrace new knowledge and have new experiences.

That is what reading this book will do for you.

Your past shortfalls can be traced, at their root, to one major oversight: you haven't committed yourself to living by the truth that *your thoughts have consequences so great that they create your reality.*

The fact is that we are all blessed; we all can reap the benefits of our constructive efforts. We don't have to settle for our present reality; we can create a new one, whenever we choose to. We all have that ability, because for better or worse, our thoughts do influence our lives.

I'm sure you've heard that before, but I wonder whether most people really believe this statement on a gut level. If we truly embraced the notion that our thoughts produce tangible effects in our lives, wouldn't we strive to never let one thought slip by us that we didn't want to experience? And wouldn't we focus our attention on what we want, instead of continually obsessing about our problems?

Think about it: if you really knew that this principle were true, would you ever miss a day in intentionally creating your desired destiny?

To Change Your Life, Change Your Beliefs about the Nature of Reality

I hope this book will shift your view of how our world operates, convince you that you are more powerful than you knew, and inspire you to demonstrate the understanding that what you think and believe has a profound effect on your world.

Until you break from the way you see your present reality, any change in your life will always be haphazard and transitory. You have to overhaul your thinking about why things happen in order to produce enduring and desired outcomes. To do that, you'll need to be open to a new interpretation of what is real and true.

To help you shift into this mode of thought and begin to create a life of your choosing, I have to begin with a bit of cosmology (the study of the structure and dynamics of the universe). But don't be alarmed—we're merely going to skim through "The Nature of Reality 101" and how some of our views about it have evolved to reach our present understanding. All of this is to explain (of necessity, in a brief and simple way) how it is possible that your thoughts shape your destiny.

This chapter just might test your willingness to abandon ideas that have in a sense been programmed into you for many years on a conscious and subconscious level. Once you gain a new conception of the fundamental forces and elements that constitute reality, it won't fit into that old perception in which the linear and the orderly rule the day. Be prepared to experience some fundamental shifts in understanding.

In fact, as you begin to embrace this new outlook, your very makeup as a human being will change. It is my wish that you will no longer be the same person you were when you began.

Obviously, I'm about to challenge you, but I want you to know that I'm entirely empathetic, because I too have had to let go of what I thought was true and leap into the unknown. To ease into this new way of thinking about the nature of our world, let's see how our worldview was shaped by the early belief that mind and matter were separate things.

Always Matter, Never Mind?
Always Mind, Never Matter?

Connecting the dots between the outer, physical world of the observable and the inner, mental world of thought has always presented quite a challenge to scientists and philosophers. To many of us, even today, the mind appears to have little or no measurable effects on the world of matter. Although we'd probably agree that the world of matter creates consequences affecting our minds, how can our minds possibly produce any physical changes affecting the solid things in our lives? Mind and matter appear to be separate . . . that is, unless there's a shift in our understanding about the way physical, solid things actually exist.

Well, there has been such a shift, and to trace its beginnings, we don't have to go back very far. For much of what historians consider modern times, humanity believed that the nature of the universe was orderly, and thus predictable and explainable. Consider 17th-century mathematician and philosopher René Descartes, who developed many concepts that still have great relevance to mathematics and other fields (does *I think, therefore I am* ring any bells?). In retrospect, however, one of his theories ultimately did more harm than good. Descartes was a proponent of the mechanistic model of the universe—a view that the universe is controlled by predictable laws.

When it came to human thought, Descartes faced a real challenge—the human mind possessed too many variables to neatly fit into any laws. Since he couldn't unify his understanding of the physical world with that of the mind, but he had to account for the presence of both, Descartes played a nifty mind game (pun intended). He said that the mind was not subject to laws of the objective, physical world, so it was completely outside the bounds of scientific inquiry. The study of matter was the jurisdiction of science (always matter, never mind)—whereas the mind was God's instrument, so the study of it fell to religion (always mind, never matter).

Essentially, Descartes started a belief system that imposed a duality between the concepts of mind and matter. For centuries, that division stood as the accepted understanding of the nature of reality.

Helping to perpetuate Descartes's beliefs were the experiments and theories of Sir Isaac Newton. The English mathematician and scientist not only solidified the concept of the universe as a machine, but he produced a set of laws stating that human beings could precisely determine, calculate, and predict the orderly ways in which the physical world would operate.

According to the "classical" Newtonian physics model, all things were considered solid. For example, energy could be explained as a force to move objects or to change the physical state of matter. But as you will see, energy is much more than an outside force exerted on material things. Energy is the very *fabric* of all things material, and is responsive to mind.

By extension, the work of Descartes and Newton established a mind-set that if reality operated on mechanistic principles, then humanity had little influence on outcomes. All of reality was predetermined. Given that outlook, is it any wonder that human beings struggled with the idea that their actions mattered, let alone entertained the notion that their *thoughts* mattered or that free will played any part in the grand scheme of things? Don't many of us still labor today (subconsciously or consciously) under the assumption that we humans are often little more than victims?

Considering that these cherished beliefs held sway for centuries, it took some revolutionary thought to counter Descartes and Newton.

Einstein: Not Just Rocking the Boat— Rocking the Universe

About 200 years after Newton, Albert Einstein produced his famous equation $E = mc^2$, demonstrating that energy and matter are so fundamentally related that they are one and the same. Essentially, his work showed that matter and energy are completely interchangeable. This directly contradicted Newton and Descartes, and ushered in a new understanding of how the universe functions.

Einstein didn't single-handedly crumble our previous view of the nature of reality. But he did undermine its foundation, and that eventually led to the collapse of some of our narrow, rigid ways of thinking. His theories set off an exploration of the puzzling behavior of light. Scientists then observed that light sometimes behaves like a wave (when it bends around a corner, for example), and at other times, it behaves like a particle. How could light be both a wave and a particle? According to the outlook of Descartes and Newton, it couldn't—a phenomenon had to be either one or the other.

Quickly, it became clear that the dualistic Cartesian/Newtonian model was flawed at the most basic level of all: the subatomic. (*Subatomic* refers to the parts—electrons, protons, neutrons, and so on—that make up atoms, which are the building blocks of all things physical.) The most fundamental components of our so-called physical world are both waves (energy) *and* particles (physical matter), depending on the mind of the observer (we'll come back to that). To understand how the world works, we had to look to its tiniest components.

Thus, out of these particular experiments, a new field of science was born, called *quantum physics*.

The Solid Ground We Stand On . . . Isn't

This change was a complete reimagining of the world we'd thought we lived in, and it led to the proverbial rug being pulled out from under our feet—feet we used to think were planted on solid ground. How so? Think back to those old toothpick-and-Styrofoam-ball models of the atom. Before quantum physics came along, people believed that an atom was made of a relatively solid nucleus with smaller, less substantial objects either located in or around it. The very idea that with a powerful enough instrument we could measure (calculate the mass of) and count (number) the subatomic particles that made up an atom made them seem as inert as cows grazing in a pasture. Atoms seemed to be made of solid stuff, right?

THE CLASSICAL ATOM

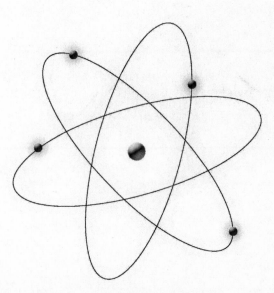

Figure 1A. The "old-school" classical Newtonian version of an atom. The focus is primarily on the material.

Nothing could be further from the truth as revealed by the quantum model. Atoms are mostly empty space; atoms are energy. Think about this: everything physical in your life is not solid matter—rather, it's all fields of energy or frequency patterns of information. All matter is more "no thing" (energy) than "some thing" (particles).

THE QUANTUM ATOM

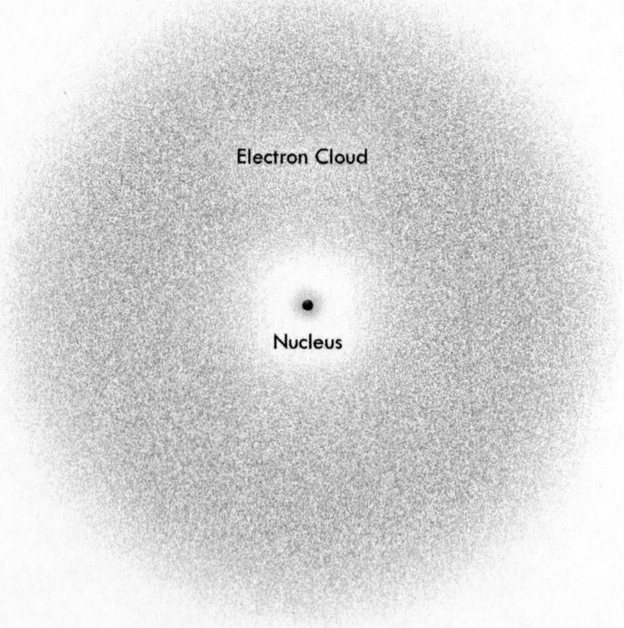

Electron Cloud

Nucleus

Figure 1B. The "new-school" quantum version of an atom with an electron cloud. The atom is 99.99999 percent energy and .00001 percent matter. It's just about nothing, materially.

THE REAL QUANTUM ATOM

Figure 1C. This is the most realistic model of any atom.
It is "no thing" materially, but all things potentially.

Another Puzzle: Subatomic Particles and Larger Objects Play by Different Rules

But this alone wasn't enough to explain the nature of reality. Einstein and others had another puzzle to solve—matter didn't always seem to behave in the same ways. When physicists began observing and measuring the tiny world of the atom, they noticed that at the subatomic level the fundamental elements of the atom didn't obey the laws of classical physics the way that larger objects did.

Events involving objects in the "large" world were predictable, reproducible, and consistent. When that legendary apple fell from a tree and moved toward the center of the earth until it collided with Newton's head, its mass accelerated with a consistent force. But electrons, as particles, behaved in unpredictable, unusual ways. When they interacted with the nucleus of the atom and moved toward its center, they gained and lost energy, appeared and disappeared, and seemed to show up all over the place without regard to the boundaries of time and space.

Did the world of the small and the world of the large operate under very different sets of rules? Since subatomic particles like electrons were the building blocks of everything in nature, how could they be subject to one set of rules, and the things they made up behave according to another set of rules?

From Matter to Energy: Particles Pull Off the Ultimate Vanishing Act

At the level of electrons, scientists can measure energy-dependent characteristics such as wavelength, voltage potentials, and the like, but these particles have a mass that is so infinitesimally small and exists so temporarily as to be almost nonexistent.

This is what makes the subatomic world unique. It possesses not just physical qualities, but also energetic qualities. In truth, matter on a subatomic level exists as a momentary phenomenon. It's so elusive that it constantly appears and disappears, appearing into three dimensions and disappearing into nothing—into the quantum field, in no space, no time—transforming from particle (matter) to wave (energy), and vice versa. But where do particles go when they vanish into thin air?

COLLAPSING the WAVE FUNCTION

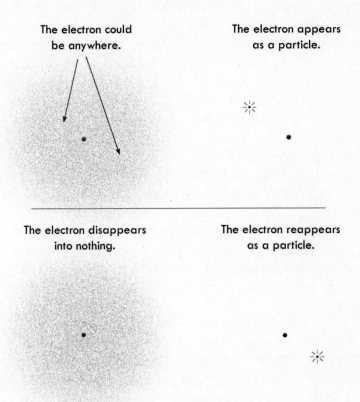

Figure 1D. The electron exists as a wave of probability in one moment, and then in the next moment appears as a solid particle, then disappears into nothing, and then reappears at another location.

The Creation of Reality:
Energy Responds to Mindful Attention

Consider again that old-school toothpick-and-Styrofoam-ball model of how atoms were constructed. Back then, weren't we led to believe that electrons orbited about the nucleus like planets around the sun? If so, we could pinpoint their location, couldn't we? The answer is yes, in a manner of speaking, but the reason is not at all what we used to think.

What quantum physicists discovered was that the person observing (or measuring) the tiny particles that make up atoms *affects* the behavior of energy and matter. Quantum experiments demonstrated that electrons exist simultaneously in an infinite array of possibilities or probabilities in an invisible field of energy. But only when an observer focuses attention on any location of any one electron does that electron appear. In other words, a particle cannot manifest in reality—that is, ordinary space-time as we know it—until we observe it.[1]

Quantum physics calls this phenomenon "collapse of the wave function" or the "observer effect." We now know that the moment the observer looks for an electron, there is a specific point in time and space when all probabilities of the electron collapse into a physical event. With this discovery, mind and matter can no longer be considered separate; they are intrinsically related, because subjective mind produces measurable changes on the objective, physical world.

Are you beginning to see why this chapter is titled "The Quantum You"? At the subatomic level, energy responds to your mindful attention and becomes matter. How would your life change if you learned to *direct* the observer effect and to collapse infinite waves of probability into the reality that *you* choose? Could you get better at observing the life you want?

An Infinite Number of Possible Realities Await the Observer

So ponder this: Everything in the physical universe is made up of subatomic particles such as electrons. By their very nature, these particles, when they exist as pure potential, are in their wave state while they are not being observed. They are potentially "every thing" and "no thing" until they are observed. They exist *everywhere* and *nowhere* until they are observed. Thus, everything in our physical reality exists as pure potential.

If subatomic particles can exist in an infinite number of possible places simultaneously, we are potentially capable of collapsing into existence an infinite number of possible realities. In other words, if you can imagine a future event in your life based on any one of your personal desires, that reality already exists as a possibility in the quantum field, waiting to be observed by you. If your mind can influence the appearance of an electron, then theoretically it can influence the appearance of *any* possibility.

This means that the quantum field contains a reality in which you are healthy, wealthy, and happy, and possess all of the qualities and capabilities of the idealized self that you hold in your thoughts. Stay with me and you will see that with willful attention, sincere application of new knowledge, and repeated daily efforts, you can use your mind, as the observer, to collapse quantum particles and organize a vast number of subatomic waves of probability into a desired physical event called an *experience* in your life.

Like clay, the energy of infinite possibilities is shaped by consciousness: your mind. And if all matter is made of energy, it makes sense that consciousness ("mind," in this case, as Newton and Descartes called it) and energy ("matter," according to the quantum model) are so intimately related that they are one. Mind and matter are completely entangled. Your consciousness (mind) has effects on energy (matter) because your consciousness *is* energy and energy *has* consciousness. You are powerful enough to influence matter because at the most elementary level, you are energy with a consciousness. You are mindful matter.

In the quantum model, the physical universe is an immaterial, interconnected, unified field of information, potentially every thing but physically no thing. The quantum universe is just waiting for a conscious observer (you or me) to come along and influence energy in the form of potential matter by using the mind and consciousness (which are themselves energy) to make waves of energetic probabilities coalesce into physical matter. Just as the wave of possibility of the electron manifests as a particle within a specific momentary event, we observers cause a particle or groups of particles to manifest physical experiences in the form of events in our lives.

This is crucial to understanding how you can cause an effect or make a change in your life. When you learn how to sharpen your skills of observation to intentionally affect your destiny, you are well on your way toward living the ideal version of your life by becoming the idealized version of your *self.*

We Are Connected to Everything in the Quantum Field

Like everything else in the universe, we are, in a sense, connected to a sea of information in a dimension beyond physical space and time. We don't need to be touching or even in close proximity to any physical elements in the quantum field to affect or be affected by them. The physical body is organized patterns of energy and information, which is unified with everything in the quantum field.

You, like all of us, broadcast a distinct energy pattern or signature. In fact, everything material is always emitting specific patterns of energy. And this energy carries information. Your fluctuating states of mind consciously or unconsciously change that signature on a moment-to-moment basis because you are more than just a physical body; you are a consciousness using a body and a brain to express different levels of mind.

Another way to look at how we humans and the quantum field are interconnected is through the concept of *quantum entanglement,* or *quantum nonlocal connection.* Essentially, once two particles can be initially linked in some way, they will always be bonded together beyond space and time. As a result, anything that is done to one will be done to the other even though they are spatially separated from one another. This means that since we too are made up of particles, we are all implicitly connected beyond space and time. What we do unto others, we do unto ourselves.

Think about the implications of this. If you can wrap your mind around this concept, then you'd have to agree that the "you" that exists in a probable future is already connected to the "you" in this now, in a dimension beyond this time and space. Stay tuned . . . by the end of this book, that idea just might seem normal to you!

Weird Science: Can We Affect the Past?

Since we're all interconnected across distance and time, does this suggest that our thoughts and feelings can influence events in our past as well as those we desire in our future?

In July 2000, Israeli doctor Leonard Leibovici conducted a double-blind, randomized controlled trial involving 3,393 hospital patients, divided into a control group and an "intercession" group. He set out to see whether prayer could have an effect on their condition.[2] Prayer experiments are great examples of mind affecting matter at a distance. But stay with me here, because everything is not always what it seems.

Leibovici selected patients who had suffered sepsis (an infection) while hospitalized. He randomly designated half the patients to have prayers said for them, while the other half were not prayed for. He compared the results in three categories: how long fever lasted, length of hospital stay, and how many died as a result of the infection.

The prayed-for benefited from an earlier decrease in fever and a shorter hospitalization time; the difference in the number of deaths among the prayed-for and not-prayed-for groups was not statistically significant, although better in the prayed-for group.

That's a powerful demonstration of the benefits of prayer and how we can send an intention out into the quantum field through our thoughts and feelings. However, there's one additional element to this story that you should know about. Did it strike you as slightly odd that in July 2000, a hospital would have more than 3,000 cases of infection at once? Was it a very poorly sterilized place, or was some kind of contagion running rampant?

Actually, those who were praying weren't praying for patients who were infected in 2000. Instead, unbeknownst to them, they were praying for lists of people who had been in the hospital from 1990 to 1996—four to ten years prior to the experiment! *The prayed-for patients actually got better during the 1990s from the experiment conducted years later.* Let me say this another way: the patients who were prayed for in 2000 all showed measurable changes in health, but *those changes took effect years before.*

A statistical analysis of this experiment proved that these effects were far beyond coincidence. This demonstrates that our intentions, our thoughts and feelings, and our prayers not only affect our present or future, but they can actually affect our past as well.

Now, this leads to the question: if you were to pray (or focus on an intention) for a better life for yourself, could it affect your past, present, *and* future?

The quantum law says that all potentials exist simultaneously. Our thinking and our feelings affect all aspects of life, beyond both space and time.

Our State of Being or State of Mind: When Mind and Body Are One

Please note: Throughout this book, I will refer interchangeably to your having and creating a *state of being* or a *state of mind.* For example, we could say that how you think and how you feel create a state of being. I want you to understand that when I use the terms *state of being* and *state of mind,* your physical body is a part of that state. In fact, as you will see later on, many people exist in a state in which the body has "become" the mind, when they are ruled almost exclusively by the body and how it feels. So when I talk about the observer having an effect, it is not just the brain that is at work influencing matter, but the body as well. It is your state of being (when mind and body are one), as an observer, which has effects on the external world.

Thoughts + Feelings Produce Test-Tube Results

We communicate with the quantum field primarily through our thoughts and feelings. Since our thoughts are themselves energy—as you know, the electrical impulses the brain generates can easily be measured by devices such as an EEG—they are one of the primary means by which we send out signals into the field.

Before I go into greater detail on how this works, I want to share with you a remarkable study that demonstrates how our thoughts and feelings influence matter.

Cellular biologist Glen Rein, Ph.D., conceived of a series of experiments to test healers' ability to affect biological systems. Since DNA is more stable than substances such as cells or bacterial cultures, he decided to have healers hold test tubes containing DNA.[3]

This study took place at the HeartMath Research Center in California. The folks there have conducted extraordinary research into the physiology of emotions, heart-brain interactions, and much more. Essentially, they and others have documented a specific link between our emotional states and our heart rhythms. When we have negative emotions (such as anger and fear), our heart rhythms become erratic and disorganized. In contrast, positive emotions (love and joy, for instance) produce highly ordered, coherent patterns that HeartMath researchers refer to as *heart coherence.*

In Dr. Rein's experiment, he first studied a group of ten individuals who were well practiced in using techniques that Heart-Math teaches to build heart-focused coherence. They applied the techniques to produce strong, elevated feelings such as love and appreciation, then for two minutes, they held vials containing DNA samples suspended in deionized water. When those samples were analyzed, no statistically significant changes had occurred.

A second group of trained participants did the same thing, but instead of just creating positive emotions (*a feeling*) of love and appreciation, they simultaneously held an intention (*a thought*) to either wind or unwind the strands of DNA. This group produced statistically significant changes in the conformation (shape) of the DNA samples. In some cases the DNA was wound or unwound as much as 25 percent!

A third group of trained subjects held a clear intent to change the DNA, but they were instructed not to enter into a positive emotional state. In other words, they were only using thought (intention) to affect matter. The result? No changes to the DNA samples.

The positive emotional state that the first group entered did nothing by itself to the DNA. Another group's clearly held intentional thought, unaccompanied by emotion, also had no impact. *Only when subjects held both heightened emotions and clear objectives in alignment were they able to produce the intended effect.*

An intentional thought needs an energizer, a catalyst—and that energy is an elevated emotion. Heart and mind working together. Feelings and thoughts unified into a state of being. If a state of being can wind and unwind strands of DNA in two minutes, what does this say about our ability to create reality?

What the HeartMath experiment demonstrates is that the quantum field doesn't respond simply to our wishes—our emotional requests. It doesn't just respond to our aims—our thoughts. It only responds when those two are aligned or coherent—that is, when they are broadcasting the same signal. When we combine an elevated emotion with an open heart and a conscious intention with clear thought, we signal the field to respond in amazing ways.

The quantum field responds not to what we want; it responds to who we are being.

Thoughts and Feelings: Broadcasting Our Electromagnetic Signal to the Quantum Field

Since every potential in the universe is a wave of probability that has an electromagnetic field and is energetic in nature, it makes sense that our thoughts and feelings are no exception.

I find it a useful model to think of thoughts as the electrical charge in the quantum field and feelings as the magnetic charge in the field.[4] The thoughts we think send an electrical signal out into the field. The feelings we generate magnetically draw events back to us. Together, how we think and how we feel produces a state of being, which generates an electromagnetic signature that influences every atom in our world. This should prompt us to ask, *What am I broadcasting (consciously or unconsciously) on a daily basis?*

All potential experiences exist as electromagnetic signatures in the quantum field. There are an infinite number of potential electromagnetic signatures—for genius, for wealth, for freedom, for health—that already exist as a frequency pattern of energy. If you could create a new electromagnetic field by changing your state of being, which matches that potential in the quantum field of information, is it possible that your body would be drawn to that event or that event would find you?

ELECTROMAGNETIC POTENTIALS
in the QUANTUM FIELD

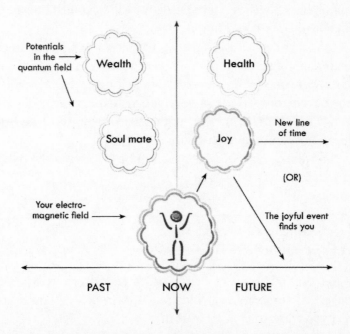

Figure 1E. All potential experiences exist in the quantum field as a sea of infinite possibilities. When you change your electromagnetic signature to match one that already exists in the field, your body will be drawn to that event, you will move into a new line of time, or the event will find you in your new reality.

To Experience Change, Observe a New Outcome with a New Mind

Quite simply, our routine, known thoughts and feelings perpetuate the same state of being, which creates the same behaviors, and creates the same reality. So if we want to change some aspect of our reality, we have to think, feel, and act in new ways; we have to "be" different in terms of our responses to experiences. We have to "become" someone else. We have to create a new state of mind . . . we need to observe a new outcome with that new mind.

From a quantum standpoint, we have to create a different state of being as an observer and generate a new electromagnetic signature. When we do, we will match a potential reality in the field that exists only as an electromagnetic potential. Once that match exists between who we are being/what we are broadcasting and the electromagnetic potential in the field, we will be pulled toward that potential reality, or it will find *us*.

I know that it's frustrating when life seems to produce an endless succession of minor variations on the same negative outcomes. But as long as you stay the same person, as long as your electromagnetic signature remains the same, you can't expect a new outcome. To change your life is to change your energy—to make an elemental change in your mind and emotions.

If you want a new outcome, you will have to break the habit of being yourself, and reinvent a *new* self.

Change Requires Coherence: Align Your Thoughts and Feelings

What do your state of being and a laser have in common? I'll make this connection to illustrate another thing you need to know if you want to change your life.

A laser is an example of a very coherent signal. When physicists talk about a coherent signal, they are referring to a signal made up of waves that are "in phase"—their troughs (low points) and crests (high points) are parallel. When those waves are coherent, they are much more powerful.

WAVE PATTERNS

Coherent Waves

Incoherent Waves

Figure 1F. When waves are in phase and rhythmic, they are more powerful than when they are out of phase.

Waves in a signal are either aligned or unaligned, coherent or incoherent. The same goes for your thoughts and feelings. How many times have you tried to create something, thinking in your mind that the end result was possible but feeling in your heart that it wasn't? What was the result of that incoherent/out-of-phase signal that you were sending? Why is it that nothing manifested? As you just saw with the HeartMath study, quantum creating only works when your thoughts and feelings are aligned.

Just as the waves in a signal are much more powerful when they are coherent, the same is true of you when your thoughts and your feelings are aligned. When you hold clear, focused thoughts about your purpose, accompanied by your passionate emotional engagement, you broadcast a stronger electromagnetic signal that pulls you toward a potential reality that matches what you want.

I frequently talk to my workshop audiences about my grandmother, a woman I adored. She was old-school Italian, as steeped in Catholic guilt as she was in the tradition of making tomato gravy to spoon on pasta. She prayed constantly for things and deliberately thought about a new life, but the guilt that had been instilled in her throughout her upbringing confused the signal she was sending. She only manifested more reasons to feel guilty.

If your intentions and desires haven't produced consistent results, you've probably been sending an incoherent, mixed message into the field. You may want wealth, you may *think* "wealthy" thoughts, but if you *feel* poor, you aren't going to attract financial abundance to yourself. Why not? Because thoughts are the language of the brain, and feelings are the language of the body. You're thinking one way and feeling another way. And when the mind is in opposition to the body (or vice versa), the field won't respond in any consistent way.

Instead, when mind and body are working together, when our thoughts and feelings are aligned, when we are in a new state of being, then we are sending a coherent signal on the airwaves of the invisible.

Why Quantum Outcomes Should Come as a Surprise

Now let's fill in another piece of the puzzle. To change our reality, those outcomes that we attract to ourselves have to surprise, even astonish, us in the way in which they come about. We should never be able to predict how our new creations will manifest; they must catch us off guard. They have to wake us up from the dream of the routine reality that we've grown accustomed to. These manifestations should leave us with no doubt that our consciousness made contact with the quantum field of intelligence, so we are inspired to do this again. That is the joy of the creative process.

Why should you want a quantum surprise? If you can predict an event, it is nothing new—it's routine, automatic; and you have experienced it many times before. If you can predict it, the same you produced the same familiar outcome. In fact, if you're try-ing to control how an outcome will occur, you just went "Newto-nian." Newtonian (classical) physics was about trying to anticipate and predict events; it was all about cause and effect.

What does "going Newtonian" mean when applied to your abil-ity to create? It's when the *external* environment is controlling your *internal* environment (thinking/feeling). That's cause and effect.

Instead, change your internal environment—the way you think and feel—and then see how the external environment is altered by your efforts. Strive to create an unknown, new future experience. Then when an unforeseen event occurs in your favor, you will be pleasantly surprised. You just became a quantum cre-ator. You just went from "cause and effect" to "causing an effect."

Hold a clear intention of what you want, but leave the "how" details to the unpredictable quantum field. Let it orchestrate an event in your life in a way that is just right for you. If you're going to expect anything, expect the unexpected. Surrender, trust, and let go of how a desired event will unfold.

This is the biggest hurdle for most to overcome, because we human beings always want to control a future reality by trying to re-create how it occurred in a past reality.

Quantum Creating: Giving Thanks Before Receiving an Outcome

I've just talked about aligning our thoughts and feelings to produce the result we want . . . yet in the process, letting go of the details surrounding how that event will come about. That's a leap of faith, and it is necessary if we are to exchange a life of hum-drum, predictable outcomes for a joyful life of new experiences and quantum surprises.

But we'll need to make yet another leap of faith to bring what we want into reality.

Under what circumstances are you typically grateful? You may answer, *I'm grateful for my family, the nice home I have, my friends, and my job.* What those things have in common is that they're *already* in your life.

Generally, we are grateful for something that already happened or is already present in our lives. You and I have been conditioned into believing that we need a reason for joy, a motivation to feel gratitude, grounds to be in a state of love. That's relying on external reality to make us feel different internally; it's Newton's model.

The new model of reality challenges us, as quantum creators, to change something within us—in mind and body, in our thoughts and feelings—*before* we can experience the physical evidence with our senses.

Can you give thanks and feel the elevated emotions associated with a desired event before it occurs? Can you imagine that reality so completely that you begin to be *in* that future life now?

In terms of quantum creating, can you give thanks for something that exists as a potential in the quantum field but has not yet happened in your reality? If so, you are moving from cause and effect (waiting for something outside of you to make a change *inside* of you) to causing an effect (changing something inside of you to produce an effect *outside* of you).

When you are in a state of gratitude, you transmit a signal into the field that an event *has already occurred.* Gratitude is more than an intellectual thought process. You have to feel as though whatever you want is in your reality at this very moment. Thus, your body (which only understands feelings) must be convinced that it has the emotional quotient of the future experience, happening to you *now.*

Universal Intelligence and the Quantum Field

I hope by now you agree on some basic underlying concepts of the quantum model—that all physical reality is primarily energy existing in a vast web that is interconnected across space and time. That web, the quantum field, holds all probabilities, which we can collapse into reality through our thoughts (consciousness), observation, feelings, and state of being.

But is reality nothing but indifferent electromagnetic forces acting on and in response to one another? Is the animating spirit within us simply a function of biology and randomness? I've had conversations with people who hold this view. Ultimately the discussion leads to a dialogue that goes something like this:

Where does the intelligence that keeps our heart beating come from?
That's a part of the autonomic nervous system.

Where is that system located?
The brain. The brain's limbic system is part of the autonomic nervous system.

And within the brain, are there specific tissues that are responsible for keeping the heart beating?
Yes.

What are those tissues made up of?
Cells.

And what are those cells made up of?
Molecules.

What are those molecules made up of?
Atoms.

And what are those atoms made up of?
Subatomic particles.

And what are those subatomic particles primarily composed of?
Energy.

When we arrive at the conclusion that our physiological vehicle is made up of the same stuff as the rest of the universe, and these folks bump up against the notion that what animates the body is a form of energy—the same 99.99999 percent "nothing" that constitutes the physical universe—they either shrug and walk away or come to realize that there is something to this notion that a unifying principle pervades all of physical reality.

Isn't it ironic, then, that we keep all of our attention on the 0.00001 percent of reality that is physical? Are we missing something?

If this nothing consists of energy waves that carry information, and this force organizes our physical structures and their functioning, then it certainly makes sense to refer to the quantum field as an invisible intelligence. And since energy is at the basis of all physical reality, that intelligence I've just described to you has organized itself into matter.

Think of the preceding conversation as a kind of template for how this intelligence has constructed reality. The quantum field is invisible potential energy that is able to organize itself from energy to subatomic particles to atoms to molecules, and on up the line to *everything*. From a physiological perspective, it organizes molecules into cells into tissues into organs into systems, and finally into the body as a whole. Put another way, this potential energy lowers itself as a frequency of wave patterns until it appears as solid.

It is this universal intelligence that gives life to that field and everything in it, including you and me. This power is the same universal mind that animates every aspect of the material universe. This intelligence keeps our hearts beating and our stomachs digesting food and oversees an incalculable number of chemical reactions per second that take place in every cell. Moreover, the same consciousness prompts trees to grow fruit and causes distant galaxies to form and collapse.

Because it exists in all places and times, and exerts its power within us and all around us, this intelligence is both personal and universal.

As an Extension of This Intelligence, We Can Emulate It

Understand that this universal intelligence possesses the same awareness that makes us individuals—consciousness or mindfulness. Even though this power is universal and objective, it does possess a consciousness—an awareness of self and its own ability to move and act within the material universe.

It is also completely mindful on all levels—not just of itself but of you and me. Because this consciousness notices everything, it observes and pays attention to us. It is aware of our thoughts, our dreams, our behaviors, and our desires. It "observes" everything into physical form.

How can a consciousness that has created all of life, that expends the energy and will to consistently regulate every function of our bodies to keep us alive, that has expressed such a deep and abiding interest in us, be anything but pure love?

We've talked about two aspects of consciousness: the objective consciousness/intelligence of the field; and the subjective consciousness that is a free-willed, self-aware individual. When we emulate the properties of this awareness, we are becoming creators. When we feel resonance with this loving intelligence, we become like it. This intelligence will orchestrate an event, an energetic response, to match whatever the subjective mind puts out into the quantum field. When our will matches its will, when our minds match its mind, when our love for life matches its love for life, we are *enacting* this universal consciousness. We *become* the elevated power that transcends the past, heals the present, and opens doors to the future.

We Get Back What We Send Out

Here's how this orchestration of events works in our lives. If we have experienced suffering, and within our minds and bodies we hold that suffering and express it through our thoughts and feelings, we broadcast that energetic signature into the field. The universal intelligence responds by sending into our lives another event that will reproduce the same intellectual and emotional response.

Our thoughts send the signal out (*I am suffering*), and our emotions (*I am suffering*) draw into our lives an event to match that emotional frequency—that is, a good reason to suffer. In a very real sense, we are asking for proof of the existence of universal intelligence at all times, and it sends us feedback in our external environment at all times. That is how powerful we are.

The question at the heart of this book is this: *Why don't we send out a signal that will produce a positive outcome for us?* How can we change so that the signal we send out matches what we intend to produce in our lives? We will change when we fully commit to the belief that by choosing the thought/signal we send out, we will produce an effect that is observable and unexpected.

With this objective intelligence, we are not punished *for* our sins (that is, our thoughts, feelings, and actions), but *by* them. When we project into the field a signal based on the thoughts and feelings (such as suffering) produced by some undesirable experience(s) in our past, is it any wonder that the field responds in the same negative way?

How many times have you uttered these words, or very similar ones: "I can't believe it . . . why does this always happen to me?"

Based on your new understanding of the nature of reality, do you now see that those statements reflect your acceptance of the Newtonian/Cartesian model in which you are a victim of cause and effect? Do you see that you are fully capable of causing an effect yourself? Do you see that instead of responding in the manner above, you could be asking yourself: *How can I think, feel, and behave differently to produce the effect/result that I want?*

Our mission, then, is to willfully move into the state of consciousness that allows us to connect to universal intelligence, make direct contact with the field of possibilities, and send out a clear signal that we truly expect to change and to see the results that we want—in the form of feedback—produced in our lives.

Ask for Quantum Feedback

When you do create purposefully, request a sign from the quantum consciousness that you have made contact with it. Dare to ask for synchronicities related to your specific desired outcomes. When you do, you are being bold enough to want to *know* that this consciousness is real and that it is aware of your efforts. Once you accept this, then you can create in a state of joy and inspiration.

This principle asks us to lay down what we think we know, surrender to the unknown, then observe the effects in the form of feedback in our lives. And that is the best way we learn. When we get positive indications (when we see our external circumstances shift in a favorable direction), we know that whatever we did inside of us was right. Naturally, we'll remember what we did so we can do it again.

So when feedback begins to occur in your life, you can choose to be like a scientist in a process of discovery. Why not monitor any changes, to see that the universe is favorable to your efforts and prove to yourself that you are that powerful?

So how can we connect with that state of consciousness?

Quantum Physics Is "Non-sense"

Newtonian physics postulated that there is always a linear series of interactions that are predictable and repeatable. You know: if $A + B = C$, then $C + D + E = F$. But in the wacky world of the quantum model of reality, everything is intercommunicating within a higher-dimensional field of information that is holistically entangled beyond space and time as we know it. Whew!

One reason why quantum physics is so elusive is that for years we have been accustomed to thinking based on our senses. If we measure and reaffirm reality with our senses, we are stuck in the Newtonian paradigm.

Instead, the quantum model demands that our understanding of reality not be based on our senses (quantum physics is non-*sense*). In the process of creating future reality via the quantum model, our senses should be the last to experience what the mind has created. The very *last* thing we experience is sensory feedback. Why?

The quantum is a multidimensional reality that exists beyond your senses, in a realm where there is no body, no thing, no time. Thus, to move into that domain and create from that paradigm, you'll need to forget about your body for a little while. You'll also have to temporarily shift your awareness away from your external environment—all those things that you identify with in your life. Your spouse, your kids, your possessions, and your problems are all part of your identity; through them, you identify with the outer world. And finally, you will have to lose track of linear time. That is, in the moment when you are intentionally observing a potential future experience, you will have to be so present that your mind no longer vacillates between memories of the past and expectations of a "same as usual" future.

Isn't it ironic that to influence your reality (environment), heal your body, or change some event in your future (time), you have to completely let go of your external world (no thing), you have to release your awareness of your body (no body) . . . you have to lose track of time (no time)—in effect, you have to become pure consciousness.

Do that, and you have dominion over the environment, your body, and time. (I affectionately call these the *Big Three*.) And since the subatomic world of the field is made purely of consciousness, you cannot enter any other way than via pure consciousness yourself. You cannot walk through the door into the quantum field as a "somebody"; you must enter as a "no body."

Your brain has the innate ability to harness this skill (stay tuned for more). When you understand that you are fully equipped to do all this, leave this world behind, and enter a new reality beyond space and time, you will be naturally inspired to apply it in your life.

Going Beyond Space and Time

What does it mean to be beyond space and time? These are constructs that humans created to explain physical phenomena involving location and our sense of the temporal. When we talk about a glass sitting on a table, we reference it in terms of location (where it is in space) and how long it has occupied that location. As humans we're obsessed with these two conceptions: Where we are. How long we've been there. How long we will remain. Where we'll go next. Even though time is not something that we can actually sense, we feel it passing in much the same way that we sense our location in space: we "feel" the seconds, minutes, and hours passing by, just as we feel our bodies pressed against our chairs and our feet planted on the ground.

In the quantum field, the infinite probabilities for materializing reality are beyond time and space, because a *potential* doesn't yet exist. If it doesn't exist, it doesn't have a location or occupy a position temporally. Anything that doesn't have material existence—that hasn't had its waves of probability collapsed into particle reality—exists beyond space and time.

Since the quantum field is nothing but immaterial probability, it is outside of space and time. As soon as we observe one of those infinite probabilities and give it material reality, it acquires those two characteristics.

To Enter the Field, Enter a Similar State

Great—we have the power to make material a reality of our own choosing by selecting it from the quantum field. But we have to somehow access that field. We're always connected to it, but how do we get the field to respond to us? If we're constantly emitting energy, and therefore sending information to the field and receiving information from it, how do we communicate more effectively with it?

In upcoming chapters I will talk at length about how to enter the field. For now, what you need to know is that to enter the field, which exists beyond space and time, you have to enter a similar state.

Do you ever have any experiences when time and space seem to disappear? Think of those moments when you're driving and your thoughts are focused on some concern you have. When that happens, you forget about your body (you are no longer aware of how you feel in space), you forget about the environment (the external world disappears), and you forget about time (you have no idea how long you are "tranced out").

At moments like these, you've been at the threshold of the door that allows you to enter the quantum field and gain access to working with universal intelligence. In essence, you've already made thought more real than anything else.

Later on, I will provide instruction on how to move into that state of consciousness regularly, to access the field and to communicate more directly with the universal intelligence that animates all things.

Change Your Mind, Change Your Life

As this chapter has progressed, I've led you from the notion that mind and matter are fully separable to the quantum model, which states that they are *in*separable. Mind is matter, and matter is mind.

So all those times in the past when you tried to change, maybe your thinking was fundamentally limited. You likely believed that it was always circumstances outside of you that needed to change: *If I didn't have so many other commitments, I could lose the excess weight, and then I'd be happy.* We've all stated some variation on that theme. If this, then that. Cause and effect.

What if you could change your mind, your thoughts, your feelings, and your way of being, outside the bounds of time and space? What if you could change *ahead* of time and see the effects of those "internal" changes in your "external" world?

You can.

What has profoundly and positively changed *my* life, and the lives of so many others, is the understanding that changing one's mind—and thereby having new experiences and gaining new insights—is simply a matter of breaking the habit of being oneself. When you overcome your senses, when you understand that you are not bound by the chains of your past—when you live a life that is greater than your body, your environment, and time—all things are possible. The universal intelligence that animates the existence of all things will both surprise and delight you. It wants nothing more than to provide you with access to all you want.

In short, when you change your mind, you change your life.

And a Child Shall Lead Them

Before we move on, I'd like to share a story that illustrates just how powerful and effective being in contact with the greater intelligence can be in making change an integral part of your life.

My children, now young adults, have used a meditation similar to the process I will describe to you in Part III of this book. As a result of practicing these techniques, they've manifested some remarkable adventures. Since their childhood, we've had an agreement that they work on creating material things or events that they want to experience. However, our rule is that I don't interfere or assist with producing the outcome. They have to create intended realities on their own, using their minds and interacting with the quantum field.

My 20-something daughter studies art in college. It was springtime, and I asked what she wanted to manifest during an upcoming summer break. She had a laundry list! Instead of the typical college-student-home-for-the-summer job, she wanted to work in Italy, learn and experience new things, visit at least six Italian cities, and spend one week in Florence, since she had friends there. She wanted to work for the first six weeks of the summer, making a decent wage, then spend the rest of the break at home.

I commended my daughter for her clear vision of what she wanted, and reminded her that universal intelligence would orchestrate the way her dream summer would manifest. She would take care of the "what"; a greater consciousness would handle the "how."

Since my daughter is practiced in the art of thinking and feeling ahead of the actual experience, I merely reminded her to not only set an intention every day with regard to what that summer would look like—what people she would see, what events would transpire, what places she would visit—but also to feel what it would be like to experience these things. I asked her to create the vision in her mind until it was so clear and real that the thought she was thinking became the experience, and her brain's synapses began to wire that information as if it was a reality.

If she was still "being" the young woman in the dorm room with a dream of going to Italy, then she was still the same person living the same reality. So while it was still March, she had to begin "being" that young woman who'd been in Italy for half the summer.

"No problem," she said. She'd had experiences like this before, when she wanted to be in a music video and when she wanted to experience an unlimited shopping spree. Both of these transpired in perfect elegance.

I then reminded my daughter, "You can't get up from your mental creation of this experience as the same person you were when you sat down. You have to get up from your seat as if you just had the most amazing summer of your life."

"I got it," she said. She understood my reminder that each day, she had to change to a new state of being. And after every mental creation, she was to go about her day living in the elevated mood of gratitude generated by having had that experience.

My daughter called a few weeks later. "Dad, the university is offering an art history summer course in Italy. I can get the cost of the program and all expenses down from $7,000 to $4,000. Can you help pay for that?"

Well, it's not that I'm an unsupportive parent, but this didn't strike me as what she had originally stated as her target. She was trying to control the outcome of this possible destiny instead of allowing the quantum field to orchestrate the events. I advised her to really inhabit that Italian trip and to think, feel, speak, and dream "in Italian" until she got lost in the experience.

A few weeks later when she called again, her excitement was palpable. She had been in the library, chatting with her art history teacher, and they eventually slipped into speaking Italian; both spoke the language fluently. At that point her teacher said, "I just remembered. One of my colleagues needs someone to teach Level I Italian to some American students who will be studying in Italy this summer."

Of course, my daughter was hired. Get this: not only would she be paid to teach (all expenses covered), but she would be in six different cities in Italy for six weeks, spend the last week in Florence, and be able to be home for the second half of the summer. She manifested her dream job and every aspect of her original vision.

This wasn't a case of a young woman pursuing this opportunity with the traditional dogged determination to find a program—searching the Internet, hounding professors, and so forth. Instead of following cause and effect, my daughter changed her state of being to the extent that she was *causing an effect*. She was living by the quantum law.

As she electromagnetically connected to an intended destiny that existed in the quantum, her body was then drawn to the future event. The experience found her. The outcome was unpredictable, it came in a way that she in no way expected, it was synchronistic, and there was no doubt that it was the result of her internal efforts.

Think about that for a moment. What opportunities are out there waiting to find you? Who are you being in this moment . . . and every other moment? Is your being that way going to attract to you all that you desire?

Can you change your state of being? And once you inhabit a new mind, can you observe a new destiny? The answers are what the rest of this book is all about.

CHAPTER TWO

OVERCOMING YOUR ENVIRONMENT

By now, I trust that you're beginning to accept the idea that the subjective mind has an effect on the objective world. You might even be keen to acknowledge that an observer can affect the subatomic world and influence a specific event, just by collapsing a single electron from a wave of energy into a particle. At this point you may also believe the scientific experiments in quantum mechanics I've discussed, which prove consciousness directly controls the tiny world of atoms because those elements fundamentally are made of consciousness and energy. That's quantum physics in action, right?

But perhaps you're still on the fence about the concept that your mind has real, measurable effects in your life. You may be asking yourself, *How can my mind influence bigger events in order to change my life? How can I collapse electrons into a specific event called a new experience that I want to embrace in some future time?* I wouldn't be surprised if you're wondering about your ability to create life-size experiences in the larger world of reality.

My goal is that you understand, and can see in action, how there might be a scientific basis for accepting that your thoughts can create your reality. For the doubter, though, I would like you to entertain the possibility that the way you think directly affects your life.

Keep Revisiting Familiar Thoughts and Feelings and You Keep Creating the Same Reality

If you can accept this paradigm as a possibility, then by pure reason, you would also have to agree that the following is possible: to create something different from what you've grown accustomed to in your personal world, you have to change the way you routinely think and feel each day.

Otherwise, by repeatedly thinking and feeling the same way you did the day before, and the day before that, you will continue to create the same circumstances in your life, which will cause you to experience the same emotions, which will influence you to think "equal to" those emotions.

Going out on a limb here, permit me to compare this situation to the proverbial hamster in a wheel. As you continually think about your problems (consciously or unconsciously), you will only create more of the same type of difficulties for yourself. And maybe you *think* about your problems so much because it was your thinking that created them in the first place. Perhaps your troubles *feel* so real because you constantly revisit those familiar feelings that initially created the problem. If you insist on thinking and feeling equal to the circumstances in your life, you will reaffirm that particular *reality*.

So in the next few chapters, I want to focus on what you need to understand in order to *change*.

To Change, Be Greater Than Your Environment, Your Body, and Time

Most people focus on three things in life: their environment, their bodies, and time. They don't just focus on those three elements, they think *equal* to them. But to break the habit of being yourself, you have to think *greater* than the circumstances of your life, be greater than the feelings that you have memorized in your body, and live in a new line of time.

If you want to change, you must have in your thoughts an idealized self—a model that you can emulate, which is different from, and better than, the "you" that exists today in your particular environment, body, and time. Every great person in history knew how to do this, and you can attain greatness in your own life once you master the concepts and techniques to come.

In this chapter, we'll focus on how you can overcome your environment, and lay some groundwork for the two chapters that follow, in which we'll discuss how to overcome your body and time.

Our Memories Make Up Our Internal Environment

Before we begin talking about how you can break the habit of being yourself, I want to appeal to your common sense for a few moments. How did this habit of thinking and feeling in the same way, over and over, begin?

I can only answer that by talking about the brain—the starting point of our thoughts and feelings. Current neuroscientific theory tells us that the brain is organized to reflect everything we *know* in our environment. All the information we have been exposed to throughout our lives, in the form of knowledge and experiences, is stored in the brain's synaptic connections.

The relationships with *people* we've known, the variety of *things* we own and are familiar with, the *places* where we've visited and lived at different *times* in our lives, and the myriad *experiences* we've embraced throughout our years are all configured in the structures of the brain. Even the vast array of actions and behaviors that we've memorized and repeatedly performed throughout our lifetimes are imprinted in the intricate folds of our gray matter.

Hence, all of our personal *experiences* with *people* and *things* at specific *times* and *places* are literally reflected within the networks of *neurons* (nerve cells) that make up our brains.

What do we collectively call all these "memories" of people and things that we experienced at different places and times in our lives? That's our *external environment*. For the most part, our brains are equal to our environment, a record of our personal past, a reflection of the life we've lived.

During our waking hours, as we routinely interact with the diverse stimuli in our world, our external environment activates various brain circuits. As a consequence of that nearly automatic response, we begin to think (and react) equal to our environment. As the environment causes us to think, familiar networks of nerve cells fire that reflect previous experiences already wired in the brain. Essentially, we automatically think in familiar ways derived from past memories.

If your thoughts determine your reality, and you keep thinking the same thoughts (which are a product and reflection of the environment), then you will continue to produce the same reality day after day. Thus, your internal thoughts and feelings exactly match your external life, because it is your outer reality—with all of its problems, conditions, and circumstances—that is influencing how you're thinking and feeling in your inner reality.

Familiar Memories "Re-mind" Us to Reproduce the Same Experiences

Every day, as you see the same people (your boss, for example, and your spouse and kids), do the same things (drive to work, perform your daily tasks, and do the same workout), go to the same places (your favorite coffee shop, the grocery store you frequent, and your place of employment), and look at the same objects (your car, your house, your toothbrush . . . even your own body), your familiar memories related to your known world "re-mind" you to reproduce the same experiences.

We could say that the environment is actually controlling your mind. Since the neuroscientific definition of *mind* is the brain in action, you repeatedly reproduce the same level of mind by "re-minding" yourself who you think you are in reference to the outer world. Your identity becomes defined by everything outside of you, because you identify with all of the elements that make up your external world. Thus, you're observing your reality with a mind that is equal to it, so you collapse the infinite waves of probabilities of the quantum field into events that reflect the mind you use to experience your life. You create more of the same.

You may not think that your environment and your thoughts are that rigidly similar and your reality so easily reproduced. But when you consider that your brain is a complete record of your past, and your mind is the product of your consciousness, in one sense you might *always be thinking in the past.* By responding with the same brain hardware that matches what you remember, you're creating a level of mind that is identical to the past, because your brain is automatically firing existing circuits to reflect everything you already know, have experienced, and thus can predict. According to quantum law (which, by the way, is still working for you), your past is now becoming your future.

Reason this: When you think from your past memories, you can only create past experiences. As all of the "knowns" in your life cause your brain to think and feel in familiar ways, thus creating knowable outcomes, you continually reaffirm your life as you know it. And since your brain is equal to your environment, then each morning, your senses plug you into the same reality and initiate the same stream of consciousness.

All of the sensory input that your brain processes from the external world (that is, seeing, smelling, hearing, feeling, and tasting) turns your brain on to think equal to everything familiar in your reality. You open your eyes and you know the person lying next to you is your spouse because of your past experiences together. You hear barking outside your door, and you know it's your dog wanting to go out. There's a pain in your back, and you remember it's the same pain you felt yesterday. You associate your outer, familiar world with who you think you are, by remembering yourself in this dimension, this particular time and space.

Our Routines: Plugging into Our Past Self

What do most of us do each morning after we've been plugged into our reality by these sensory reminders of who we are, where we are, and so forth? Well, we remain plugged into this past self by following a highly routine, unconscious set of automatic behaviors.

For example, you probably wake up on the same side of the bed, slip into your robe the same way as always, look into the mirror to remember who you are, and shower following an automatic routine. Then you groom yourself to look like everyone expects you to look, and brush your teeth in your usual memorized fashion. You drink coffee out of your favorite mug and eat your customary breakfast cereal. You put on the jacket you always wear and unconsciously zip it up.

Next, you automatically drive to work along your accustomed, convenient route. At work you do the familiar things that you have memorized how to do so well. You see the same people, who push your same emotional buttons, which causes you to think the same thoughts about those people and your work and your life.

Later, you hurry up and go home, so you can hurry up and eat, so you can hurry up and watch your favorite TV show, so you can hurry up and go to bed, so you can hurry up and do it all over again. Has your brain changed at all that day?

Why are you secretly expecting something different to show up in your life, when you think the same thoughts, perform the same actions, and experience the same emotions every single day? Isn't that the definition of insanity? All of us have fallen prey to this type of limited life, one time or another. By now, you understand the reason why.

In the preceding example, it is safe to say that you're reproducing the same level of mind, every day. And if the quantum world shows that the environment is an extension of your mind (and that mind and matter are one), then as long as your mind remains the same, your life will stay "status quo."

Thus, if your environment remains the same and you react by thinking in the same way, then according to the quantum model of reality, shouldn't you create more of the same? Think of it this way: the input remains the same, so the output has to remain the same. How, then, can you ever create anything *new?*

Hardwired to Hard Times

There is another possible consequence that I should mention, if you keep firing the same neural patterns by living your life the same way each day. Every time you respond to your familiar reality by re-creating the same mind (that is, turning on the same nerve cells to make the brain work in the same way), you "hardwire" your brain to match the customary conditions in your personal reality, be they good or bad.

There is a principle in neuroscience called *Hebb's law.* It basically states that "nerve cells that fire together, wire together." Hebb's credo demonstrates that if you repeatedly activate the same nerve cells, then each time they turn on, it will be easier for them to fire in unison again. Eventually those neurons will develop a long-term relationship.[1]

So when I use the word *hardwired,* it means that clusters of neurons have fired so many times in the same ways that they have organized themselves into specific patterns with long-lasting connections. The more these networks of neurons fire, the more they wire into static routes of activity. In time, whatever the oft-repeated thought, behavior, or feeling is, it will become an automatic, unconscious habit. When your environment is influencing your mind to that extent, *your habitat becomes your habit.*

So if you keep thinking the same thoughts, doing the same things, and feeling the same emotions, you will begin to hardwire your brain into a finite pattern that is the direct reflection of your finite reality. Consequently, it will become easier and more natural for you to reproduce the same mind on a moment-to-moment basis.

This innocent response cycle causes your brain and then your mind to reinforce even further the particular reality that is your external world. The more you fire the same circuits by reacting to your external life, the more you'll wire your brain to be equal to your personal world. You'll become neurochemically attached to the conditions in your life. In time, you'll begin to think "in the box," because your brain will fire a finite set of circuits that then creates a very specific mental signature. This signature is called your *personality.*

How You Form the Habit of Being Yourself

As an effect of this neural habituation, the two realities of the inner mind and the outer world seem to become almost insep-arable. For instance, if you can never stop thinking about your problems, then your mind and your life will merge together as one. The objective world is now colored by the perceptions of your subjective mind, and thus reality continuously conforms. You be-come lost in the illusion of the dream.

You could call this a rut, and we all fall into them, but it goes much deeper than that: not just your actions, but also your at-titudes and your feelings become repetitive. You have formed the habit of being yourself by becoming, in a sense, enslaved to your environment. Your thinking has become equal to the conditions in your life, and thus you, as the quantum observer, are creating a mind that only reaffirms those circumstances into your specific reality. All you are doing is reacting to your external, known, un-changing world.

In a very real way, you have become an effect of circumstances outside of yourself. You have allowed yourself to give up control of your destiny. Unlike Bill Murray's character in the movie *Ground-hog Day,* you're not even fighting against the ceaseless monotony of what you are like and what your life has become. Worse, you aren't the victim of some mysterious and unseen force that has placed you in this repetitive loop—*you* are the creator of the loop.

The good news is that since you created this loop, you can choose to end it.

The quantum model of reality tells us that to change our lives, we must fundamentally change the ways we think, act, and feel. We must change our state of being. Because how we think, feel, and behave is, in essence, our personality, it is our *personality* that creates our *personal reality*. So to create a new personal reality, a new life, we must create a new personality; we must become someone else.

To change, then, is to think and act greater than our present circumstances, greater than our environment.

Greatness Is Holding Fast to a Dream, Independent of the Environment

Before I begin to explore the ways in which you can think greater than your environment and thus break the habit of being yourself, I want to remind you of something.

It is possible to think greater than your present reality, and history books are filled with names of people who have done so, men and women such as Martin Luther King, Jr., William Wallace, Marie Curie, Mahatma Gandhi, Thomas Edison, and Joan of Arc. Every one of these individuals had a concept in his or her mind of a future reality that existed as a potential in the quantum field. This vision was alive in an inner world of possibilities beyond the senses, and in time, each of these people made those ideas a reality.

As a common thread, they all had a dream, vision, or objective that was much larger than they were. They all believed in a future destiny that was so real in their minds that they began to live as if that dream were already happening. They couldn't see, hear, taste, smell, or feel it, but they were so possessed by their dream that they acted in a way that corresponded to this potential reality ahead of time. In other words, they behaved as if what they envisioned was already a reality.

For example, the imperialist dictum that had India under colonial rule in the early 1900s was demoralizing to Indians. Despite that, Gandhi believed in a reality that wasn't yet present in his people's lives. He wholeheartedly endorsed the concepts of equality, freedom, and nonviolence with undying conviction.

Even though Gandhi endorsed liberty for all, the reality of tyranny and British control at that time was quite different. The conventional beliefs of that era were in contrast to his hopes and aspirations. Although the experience of liberty was not a reality while he was initially engaged in changing India, he did not let outward evidence of adversity sway him to give up this ideal.

For a long time, much of the feedback from the external world didn't show Gandhi that he was making a difference. But seldom did he allow the conditions in his environment to control his way of being. He believed in a future that he could not yet see or experience with his senses, but which was so alive in his mind that he could not live any other way. He embraced a new future life while physically living his present life. He understood that the way he was thinking, acting, and feeling would change the current conditions in his environment. And eventually, reality began to change as a result of his efforts.

When our behaviors match our intentions, when our actions are equal to our thoughts, when our minds and our bodies are working together, when our words and our deeds are aligned . . . there is an immense power behind any individual.

History's Giants:
Why Their Dreams Were "Unrealistic Nonsense"

The greatest individuals in history were unwaveringly committed to a future destiny without any need for immediate feedback from the environment. It didn't matter to them if they hadn't yet received any sensory indication or physical evidence of the change they wanted; they must have reminded themselves daily of the reality *they* were focused upon. Their minds were *ahead* of their present environment, because their environment no longer controlled their thinking. Truly, they were ahead of their time.

Another fundamental element shared by each of these celebrated beings was that they were clear in their minds about exactly what they wanted to happen. (Remember, we leave the *how* to a greater mind, and they must have known this.)

Now, some in their day might have called them unrealistic. In fact, they *were* completely unrealistic, and so were their dreams. The event they were embracing in thought, action, and emotion was not realistic, because the reality had not yet occurred. The ignorant and the cynical might also have said their vision was nonsense, and such naysayers would have been right—a vision of future reality was "non-sense"; it existed in a reality beyond the senses.

As another example, Joan of Arc was considered foolhardy, even insane. Her ideas challenged the beliefs of her time and made her a threat to the present political system. But once her vision was made manifest, she was considered profoundly virtuous.

When one holds a dream independent of the environment, that's greatness. Coming up, we'll see that overcoming the environment is inextricably linked with overcoming the body and time. In Gandhi's case, he was not swayed by what was happening in his outer world (environment), he didn't worry about how he felt and what would happen to him (body), and he didn't care how long it would take to realize the dream of freedom (time). He simply knew that all of these elements would sooner or later bend to his intentions.

For all of the giants in history, is it possible that their ideas were thriving in the laboratory of their minds to such an extent that to their brains, it was as though the experience had already happened? Can you, too, change who you are by thought alone?

Mental Rehearsal:
How Our Thoughts Can Become Our Experience

Neuroscience has proven that we can change our brains—and therefore our behaviors, attitudes, and beliefs—just by thinking differently (in other words, without changing anything in our environment). Through *mental rehearsal* (repeatedly imagining performing an action), the circuits in the brain can reorganize themselves to reflect our objectives. We can make our thoughts so real that the brain changes to look like the event has already become a physical reality. We can change it to be ahead of any actual experience in our external world.

Here's an example. In *Evolve Your Brain,* I discussed how research subjects who *mentally* rehearsed one-handed piano exercises for two hours a day for five days (never actually touching any piano keys) demonstrated almost the same brain changes as people who *physically* performed the identical finger movements on a piano keyboard for the same length of time.[2] Functional brain scans showed that all the participants activated and expanded clusters of neurons in the same specific area of the brain. In essence, the group who mentally rehearsed practicing scales and chords grew nearly the same number of brain circuits as the group who physically engaged in the activity.

This study demonstrates two important points. Not only can we change our brains just by thinking differently, but when we are truly focused and single-minded, the brain does not know the difference between the internal world of the mind and what we experience in the external environment. Our thoughts can become our experience.

This notion is critical to your success or failure in your endeavor to replace old habits (prune old neural connections) with new ones (sprout new neural networks). So let's look more closely at how the same learning sequence took place in those people who mentally practiced but never physically played any notes.

❁❁❁

Whether we physically or mentally acquire a skill, there are four elements that we all use to change our brains: learning knowledge, receiving hands-on instruction, paying attention, and repetition.

Learning is making synaptic connections; *instruction* gets the body involved in order to have a new experience, which further enriches the brain. When we also *pay attention* and *repeat* our new skill over and over again, our brains will change.

The group who physically played the scales and chords grew new brain circuits because they followed this formula.

The participants who mentally rehearsed also followed this formula, except that they never got their bodies physically involved. In their minds they were easily able to conceive of themselves playing the piano.

Remember, after these subjects repeatedly mentally practiced, their brains showed the same neurological changes as the participants who actually played the piano. New networks of neurons (neural networks) were forged, demonstrating that in effect, they had already engaged in practicing piano scales and chords without actually having that physical experience. We could say that their brains "existed in the future" ahead of the physical event of playing the piano.

Because of our enlarged human frontal lobe and our unique ability to make thought more real than anything else, the forebrain can naturally "lower the volume" from the external environment so that nothing else is being processed but a single-minded thought. This type of internal processing allows us to become so involved in our mental imaging that the brain will modify its wiring without having experienced the actual event. When we can change our minds independent of the environment and then steadfastly embrace an ideal with sustained concentration, the brain will be *ahead* of the environment.

That is mental rehearsal, an important tool in breaking the habit of being ourselves. If we repeatedly think about something to the exclusion of everything else, we encounter a moment when the thought becomes the experience. When this occurs, the neural hardware is rewired to reflect the thought as the experience. This is the moment that our thinking changes our brains and thus, our minds.

To understand that neurological change can take place in the absence of physical interactions in the environment is crucial to our success in breaking the habit of being ourselves. Consider the larger implications of the finger-exercise experiment. If we apply the same process—mental rehearsal—to anything that we want to do, we can change our brains ahead of any concrete experience.

If you can influence your brain to change *before* you experience a desired future event, you will create the appropriate neural circuits that will enable you to behave in alignment with your intention before it becomes a reality in your life. Through your own repeated mental rehearsal of a better way to think, act, or be, you will "install" the neural hardware needed to physiologically prepare you for the new event.

In fact, you'll do more than that. The brain's hardware, as I use the analogy in this book, refers to its physical structures, its anatomy, right down to its neurons. If you keep installing, reinforcing, and refining your neurological hardware, the end result of that repetition is a neural network—in effect, a new software program. Just like computer software, this program (for example, a behavior, an attitude, or an emotional state) now runs automatically.

Now you've cultivated the brain to be ready for your new experience, and frankly, you have the mind in place so that you can handle the challenge. When you change your mind, your brain changes; and when you change your brain, your mind changes.

So when the time comes to demonstrate a vision contrary to the environmental conditions at hand, it is quite possible for you to be already prepared to think and act, with a conviction that is steadfast and unwavering. In fact, the more you formulate an image of your behavior in a future event, the easier it will be for you to execute a new way of being.

So can you believe in a future you cannot yet see or experience with your senses but have thought about enough times in your mind that your brain is actually changed to look like the experience has already happened ahead of the physical event in your external environment? If so, then your brain is no longer a record of the past, but has become a map to the future.

Now that you know you can change your brain by thinking differently, is it possible to change your body to "look like" it too has had an experience ahead of the actual intended circumstances? Is your mind that powerful? Stay tuned.

CHAPTER THREE

OVERCOMING YOUR BODY

You do not think in a vacuum. Every time you have a thought, there is a biochemical reaction in the brain—you make a chemical. And as you'll learn, the brain then releases specific chemical signals to the body, where they act as messengers of the thought. When the body gets these chemical messages from the brain, it complies instantly by initiating a matching set of reactions directly in alignment with what the brain is thinking. Then the body immediately sends a confirming message back up to the brain that it's now *feeling* exactly the way the brain is *thinking*.

To understand this process—how you typically think equal to your body, and how to form a new mind—you first need to appreciate the role that your brain and its chemistry plays in your life. In the last few decades, we've discovered that the brain and the rest of the body interact via powerful electrochemical signals. There is an extensive chemical factory between our ears that orchestrates a myriad of bodily functions. But relax, this is going to be "Brain Chemistry 101," and a few terms are all that you need to know.

All cells have receptor sites on their exterior surface that receive information from outside their boundaries. When there is a match in chemistry, frequency, and electrical charge between a receptor site and an incoming signal from the outside, the cell gets "turned on" to perform certain tasks.

CELL ACTIVITIES

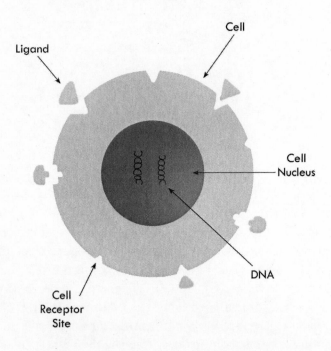

Figure 3A. A cell with receptor sites that receive vital incoming information from outside the cell. The signal can influence the cell to perform myriad biological functions.

Neurotransmitters, neuropeptides, and *hormones* are the cause-and-effect chemicals for brain activity and bodily functioning. These three different types of chemicals, called *ligands* (the word *ligare* means "to bind" in Latin), connect to, interact with, or influence the cell in a matter of milliseconds.

— **Neurotransmitters** are chemical messengers that primarily send signals between nerve cells, allowing the brain and nervous system to communicate. There are different types of neurotransmitters, and each is responsible for a particular activity. Some excite the brain, others slow it down, while still others make us sleepy or awake. They can tell a neuron to unhook from its current connection or make it stick better to its present connection. They can even change the message as it is being sent to a neuron, rewriting it so that a different message is delivered to all the connected nerve cells.

— **Neuropeptides**, the second type of ligand, make up the majority of these messengers. Most are manufactured in a structure of the brain called the hypothalamus (recent studies show that our immune system also makes them). These chemicals are passed through the pituitary gland, which then releases a chemical message to the body with specific instructions.

— As neuropeptides make their way through the bloodstream, they attach to the cells of various tissues (primarily glands) and then turn on the third type of ligand, **hormones**, which further influence us to feel certain ways. Neuropeptides and hormones are the chemicals responsible for our feelings.

For our purposes, think of neurotransmitters as chemical messengers primarily from the brain and mind, neuropeptides as chemical signalers that serve as a bridge between the brain and the body to make us feel the way we think, and hormones as the chemicals related to feelings primarily in the body.

OVERVIEW of the ROLE of LIGANDS in the BRAIN and BODY

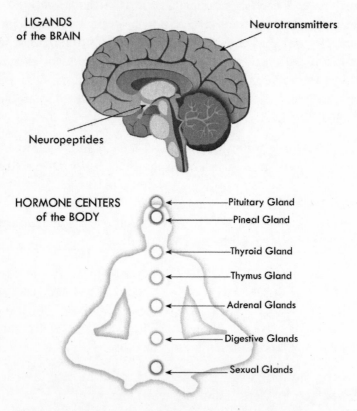

LIGANDS of the BRAIN

Neurotransmitters

Neuropeptides

HORMONE CENTERS of the BODY

Pituitary Gland
Pineal Gland
Thyroid Gland
Thymus Gland
Adrenal Glands
Digestive Glands
Sexual Glands

Figure 3B. Neurotransmitters are diverse chemical messengers between neurons. Neuropeptides are chemical couriers that signal different glands of the body to make hormones.

For example, when you have a sexual fantasy, all three of these factors are called to action. First, as you start to think a few thoughts, your brain whips up some neurotransmitters that turn on a network of neurons, which creates pictures in your mind. These chemicals then stimulate the release of specific neuropeptides into your bloodstream. Once they reach your sexual glands, those peptides bind to the cells of those tissues; they turn on your hormonal system, and—*presto*—things start happening.

You've made your fantasy thoughts so real in your mind that your body starts to get prepared for an actual sexual experience (ahead of the event). That's how powerfully mind and body are related.

By the same means, if you start to think about confronting your teenager over the new dent in the car, your neurotransmitters would start the thought process in your brain to produce a specific level of mind, your neuropeptides would chemically signal your body in a specific way, and you would begin to feel a bit riled up. As the peptides find their way to your adrenal glands, they would then be prompted to release the hormones adrenaline and cortisol—and now you are definitely feeling fired up. Chemically, your body is ready for battle.

The Thinking and Feeling Loop

As you think different thoughts, your brain circuits fire in corresponding sequences, patterns, and combinations, which then produce levels of mind equal to those thoughts. Once these specific networks of neurons are activated, the brain produces specific chemicals with the exact signature to match those thoughts so that you can feel the way you were just thinking.

Therefore, when you have great thoughts or loving thoughts or joyous thoughts, you produce chemicals that make you feel great or loving or joyful. The same holds true if you have negative, fearful, or impatient thoughts. In a matter of seconds, you begin to feel negative or anxious or impatient.

There's a certain synchronicity that takes place moment by moment between the brain and the body. In fact, as we begin to feel the way we are thinking—because the brain is in constant communication with the body—we begin to think the way we are feeling. The brain constantly monitors the way the body is feeling. Based on the chemical feedback it receives, it will generate more thoughts that produce chemicals corresponding to the way the body is feeling, so that we first begin to *feel* the way we *think* and then to *think* the way we *feel*.

CYCLE of THINKING and FEELING

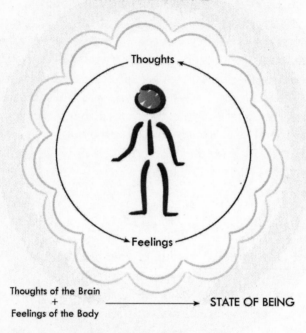

Thoughts

Feelings

Thoughts of the Brain
+   ──────────────▶ STATE OF BEING
Feelings of the Body

Figure 3C. The neurochemical relationship between the brain and the body. As you think certain thoughts, the brain produces chemicals that cause you to feel exactly the way you were thinking. Once you feel the way you think, you begin to think the way you feel. This continuous cycle creates a feedback loop called a "state of being."

We will delve deeper into this idea throughout the book, but consider that thoughts are primarily related to the mind (and the brain), and feelings are connected to the body. Therefore, as the feelings of the *body* align to thoughts from a particular state of *mind*, mind and body are now working together as one. And as you'll recall, when the mind and body are in unison, the end product is called a "state of being." We could also say that the process of continuously thinking and feeling and feeling and thinking creates a state of being, which produces effects on our reality.

A state of being means we have become familiar with a mental-emotional state, a way of thinking and a way of feeling, which has become an integral part of our self-identity. And so we describe who we are by how we are thinking (and thus feeling) or being in the present moment. *I am angry; I am suffering; I am inspired; I am insecure; I am negative. . . .*

But years of thinking certain thoughts, and then feeling the same way, and then thinking equal to those feelings (the hamster in the wheel) creates a *memorized* state of being in which we can emphatically declare our *I am* statement as an absolute. That means we're now at the point when *we define ourselves as this state of being.* Our thoughts and feelings have merged.

For example, we say: *I have always been lazy; I am an anxious person; I am typically uncertain of myself; I have worthiness issues; I am short-tempered and impatient; I am really not that smart;* and so on. And those particular memorized feelings contribute to all our personality traits.

Warning: when feelings become the means of thinking, or if we cannot think greater than how we feel, we can never change. *To change is to think greater than how we feel.* To change is to act greater than the familiar feelings of the memorized self.

As a practical example, let's say you're driving to work this morning and you begin to think about the heated encounter you had a few days ago with a co-worker. As you think the thoughts associated with that person and that particular experience, your brain starts releasing chemicals that circulate through your body. Very quickly, you begin to *feel* exactly the way you were *thinking.* You probably become angry.

Your body sends a message back to your brain, saying, *Yup, I'm feeling really ticked off.* Of course, your brain, which constantly communicates with the body and monitors its internal chemical order, is influenced by the sudden change in the way you're feeling. As a result, you begin to think differently. (The moment you begin to *feel* the way you *think,* you begin to *think* the way you *feel.*) You unconsciously reinforce the same feeling by continuing to think angry and frustrated thoughts, which then make you feel more angry and frustrated. In effect, your feelings are now controlling your thinking. Your body is now driving your mind.

As the cycle goes on, your angry thoughts produce more chemical signals to your body, which activate the adrenal chemicals associated with your angry feelings. Now you become enraged and aggressive. You feel flushed, your stomach is twisted into a knot, your head pounds, and your muscles start to clench. As all those heightened feelings flood the body and change its physiology, this chemical cocktail fires up a set of circuits in the brain, causing you to think equal to those emotions.

Now you're telling your associate off ten different ways in the privacy of your own mind. You indignantly conjure up a litany of past events that validate your present upset, brainstorming through a letter recounting all those complaints you've always wanted to lodge. In your mind, you've already forwarded it to your boss before you even arrive at work. You exit the car dazed and crazed and a breath away from homicidal. Hello, walking, talking model of an angry person . . . and all of this started with a single thought. In this moment, it seems impossible to think greater than you feel—and that's why it's so hard to change.

The result of this cyclic communication between your brain and body is that you tend to react predictably to these kinds of situations. You create patterns of the same familiar thoughts and feelings, you unconsciously behave in automatic ways, and you are mired in these routines. This is how the chemical "you" functions.

Does Your Mind Control Your Body?
Or Does Your Body Control Your Mind?

Why is it so hard to change?

Imagine that your mother loved to suffer, and through long observation, you unconsciously saw that this behavior pattern enabled her to get what she wanted in life. Let's also say that you've had a few tough experiences in your own life, which created quite a bit of suffering for you. Those memories still elicit an emotional reaction, centered around a specific person at a particular place at a certain time in your life. You've thought about the past often enough, and somehow, those memories are easy to recall, even automatic. Now imagine that for more than 20 years, you've practiced thinking and feeling, feeling and thinking, about suffering.

Actually, you no longer need to think about the past event to create the feeling. You can't seem to think or act any other way than how you always feel. You've memorized suffering by your recurrent thoughts and feelings—those related to that incident, as well as other events in your life. Your thoughts about yourself and your life tend to be colored by feelings of victimization and self-pity. Repeating the same thoughts and feelings you've courted for more than 20 years has conditioned your body to remember the feeling of suffering without much conscious thought. This seems so natural and normal now. It's who you are. And anytime you try to change anything about yourself, it's like the road turns back on you. You're right back to your old self.

What most people don't know is that when they think about a highly charged emotional experience, they make the brain fire in the exact sequences and patterns as before; they are firing and wiring their brains to the past by reinforcing those circuits into ever more hardwired networks. They also duplicate the same chemicals in the brain and body (in varying degrees) as if they were experiencing the event again in that moment. Those chemicals begin to train the body to further memorize that emotion. Both the chemical results of thinking and feeling, feeling and thinking, as well as the neurons firing and wiring together, condition the mind and the body into a finite set of automatic programs.

We are capable of reliving a past event over and over, perhaps thousands of times in one lifetime. It is this unconscious repetition that trains the body to remember that emotional state, equal to or better than the conscious mind does. When the body remembers better than the conscious mind—that is, when the body *is* the mind—that's called a *habit*.

Psychologists tell us that by the time we're in our mid-30s, our identity or personality will be completely formed. This means that for those of us over 35, we have memorized a select set of behaviors, attitudes, beliefs, emotional reactions, habits, skills, associative memories, conditioned responses, and perceptions that are now subconsciously programmed within us. Those programs are running us, because the body has become the mind.

This means that we will think the same thoughts, feel the same feelings, react in identical ways, behave in the same manner, believe the same dogmas, and perceive reality the same ways. About 95 percent of who we are by midlife[1] is a series of subconscious programs that have become automatic—driving a car, brushing our teeth, overeating when we're stressed, worrying about our future, judging our friends, complaining about our lives, blaming our parents, not believing in ourselves, and insisting on being chronically unhappy, just to name a few.

Often We Only Appear to Be Awake

Since the body becomes the *subconscious* mind, it's easy to see that in situations when the body becomes the mind, the *conscious* mind no longer has much to do with our behavior. The instant we have a thought, feeling, or reaction, the body runs on automatic pilot. We go unconscious.

Take, for example, a mother driving a minivan to drop her kids off at school. How is she able to navigate traffic, break up arguments, drink her coffee, shift gears, and help her son blow his nose . . . all at once? Much like a computer program, these actions have become automatic functions that can run very fluidly and easily. Mom's body is skillfully doing everything because it has memorized *how* to do all these deeds through much repetition. She no longer has any conscious thought about *how* she does them; they are habitual.

Think about that: 5 percent of the mind is conscious, struggling against the 95 percent that is running subconscious automatic programs. We've memorized a set of behaviors so well that we have become an automatic, habitual body-mind. In fact, when the body has memorized a thought, action, or feeling to the extent that the body *is* the mind—when mind and body are one—we are (in a state of) being the memory of ourselves. And if 95 percent of who we are by age 35 is a set of involuntary programs, memorized behaviors, and habitual emotional reactions, it follows that 95 percent of our day, we are unconscious. We only appear to be awake. Yikes!

So a person may consciously want to be happy, healthy, or free, but the experience of hosting 20 years of suffering and the repeated cycling of those chemicals of pain and pity have subconsciously conditioned the body to be in a habitual state. We live by habit when we're no longer aware of what we're thinking, doing, or feeling; we become unconscious.

The greatest habit we must break is the habit of being ourselves.

When the Body Is Running the Show

Here are some practical illustrations of the body being in a habitual state. Have you ever been unable to consciously remember a phone number? Try as you may, you can't even recall three digits out of the string of numbers required to make the call. And yet, you can pick up the phone and watch as your fingers dial the number. Your conscious, thinking brain can't remember the number, but you've practiced this action so many times with your fingers that your body now knows and remembers better than your brain. (That example was for those of us who grew up before speed dial or cell phones came along; perhaps you've had the same experience with typing your PIN into an ATM or entering a password online.)

Similarly, I can recall times when I worked out at a gym and had a locker with a combination lock. I was so tired after the workout that I couldn't remember the combination. I'd stare at that dial, trying to recall the sequence of three numbers, and they wouldn't surface. However, when I started to twirl the dial, the combination would come back to me, almost as if by magic. Again, this happens because we practiced something so many times that our bodies know better than our conscious minds. The body subconsciously has become the mind.

Remember that 95 percent of who we are by age 35 sits in the same subconscious memory system, in which the body automatically runs a programmed set of behaviors and emotional reactions. In other words, the body is running the show.

When the Servant Becomes the Master

In truth, the body is the servant of the mind. It follows that if the body has become the mind, the servant has become the master. And the former master (the conscious mind) has gone to sleep. The mind might *think* it's still in charge, but the body is influencing decisions equal to its memorized emotions.

Now, let's say the mind wants to get back in control. What do you think the body is going to say?

Where have you been? Go back to sleep. I've got it together here. You don't have the will, the persistence, or the awareness to do what I have been doing all this time while you were unconsciously following my orders. I even modified my receptor sites over the years in order to serve you better. You thought you were running things, while I have been influencing you all along and urging you to make all of your decisions equal to what feels right and familiar.

And when the 5 percent that is conscious is going against 95 percent that is running subconscious automatic programs, the 95 percent is so reflexive that it only takes one stray thought or a single stimulus from the environment to turn on the automatic program again. Then we're back to same old, same old—thinking the same thoughts, performing the same actions, *but expecting something different to happen in our lives.*

When we try to regain control, this is when the body signals the brain to begin talking us out of our conscious goals. Our internal chatter comes up with a battery of reasons why we should not attempt to do anything out of the ordinary, not break out of the habituated state of being that we're used to. It will pick up all of our weaknesses, which it knows and fosters, and hurl them at us one by one.

We create worst-case scenarios in our minds so that we don't have to rise above those familiar feelings. Because when we try to break the internal chemical order we have made so second nature, the body goes into chaos. Its internal badgering feels nearly irresistible—and plenty of times, we succumb.

Enter into the Subconscious to Change It

The subconscious mind only knows what you have programmed it to do. Have you ever been typing along on your laptop, and all of a sudden your computer starts running automatic programs that you have no control over? When you try to use the conscious mind to stop the automatic, subconscious programs stored in your body, it's like yelling at a computer that's gone rogue, with several programs running while windows are popping up and showing more than you can handle. *Hey! Stop that!* The computer isn't even going to register that. It's going to keep doing what it does until there is some sort of intervention—until you get into its operating system and change some settings.

In this book, you will learn how to get into the subconscious, and reprogram it with a new set of strategies. In effect, you have to *unlearn,* or unwire, your old thinking and feeling patterns and then *relearn,* or rewire, your brain with new patterns of thinking and feeling, based on who you want to be instead. When you condition the body with a new mind, the two can no longer work in opposition, but must be in harmony. This is the point of change . . . of self-creation.

Guilty Until Proven Innocent

Let's use a real-life situation to illustrate what happens when we decide to break from some memorized emotional state and change our minds. I think we can all relate to one common state of being: *guilt.* So I'm going to use that to illustrate in practical terms how this cycle of thinking and feeling works against us. Then we'll identify some of the efforts the brain-body system is going to make to remain in control and preserve that negative state of being.

Imagine that you frequently feel guilty about one thing or another. If something goes wrong in a relationship—a simple miscommunication, someone unreasonably misplacing his or her anger on you, or whatever—you wind up taking the blame and feeling bad. Picture yourself as one of those people who repeatedly say or think, *It was my fault.*

After 20 years of doing this to yourself, you feel guilty and think guilty thoughts automatically. You have created an environment of guilt for yourself. Other factors have contributed to this, but for now, let's stay with this notion of how your thinking and feeling have created your state of being and your environment.

Every time you think a guilty thought, you've signaled your body to produce the specific chemicals that make up the feeling of guilt. You've done this so often that your cells are swimming in a sea of guilt chemicals.

The receptor sites on your cells adapt so that they can better take in and process this particular chemical expression, that of guilt. The enormous amount of guilt bathing the cells begins to feel normal to them, and eventually, what the body perceives as normal starts to be interpreted as pleasurable. It's like living for years near an airport. You get so used to the noise that you no longer hear it consciously, unless one jet flies lower than usual and the roar of its engines is so much louder that it gets your attention. The same thing happens to your cells. As a result, they literally become desensitized to the chemical feeling of guilt; they will require a stronger, more powerful emotion from you—a higher threshold of stimuli—to turn on the next time. And when that stronger "hit" of guilt chemicals gets the body's attention, your cells "perk up" at that stimulation, much like that first cup of java feels to a coffee drinker.

And when each cell divides at the end of its life and makes a daughter cell, the receptor sites on the outside of the new cell will require a higher threshold of guilt to turn them on. Now the body demands a stronger emotional rush of feeling bad in order to feel *alive.* You become addicted to guilt by your own doing.

When anything goes wrong or is awry in your life, you automatically assume that you're the guilty party. But that seems normal to you now. You don't even have to think about feeling guilty—you just *are* that way. Not only is your mind not conscious of how you express your guilty state by way of the things you say and do, but your body wants to feel its accustomed *level* of guilt, because that's what you have trained it to do. You have become unconsciously guilty most of the time—your body has become the mind of guilt.

Only when, say, a friend points out that you needn't have apologized to the store clerk for giving you the wrong change do you realize how pervasive this aspect of your personality has become. Let's say that this triggers one of those moments of enlightenment—an epiphany—and you think, *She's right. Why do I apologize all the time? Why do I take responsibility for everyone else's missteps?* After you reflect on your history of constantly "pleading guilty," you say to yourself, *Today I'm going to stop blaming myself and making excuses for other people's bad behavior. I'm going to change.*

Because of your decision, you're no longer going to think the same thoughts that produce the same feelings, and vice versa. And if you falter, you've made a deal with yourself that you're going to stop and remember your intention. Two hours go by and you feel really good about yourself. You think, *Wow, this is actually working.*

Unfortunately, your body's cells aren't feeling so good. Over the years, you've trained them to demand more molecules of emotion (guilt, in this case) in order to fulfill their chemical needs. You had trained your body to live as a memorized chemical continuity, but now you're interrupting that, denying it its chemical needs and going contrary to its subconscious programs.

The body becomes addicted to guilt or any emotion in the same way that it would get addicted to drugs.[2] At first you only need a little of the emotion/drug in order to feel it; then your body becomes desensitized, and your cells require more and more of it just to feel the same again. Trying to change your emotional pattern is like going through drug withdrawal.

Once your cells are no longer getting the usual signals from the brain about feeling guilty, they begin to express concern. Before, the body and the mind were working together to produce this state of being called guilt; now you are no longer thinking and feeling, feeling and thinking, in the same way. Your intention is to produce more positive thoughts, but the body is still all revved up to produce feelings of guilt based on guilty thoughts.

Think of this as a kind of highly specialized assembly line. Your brain has programmed the body to expect one part that will fit into this larger assembly. All of a sudden, you've sent it another part that doesn't fit into the space where the old "guilty" part once did. An alarm goes off, and the whole operation comes to a standstill.

Your cells are always spying on what is happening in the brain and the mind; your body is the best mind reader ever. So they all stop what they are doing, look up toward the brain, and think:

What are you doing up there? You insisted on being guilty, and we loyally followed your commands for years! We subconsciously memorized a program of guilt from your repetitive thoughts and feelings. We changed our receptor sites to reflect your mind—modified our chemistry so that you could automatically feel guilty. We have maintained your internal chemical order, independent of any external circumstances in your life. We are so used to the same chemical order that your new state of being feels uncomfortable, unfamiliar. We want the familiar, the predictable, and what feels natural. All of a sudden you're going to change? We can't have that!

So the cells huddle up and say: *Let's send a protest message to the brain. But we have to be sneaky, because we want her to think that she's actually responsible for these thoughts. We don't want her to know they came from us.* So now the cells send a message marked URGENT right up the spinal cord to the surface of the thinking brain. I call that the "fast track," because the message goes straight up the central nervous system in a matter of seconds.

At the same time this is happening, the chemistry of the body—the chemistry of guilt—is now at a lower level, because you're not thinking and feeling the same way. But this drop does not go unnoticed. A thermostat in the brain called the hypothalamus also sends out an alarm that says: *Chemical values are going down. We've got to make more!*

So the hypothalamus signals the thinking brain to revert back to its old habitual ways. This is the "slow track," because it takes longer for the chemicals to circulate through the bloodstream. The body wants you to return to your memorized chemical self, so it influences you to think in familiar, routine ways.

These "fast track" and "slow track" cellular responses occur simultaneously. And the next thing you know, you start to hear the chatter of thoughts like these in your head: *You're too tired today. You can start tomorrow. Tomorrow's a better day. Really, you can do it later.* And my favorite: *This doesn't feel right.*

If that doesn't work, a second sneak attack occurs. The body-mind wants to be in control again, so it starts picking on you a bit: *It's okay for you to feel a little bad right now. It's your father's fault. Don't you feel bad about what you did in your past? In fact, let's take a look at your past so we can remember why you are this way. Look at you—you're a mess, a loser. You're pathetic and weak. Your life is a failure. You'll never change. You're too much like your mother. Why don't you just quit.* As you continue this "awfulizing," the body is tempting the mind to return to the state it has unconsciously memorized. On a rational level, that is absurd. But obviously, on some level it feels good to feel bad.

The moment we listen to those subvocalizations, believe those thoughts, and respond by feeling the same familiar feelings, mental amnesia sets in and we forget our original aim. The funny thing is that we actually begin to *believe* what the body is telling the brain to say to us. We immerse ourselves back into that automatic program and return to being our old self.

Most of us can relate to this little scenario. It's no different from any habit we've tried to break. Whether we're addicted to cigarettes, chocolate, alcohol, shopping, gambling, or biting our nails, the moment we cease the habitual action, chaos rages between the body and the mind. The thoughts we embrace are intimately identified with the feelings of what it would be like to experience the indulgence. When we give in to the cravings, we will keep producing the same outcomes in our lives, because the mind and body are in opposition. Our thoughts and feelings are working against each other, and if the body has become the mind, we will always fall prey to how we feel.

As long as we use familiar feelings as a barometer, as feedback on our efforts to change, we'll always talk ourselves out of greatness. We will never be able to think greater than our internal environment. We will never be able to see a world of possible outcomes other than the negative ones from our past. Our thoughts and feelings have that much power over us.

Help Is Only a Thought Away

The next step in breaking the habit of being ourselves is understanding how important it is to get the mind and body working together and to break the chemical continuity of our guilty, ashamed, angry, depressed state of being. Resisting the body's demand to restore that old unhealthy order isn't easy, but help is only a thought away.

You will learn in the following pages that for true change to occur, it is essential to "unmemorize" an emotion that has become part of your personality, and then to recondition the body to a new mind.

It's easy to feel hopeless when we realize that the chemistry of our emotions has habituated our bodies to a state of being that is too often a product of anger, jealousy, resentment, sadness, and so forth. After all, I've said that these programs, these propensities, are buried in our subconscious.

The good news is that we can become consciously aware of these tendencies. I'll deal more with this concept in the pages ahead. For now, I hope you can accept that to change your personality, you need to change your state of being, which is intimately connected to feelings that you've memorized. Just as negative emotions can become embedded in the operating system of your subconscious, so can positive ones.

By Itself, Conscious Positive Thinking Cannot Overcome Subconscious Negative Feelings

At one time or another, we've all consciously declared: *I want to be happy.* But until the body is instructed otherwise, it's going to continue expressing those programs of guilt or sadness or anxiety.

The conscious, intellectual mind may reason that it wants joy, but the body has been programmed to feel otherwise for years. We stand on a soapbox proclaiming change to be in our best interests, but on a visceral level we can't seem to bring up the feeling of true happiness. That's because mind and body aren't working together. The conscious mind wants one thing, but the body wants another.

If you've been devoted to feeling negatively for years, those feelings have created an automatic state of being. We could say that you are subconsciously unhappy, right? Your body has been conditioned to be negative; it knows how to be unhappy better than your conscious mind knows otherwise. You don't even have to think about how to be negative. You just know that it's how you are. How can your conscious mind control this attitude in the subconscious body-mind?

Some maintain that "positive thinking" is the answer. I want to be clear that *by itself,* positive thinking never works. Many so-called positive thinkers have felt negative most of their lives, and now they're trying to think positively. They are in a polarized state in which they are *trying* to think one way in order to override how they feel inside of them. They consciously think one way, but they are *being* the opposite. *When the mind and body are in opposition, change will never happen.*

Memorized Feelings Limit Us to Re-creating the Past

By definition, emotions are the end products of past experiences in life.

When you're in the midst of an experience, the brain receives vital information from the external environment through five different sensory pathways (sight, smell, sound, taste, and touch). As that cumulative sensory data reaches the brain and is processed, networks of neurons arrange themselves into specific patterns reflecting the external event. The moment those nerve cells string into place, the brain releases chemicals. Those chemicals are called an "emotion" or a "feeling." (In this book, I use the words *feelings* and *emotions* interchangeably because they are close enough for our understanding.)

When those emotions begin to chemically flood your body, you detect a change in your internal order (you're thinking and feeling differently than you were moments before). Naturally, when you notice this change in your internal state, you'll pay attention to whoever or whatever in your external environment caused that change. When you can identify whatever it was in your outer world that caused your internal change, that event in and of itself is called a *memory*. Neurologically and chemically, you encode that environmental information into your brain and body. Thus you can remember experiences better because you recall how they felt at the time they happened—feelings and emotions are a chemical record of past experiences.

For example, your boss arrives for your performance review. You notice immediately that he looks red faced, even irritated. As he starts speaking in a loud voice, you smell garlic on his breath. He accuses you of undermining him in front of other employees, and says he has passed you over for a promotion. In this moment you feel jittery, weak in the knees, and queasy; and your heart is racing. You feel fearful, betrayed, and angry. All of the cumulative sensory information—everything you're smelling, seeing, feeling, and hearing—is changing your internal state. You associate that external experience with a change in how you're feeling internally, and it brands you emotionally.

You go home and repeatedly review this experience in your mind. Every time you do, you remind yourself of the accusing, intimidating look on your employer's face, how he yelled at you, what he said, and even how he smelled. Then you once again feel fearful and angry; you produce the same chemistry in your brain and body as if the performance review is still happening. Because your body believes it is experiencing the same event again and again, you are conditioning it to live in the past.

Let's reason this a bit further. Think of your body as the unconscious mind, or as an objective servant that takes orders from your consciousness. It is so objective that it doesn't know the difference between the emotions that are created from experiences in your external world and those you fabricate in your internal world by thought alone. To the body, they are the same.

What if this cycle of thinking and feeling that you were betrayed continues for years on end? If you keep dwelling on that experience with your boss or reliving those familiar feelings, day in and day out, you continually signal your body with chemical feelings that it associates with the past. This chemical continuity fools the body into believing that it is still reexperiencing the past, so the body keeps reliving the same emotional experience. When your memorized thoughts and feelings consistently force your body to "be in" the past, we could say that the body becomes the memory of the past.

If those memorized feelings of betrayal have been driving your thoughts for years, then your body has been living in the past 24 hours a day, 7 days a week, 52 weeks a year. In time, your body is anchored in the past.

You know that when you repeatedly re-create the same emotions until you cannot think any greater than how you feel, your feelings are now the means of your thinking. And since your feelings are a record of previous experiences, you're thinking in the past. And by quantum law, you create more of the past.

Bottom line: Most of us live in the past and resist living in a new future. Why? The body is so habituated to memorizing the chemical records of our past experiences that it grows attached to these emotions. In a very real sense, we become addicted to those familiar feelings. So when we want to look to the future and dream of new vistas and bold landscapes in our not-too-distant reality, the body, whose currency is feelings, resists the sudden change in direction.

Accomplishing this about-face is the great labor of personal change. So many people struggle to create a new destiny, but find themselves unable to overcome the past memory of who they feel they are. Even if we crave unknown adventures and dream of new possibilities ahead in the future, we seem to be compelled to re-visit the past.

Feelings and emotions are not bad. They are the end products of experience. But if we always relive the same ones, we can't embrace any *new* experiences. Have you known people who always seem to talk about "the good old days"? What they're really saying is: *Nothing new is happening in my life to stimulate my feelings; therefore I'll have to reaffirm myself from some glorious moments in the past.* If we believe that our thoughts have something to do with our destiny, then as creators, most of us are only going in circles.

Controlling Our Inner Environment: The Genetic Myth

So far, in discussing how the quantum model of reality relates to change, I've spent most of the time talking about our emotions, the brain, and the body. We've seen that overcoming the recurring thoughts and feelings that the body memorizes is a must if we are to break the habit of being ourselves.

Another major aspect of breaking this habit has to do with our physical health. Certainly, in the hierarchy of things that most of us want to change about our lives, health issues rank way up there. And when it comes to what we'd like to change about our health, there is one set of dogmas that we're going to have to examine and dispel—the myth that genes create disease and the fallacy of genetic determinism. We will also look at a scientific understanding that may be new to you, called *epigenetics:* the control of genes from outside the cell, or more precisely, the study of changes in gene function that occur without a change in DNA sequence.[3]

Just as we can create new experiences for ourselves, like my daughter did, we can also gain control of a very important part of our lives—what we commonly think of as our genetic destiny. As we go along, you will see that knowing something about your genes and what signals them to be expressed or not is crucial to understanding why you have to change from the inside out.

Scientific dictum used to declare that our genes were responsible for most diseases. Then a couple of decades ago, the scientific community casually mentioned that they had been in error, and announced that the environment, by activating or deactivating particular genes, is the most causative factor in producing disease. We now know that less than 5 percent of all diseases today stem from single-gene disorders (such as Tay-Sachs and Huntington's chorea), whereas around 95 percent of all illnesses are related to lifestyle choices, chronic stress, and toxic factors in the environment.[4]

Yet factors in the outer environment are only part of the picture. What explains why two people can be exposed to the same toxic environmental conditions and one gets sick or diseased while the other doesn't? How is it that when someone has multiple personality disorder, one personality can demonstrate a severe allergy to something, while another personality in that same body can be immune to the same antigen or stimulus? Why, when most health-care providers are exposed to pathogens on a daily basis, aren't doctors and others in the medical community continually ill?

There are also numerous case studies documenting identical twins (who share the same genes) who have had very different experiences when it came to their health and longevity. For example, if both shared a family history of a particular disease, that illness often manifested in one twin but not the other. Same genes, different outcomes.[5]

In all these cases, could the person who remains healthy have such a coherent, balanced, vital internal order that even when his or her body is exposed to the same hazardous environmental conditions, the external world does nothing to his or her gene expression, and so doesn't signal the genes to create disease?

It's true that the external environment influences our internal environment. However, by changing our internal state of being, can we overcome the effects of a stressful or toxic environment so that certain genes do not become activated? We may not be able to control all the conditions in our external environment, but we certainly have a choice in controlling our *inner* environment.

Genes: Memories of the Past Environment

To explain how we can control our inner environment, I need to talk a bit about the nature of genes, which are expressed in the body when cells manufacture specific proteins, the building blocks of life.

The body is a protein-producing factory. Muscle cells make muscle proteins that are called *actin* and *myosin,* skin cells make skin proteins called *collagen* and *elastin,* and stomach cells make stomach proteins called *enzymes.* Most of the cells of the body make proteins, and genes are the way we make them. We express particular genes via certain cells making particular proteins.

The way most organisms adapt to conditions in their environment is through gradual genetic modifications. For example, when an organism is faced with tough environmental conditions such as temperature extremes, dangerous predators, fast prey, destructive winds, strong currents, and so on, it is forced to overcome the adverse aspects of its world in order to survive. As organisms record those experiences, in the wiring in their brains and the emotions in their bodies, they will change over time. If lions are chasing prey that can outrun them, then by actively engaging the same experiences for generations, they will develop longer legs, sharper teeth, or bigger hearts. All of these changes are the result of genes making proteins that modify the body to adapt to its environment.

Let's stay with the animal world to look at how this works in terms of adaptation or evolution. A hypothetical group of mammals migrated to an environment in which the temperature ranged from –15 to 40 degrees Fahrenheit. The genes in those mammals, over many generations of living under extremely cold conditions, would eventually be triggered to produce a new protein, which would produce thicker and greater amounts of fur (hair and fur are proteins).

Numerous insect species have evolved the ability to camouflage themselves. Some that live in trees or other foliage have adapted to look like twigs or thorns, enabling them to escape the notice of birds. The chameleon is probably the best known of the "camouflagers," and it owes its color-changing abilities to the genetic expression of proteins. In these processes, genes encode the conditions of the external world. That's evolution, right?

Epigenetics Suggests That We Can Signal Our Genes to Rewrite Our Future

Our genes are as changeable as our brains. The latest research in genetics shows that different genes are activated at different times—they are always in flux and being influenced. There are experience-dependent genes that are activated when there is growth, healing, or learning; and there are behavioral-state-dependent genes that are influenced during stress, emotional arousal, or dreaming.[6]

One of the most active areas of research today is *epigenetics* (literally, "above genetics"), the study of how the environment controls gene activity. Epigenetics flies in the face of the conventional genetic model, which stated that DNA controls all of life and that all gene expression takes place inside the cell. This old understanding doomed us to a predictable future in which our destiny fell prey to our genetic inheritance, and all cellular life was predetermined, like an automatic "ghost in the machine."

In fact, epigenetic changes in DNA expression can be passed on to future generations. But how do they get passed on if the DNA code stays the same?

While a scientific explanation is beyond the scope of this book, we can use an analogy. Let's compare a genetic sequence to a blueprint. Imagine that you start with a blueprint for a house, and scan it into your computer. Then, using Photoshop, you could alter its appearance on the screen, changing a number of characteristics without changing the blueprint. For example, you could change the expression of variables such as color, size, scale, dimensions, materials, and so on. Thousands of people (representing environmental variables) could produce different images, but they would all be expressions of that same blueprint.

Epigenetics empowers us to think about change more profoundly. The epigenetic paradigm shift gives us free will to activate our own gene activity and modify our genetic destiny. For the sake of example and simplification, when I talk about activating a gene by expressing it in different ways, I will refer to "turning it on." In reality, genes don't turn on or off; they are activated by chemical signals, and they express themselves in specific ways by making various proteins.

Just by changing our thoughts, feelings, emotional reactions, and behaviors (for example, making healthier lifestyle choices with regard to nutrition and stress level), we send our cells new signals, and they express new proteins without changing the genetic blueprint. So while the DNA code stays the same, once a cell is activated in a new way by new information, the cell can create thousands of variations of the same gene. We can signal our genes to rewrite our future.

Perpetuating Old States of Being Sets Us Up for an Undesirable Genetic Destiny

Just as certain areas of the brain are hardwired, whereas other areas are more *plastic* (able to be changed by learning and experience), I believe genes are the same way. There are certain parts of our genetics that are more easily turned on; while other genetic sequences are somewhat more hardwired, which means they are harder to activate, because they have been around longer in our genetic history. At least, that's what science says right now.

How do we keep certain genes turned on and others turned off? If we stay in the same toxic state of anger, the same melancholy state of depression, the same vigilant state of anxiety, or the same low state of unworthiness, those redundant chemical signals we have talked about keep pushing the same genetic buttons, which ultimately cause the activation of certain diseases. Stressful emotions, as you will learn, actually pull the genetic trigger, dysregulating the cells (*dysregulation* refers to impairment of a physiological regulatory mechanism) and creating disease.

When we think and feel in the same ways for most of our lives and memorize familiar states of being, our internal chemical state keeps activating the same genes, meaning that we keep making the same proteins. But the body cannot adapt to these repeated demands, and it begins to break down. If we do that for 10 or 20 years, the genes begin to wear out, and they start making "cheaper" proteins. What do I mean? Think about what happens when we age. Our skin sags because its collagen and elastin come to be made of cheaper proteins. What happens to our muscles? They atrophy. Well, no surprise there—actin and myosin, too, are proteins.

Here's an analogy. When a metal part for your car is manufactured, it is produced in a die or a mold. Each time that mold or die is used, it is subjected to certain forces, including heat and friction, which begin to wear it down. As you might guess, car parts are built to very close tolerances (referring to the permitted variation in a workpiece's dimensions). Over time, that die or mold wears to the point that it produces parts that won't fit properly to other parts. This is similar to what happens to the body. As a result of stress or a habit of being repeatedly and consistently angry, fearful, sad, and so on, the DNA that the peptides use to produce proteins will start to malfunction.

What is the genetic impact if we stay in routine, familiar conditions—creating the same emotional reactions by doing the same things, thinking the same thoughts, seeing the same people, and memorizing our lives into a predictable pattern? We are now headed for an undesirable genetic destiny; we are locked into the same patterns as generations before us, which confronted the same or similar situations. And if we are only reliving our emotional memories of the past, then we are headed for a predictable end— our bodies will begin to create the same genetic conditions that previous generations faced.

Thus, the body will stay the same as long as we are feeling the same way, day in and day out. And if science tells us that it is the environment that signals the genes involved in evolution, what if our environment never changes? What if we've memorized the same conditions in our outer world and we're living by the same thoughts, behaviors, and feelings? What if everything in our lives stays the same?

⚬⚬⚬

You just learned that the external environment chemically signals genes through the emotions of an experience. So if the experiences in your life aren't changing, the chemical signals going to your genes aren't changing. No new information from the outer world is reaching your cells.

The quantum model asserts that we can signal the body emotionally and begin to alter a chain of genetic events without first having any actual physical experience that correlates to that emotion. We don't need to win the race, the lottery, or the promotion before we experience the emotions of those events. Remember, we can create an emotion by thought alone. We can experience joy or gratitude ahead of the environment to such an extent that the body begins to believe that it is already "in" that event. As a result, we can signal our genes to make new proteins to change our bodies to be ahead of the present environment.

Can Elevated States of Mind Produce Healthier Expression of Genes?

Here's an example of how we can signal new genes in new ways when we begin to emotionally embrace an event in the future before it is made manifest.

In Japan, a study was conducted to find out what effect one's state of mind might have on disease. The subjects were two groups of patients with type 2 diabetes, all of whom were dependent on insulin. Keep in mind that most diabetics medicate with insulin to remove sugar (glucose) out of the bloodstream and deposit it in the cells, where it can be used for energy. At the time of this study, the people involved were being treated with insulin pills or injections to help control their elevated blood-sugar levels.[7]

Each group had their fasting blood-sugar level tested to establish a baseline. Next, one set of subjects watched a comedy show for an hour, while the control group watched a boring lecture. The test subjects then ate a delicious meal, after which their blood-glucose levels were checked again.

There was a significant discrepancy between the subjects who enjoyed the comedy show and those who viewed the uneventful lecture. On average, those who watched the lecture had their blood-sugar levels rise 123 mg/dl—high enough that they would need to take insulin to keep themselves out of the danger zone. In the joyful group, who had laughed for one hour, their after-dinner blood-sugar values rose about half that amount (slightly outside of normal range).

Initially, the researchers who performed the experiment thought that the lighthearted subjects had lowered their sugar levels by contracting their abdominal and diaphragm muscles when they laughed. They reasoned that when a muscle contracts, it uses energy—and circulating energy is glucose.

But the research went further. They examined the gene sequences of the jovial individuals and discovered that these diabetics had altered 23 different gene expressions just by laughing at the comedy show they'd seen. Their elevated state of mind apparently triggered their brains to send new signals to their cells, which turned on those genetic variations that allowed their bodies to naturally begin to regulate the genes responsible for processing blood sugar.

Our emotions can turn on some gene sequences and turn off others, this study clearly showed. Just by signaling the body with a new emotion, the laughing subjects altered their internal chemistry to change the expression of their genes.

Sometimes a change in genetic expression can be sudden and dramatic. Have you ever heard of people, after being subjected to extremely stressful conditions, whose hair turned gray overnight? That's an example of genes at work. They experienced such a strong emotional reaction that their altered body chemistry both turned on the gene for the expression of gray hair and shut off the genetic expression for their normal hair color, within a matter of hours. They signaled new genes in new ways by emotionally, and thus chemically, altering their internal environment.

As I discussed in the last chapter, when you've "experienced" an event numerous times by mentally rehearsing every aspect of it in your mind, you feel what that event would feel like, before it unfolds. Then as you change the circuitry in your brain by thinking in new ways, and you embrace the emotions of an event ahead of its physical manifestation, it's possible that you can change your body genetically.

Can you pick a potential from the quantum field (every potential already exists, by the way) and emotionally embrace a future event before the actual experience? Can you do this so many times that you emotionally condition the body to a new mind, thus signaling new genes in new ways? If you can, it is highly possible that you will begin to shape and mold your brain and body into a new expression . . . so that they physically change before the desired potential reality is made manifest.

Changing Your Body: Why Lift a Finger?

We may believe that we can change our brains by thinking, but what effects, if any, will this have on the body? Through the simple process of mentally rehearsing an activity, we can derive great benefits without lifting a finger. Here's an example of how that *literally* happened.

As described in an article published in the 1992 *Journal of Neurophysiology*,[8] subjects were divided into three groups:

- The first group was asked to exercise by contracting and relaxing one finger on their left hand, for five one-hour training sessions per week for four weeks.

- A second group *mentally rehearsed* the same exercises, on the same timetable, without physically activating any muscles in the finger.

- People in a control group exercised neither their fingers nor their minds.

At the end of the study, the scientists compared the findings. The first set of participants had their finger strength tested against the control group. A no-brainer, right? The group who did the actual exercises exhibited 30 percent greater finger strength than those in the control group. We all know that if we repeatedly put a load on a muscle, we will increase the strength of that muscle. What we probably wouldn't anticipate is that the group who mentally rehearsed the exercises demonstrated a 22 percent increase in muscle strength! The mind, then, produced a quantifiable physical effect on the body. In other words, the body changed without having an actual physical experience.

Just as researchers have worked with test subjects who mentally rehearsed finger exercises and others who imagined playing piano scales, experiments have compared practical experience versus mental rehearsal for individuals doing bicep curls. The results were the same. Whether the participants physically performed bicep curls or mentally rehearsed those activities, they all increased their bicep strength. The mental exercisers, though, demonstrated physiological changes without ever having the physical experience.[9]

When the body has changed physically/biologically to look like an experience has happened just by thought or mental efforts alone, then from a quantum perspective, this offers evidence that the event has already transpired in our reality. If the brain upgrades its hardware to look like the experience physically occurred and the body is changed genetically or biologically (it is showing evidence that it happened), and both are different without our "doing" anything in three dimensions, then the event has occurred both in the quantum world of consciousness *and* in the world of physical reality.

When you have thoughtfully rehearsed a future reality until your brain has physically changed to look like it has had the experience, and you have emotionally embraced a new intention so many times that your body is altered to reflect that *it* has had the experience, hang on . . . because this is the moment the event finds you! And it will arrive in a way that you least expect, which leaves no doubt that it came from your relationship to a greater consciousness—so that it inspires you to do it again and again.

❀❀❀❀

CHAPTER FOUR

OVERCOMING TIME

So much has been written about the importance of staying present. I could cite statistics on everything from distracted driving to divorce to support the notion that people have a really hard time staying in the present moment. Let me add to that body of knowledge by expressing this concept in quantum terms. In the present, all potentials exist simultaneously in the field. When we stay present, when we are "in the moment," we can move beyond space and time, and we can make any one of those potentials a reality. When we are mired in the past, however, none of those new potentials exist.

You've learned that when human beings try to change, we react much like addicts, because we become addicted to our familiar chemical states of being. You know that when you have an addiction, it is almost as if your body has a mind of its own. As past events trigger the same chemical response as the original incident, your body thinks it is reexperiencing the same event. Once conditioned to *be* the subconscious mind through this process, the body has taken over for the mind—it has become the mind and therefore can, in a sense, think.

I just touched upon how the body becomes the mind by the cycle of thinking and feeling, feeling and thinking. But there is another way in which this occurs, based on past memories.

Here is how it works: You have an experience, which has an emotional charge. Then you have a thought about that particular past event. The thought becomes a memory, which then reflexively reproduces the emotion of the experience. If you keep thinking about that memory repeatedly, the thought, the memory, and the emotion merge as one, and you "memorize" the emotion. Now living in the past becomes less of a conscious process and more of a *subconscious* one.

MEMORIZING EMOTIONS

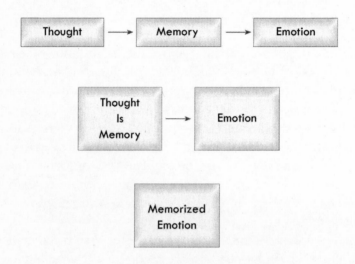

Figure 4A. The thought produces a memory, which creates an emotion. In time, the thought becomes the memory, and an emotion follows. If this process is repeated enough times, the thought is the memory, which is the emotion. We memorize the emotion.

The subconscious comprises most physical and mental processes that take place below our conscious awareness. Much of its activity is involved in keeping the body functioning. Scientists refer to this regulatory system as the *autonomic nervous system.* We don't have to consciously think about breathing, keeping our hearts beating, raising and lowering our body temperature, or any of the other millions of processes that help the body maintain order and heal itself.

I think that you can see how potentially dangerous it is for us to cede control over our daily emotional responses to our memories and environment—to this automatic system. This subconscious set of routine responses has been variously compared to an autopilot system and to programs running in the background of a computer. What those analogies are trying to convey is the sense that there is something below the surface of our awareness that is in control of how we behave.

Here's an example to reinforce these points. Imagine that in your youth, you came home one day and discovered your favorite pet lying dead on the floor. Every sensory impression of that experience would be, as the expression goes, burned into your brain. That experience would scar you.

With traumatic experiences like that, it's easy to understand how those emotions can become unconscious, memorized responses to reminders from your environment that you lost a loved one. You know by now that when you think about that experience, you create the same emotions in your brain and body as if the event was occurring all over again. All it takes is one stray thought, or one reaction to some event in the external world, to activate that program—and you start feeling the emotion of your past grief. The trigger could be seeing a dog that looks like yours, or visiting a place you once took him as a puppy. Regardless of the sensory input, it activates an emotion. Those emotional triggers can be obvious or subtle, but they all affect you at a subconscious level, and before you can process what has happened, you're back in that emotional/chemical state of grief, anger, and sadness.

Once that happens, the body runs the mind. You can use your conscious mind to try to get out of that emotional state, but invariably you feel like you're out of control.

Think of Pavlov and his dogs. In the 1890s, the young Russian scientist strapped a few dogs to a table, rang a bell, and then fed the canines a hearty meal. Over time, after repeatedly exposing the dogs to the same stimulus, he simply rang the bell, and the dogs automatically salivated in anticipation.

This is called a *conditioned response,* and the process occurs automatically. Why? Because the body begins to respond autonomically (think of our *autonomic* nervous system). The cascade of chemical reactions that is triggered within moments changes the body physiologically, and it happens quite subconsciously—with little or no conscious effort.

This is one of the reasons why it is so hard to change. The conscious mind may be in the present, but the subconscious body-mind is living in the past. If we begin to expect a predictable future event to occur in reference to a memory of the past, we are just like those canines. One experience of a particular person or thing at a specific time and place from the past automatically (or autonomically) causes us to respond physiologically.

Once we break the emotional addictions rooted in our past, there will no longer be any pull to cause us to return to the same automatic programs of the old self.

It begins to make sense that although we "think" or "believe" we are living in the present, there is a good possibility that our bodies are in the past.

Emotions to Moods to Temperaments to Personality Traits: Conditioning the Body to Live in the Past

Unfortunately for most of us, because the brain always works by repetition and association, it doesn't take a major trauma to produce the effect of the body becoming the mind.[1] The most minor triggers can produce emotional responses that feel as though they are beyond our control.

For instance, you're driving to work and you stop at your usual coffee shop, which is all out of your favorite, hazelnut coffee. Disappointed, you grumble to yourself why a major enterprise like this one can't keep in stock such a very popular flavor. At work, you're irritated to see another car in your preferred parking spot.

Stepping into an empty elevator, you are exasperated to discover that someone ahead of you pushed all the buttons.

When you finally walk into the office, someone comments, "What's up? You seem kind of down."

You tell your story, and the person sympathizes. You sum it up: "I'm in a bad mood. I'll get over it."

The thing is, you don't.

A *mood* is a chemical state of being, generally short-term, that is an expression of a prolonged emotional reaction. Something in your environment—in this case, the failure of your barista to meet your needs, followed by a few other minor annoyances—sets off an emotional response. The chemicals of that emotion don't get used up instantly, so their effect lingers for a while. I call that the *refractory period*—the time after their initial release and until the effect diminishes.[2] The longer the refractory period, obviously, the longer you experience those feelings. When the chemical refractory period of an emotional reaction lasts for hours to days, that's a mood.

What happens when that recently triggered mood lingers? You've been in a bit of a funk since that day, and now you look around the room during a staff meeting and all you think of is that this person's tie is hideous, and the nasally tone of your boss is worse than nails on a chalkboard.

At this point, you're not just in a mood. You're reflecting a *temperament,* a tendency toward the habitual expression of an emotion through certain behaviors. A temperament is an emotional reaction with a refractory period that lasts from weeks to months.

Eventually, if you keep the refractory period of an emotion going for months and years, that tendency turns into a *personality trait*. At that point others will describe you as "bitter" or "resentful" or "angry" or "judgmental."

Our personality traits, then, are frequently based in our past emotions. Most of the time, personality (how we think, act, and feel) is anchored in the past. So to change our personalities, we have to change the emotions that we memorize. We have to move out of the past.

CREATE DIFFERENT STATES of BEING

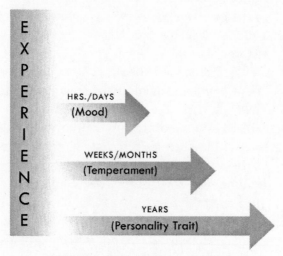

TIME OF REFRACTORY PERIOD
(Length of emotional reaction)

Figure 4B. The progression of different refractory periods. An experience creates an emotional reaction, which then can turn into a mood, then into a temperament, and finally into a personality trait. We, as personalities, memorize our emotional reactions and live in the past.

We Can't Change When Living in the Predictable Future

There is yet another way that we get stuck and keep ourselves from changing. We may also train the body to be the mind in order to live in a predictable future, based on the memory of the known past—and thus we miss the precious "now" moment again.

As you know, we can condition the body to live in the future. Of course, that can be a means to change our lives for the better, when we make a conscious choice to focus on a desired new experience, as my daughter did when she created her summer job in Italy. As her story demonstrates, if we focus on an intended future event and then plan how we will prepare or behave, there will be a moment when we are so clear and focused on that possible future that the thoughts we are thinking will begin to become the experience itself. Once the thought becomes the experience, its end product is an emotion. When we begin to experience the emotion of that event ahead of its possible occurrence, the body (as the unconscious mind) begins to respond as though the event is actually unfolding.

On the other hand, what happens if we begin to anticipate some unwanted future experience, or even obsess about a worst-case scenario, based on a memory from our past? We are still pro-gramming the body to experience a future event before it occurs. Now the body is no longer in the moment or in the past; it is living in the future—but a future based on some construct of the past.

When this occurs, the body does not know the difference be-tween the actual event transpiring in reality and what we are en-tertaining mentally. Because we are priming it to be juiced up for whatever we think might be coming, the body begins to get ready. And in a very real way, the body is in the event.

Here's an example of living in the future, based on the past. Imagine that you've been asked to give a lecture in front of 350 people, but you fear being onstage, based on memories of previous public-speaking disasters from your distant past. Whenever you think about the coming talk, you envision yourself standing there stammering and losing your train of thought. Your body begins to respond as if that future event is unfolding now; your shoulders tense, your heart races, and you perspire heavily. As you anticipate that dreaded day, you cause your body to already be living in that stressful reality.

Caught up in and obsessed with the possibility of failing again, you are so intent on that expected reality that you can't concen-trate on anything else. Your mind and body are polarized, moving from the past to the future and back again. As a result, you deny yourself the novelty of a wonderful future outcome.

As a more universal example of living in a predictable future, let's say that for many years you wake up to each new day, only to slide automatically into the same old set of unconscious actions. The body is so used to anticipating performing your daily behaviors that it goes almost mechanically from one task to the next. There's feeding the dog, brushing your teeth, putting on your clothes, making tea, taking the garbage out, getting the mail . . . you get the idea. Although you may wake up with a thought to do something different, somehow you find yourself doing those same-old, same-old things as if you are just along for the ride.

After you have memorized these types of actions for a decade or two, your body has been trained to continuously "look forward" to doing these things. In fact, it's been subconsciously programmed to live in the future and thus allow you to go to sleep behind the wheel . . . we could even say that you're no longer even driving the car. Now your body cannot exist in the present moment. It is primed to control you by running a host of unconscious programs while you sit back and allow it to head toward some humdrum, known destiny.

Overcoming your nearly automatic habits, and no longer anticipating the future, requires the ability to live greater than time. (More on that to come.)

Living in the Past, Which Is Your Future

Here's another example that demonstrates how familiar emotions create a corresponding future. You are invited to a co-worker's 4th of July barbecue. Everyone from your department is expected to attend. You don't like the host. He's always number one, and he doesn't mind letting everyone know it.

Every time he's hosted an event before, you've wound up having a miserable time, with this guy pushing every single one of your buttons. As you're driving to his place now, all you can think about is how at the last party, he interrupted everyone's meal so he could present his wife with a new BMW. You're certain, as you've told your partner the whole week leading up to the cookout, that this is going to be one miserable day. And it becomes exactly that.

You run a stop sign and get a ticket. One of your co-workers spills a beer on your pants and shirt. The hamburger that you requested be done medium-well comes to you barely beyond raw.

Given your attitude (your state of being) going in, how could you have expected things to turn out any other way? You woke up anticipating that this day was slated to be a horror show, and it turned out that way. You alternated between obsessing about an unwanted future (anticipating what would come next) and living in the past (comparing stimuli you were receiving to what you received previously), so you created more of the same.

If you start keeping track of your thoughts and write them down, you'll find that most of the time, you are either thinking ahead or looking back.

Live Your Desired New Future in the Precious Present

So here's another of those big questions: If you know that by staying present and severing or pruning your connections with the past, you can have access to all the possible outcomes in the quantum field, why would you choose to live in the past and keep creating the same future for yourself? Why wouldn't you do what is already in your power to do—to mentally alter the physical makeup of your brain and body so that you can be changed ahead of any actual desired experience? Why wouldn't you opt for living in the future *of your choice*—now, ahead of time?

Instead of obsessing about some traumatic or stressful event that you fear is in your future, based on your experience of the past, obsess about a new, desired experience that you haven't yet embraced emotionally. Allow yourself to live in that potential new future *now,* to the extent that your body begins to accept or believe that you're experiencing the elevated emotions of that new future outcome in the present moment. (You're going to learn how to do this.)

Remember when I said that my daughter needed to live her present life like she'd already had the experiences of the great summer in Italy? By doing that, she was broadcasting into the quantum field that the event had already physically occurred.

The greatest people in the world have demonstrated this, thousands of so-called ordinary people have done it, and you can as well. You have all the neurological machinery to transcend time, to make this a skill. What some might call miracles, I describe as cases of individuals working toward changing their state of being, so that their bodies and minds are no longer merely a record of their past but become active partners, taking steps to a new and better future.

Transcending the Big Three: Peak Experiences and Ordinary Altered States of Consciousness

At this point, you understand that the main obstacle to breaking the habit of being yourself is thinking and feeling *equal to* your environment, your body, and time. Obviously, then, learning to think and feel (be) *greater than* the "Big Three" is your first goal as you prepare for the meditation process you will learn in this book.

I'd bet that at some point in your life (perhaps even frequently) you've already been able to think greater than your environment, your body, and time. These moments when you transcend the Big Three are what some people call being "in the flow." There are a number of ways to describe what happens when our surroundings, our bodies, and our sense of time's passage disappear and we are "lost" to the world. In speaking to groups across the globe, I've asked audience members to describe *creative* moments when they were so consumed by what they were doing, or were so relaxed and at ease, that they seemed to enter an altered state of consciousness.

These experiences generally fall into two categories. The first of these are the so-called peak experiences, what we think of as transcendent moments, when we attain a state of being that we associate with monks and mystics. Compared to those highly spiritual events, the others may be more mundane, ordinary, and prosaic—but that doesn't mean that they are any less important.

These ordinary moments happened to me many times (although not as often as I would like) while in the process of writing this book. When I first sit down to write, I often have many other things on my mind—my busy travel schedule, my patients, my kids, my staff, how hungry/sleepy/happy I am. On good days, when the words seem to flow out of me, it is as though my hands and my keyboard are an extension of my mind. I'm not consciously aware of my fingers moving or my back resting against the chair. The trees swaying in the breeze outside my office disappear, that bit of stiffness in my neck no longer nudges for my attention, and I am completely focused on and absorbed by the words on my computer screen. At some point, I realize that an hour or more has gone by in what seemed an instant.

This kind of thing has likely happened to you—perhaps while you were driving, watching a movie, enjoying a dinner with good company, reading, knitting, practicing piano, or simply sitting in a quiet spot in nature.

I don't know about you, but I often feel amazingly refreshed after experiencing one of those moments when my environment, my body, and time seemed to disappear. They don't always happen when I'm writing, but after completing my second book, I find that they occur with greater frequency. With practice, I've been able to take control so that these experiences of being in the flow are not as accidental or serendipitous as they were at first.

Overcoming the Big Three to facilitate the occurrence of such moments is essential for losing your mind and creating a new one.

CHAPTER FIVE

SURVIVAL vs. CREATION

In the last chapter, I purposely used the example of my writing to illustrate my point about transcending the Big Three, because when you write, you are *creating* words (whether on the physical page or in a digital document). The same creativity is operating when you paint, play a musical instrument, turn wood on a lathe, or engage in any other activity that has the effect of breaking the bonds that the Big Three hold over you.

Why is it so hard to live in these creative moments? If we focus on an unwanted past or a dreaded future, that means that we live mostly in stress—in survival mode. Whether we're obsessing over our health (the survival of the *body*), paying our mortgage (the survival need for shelter from our external *environment*), or not having enough *time* to do what we need to do to survive, most of us are much more familiar with the addictive state of mind we'll call "survival" than we are with living as creators.

In my first book, I went into great detail about the difference between living in creation versus living in survival. So for a fuller explanation of this difference, you may want to read Chapters 8 through 11 in *Evolve Your Brain*. In the pages that follow, I'm going to briefly outline the difference between the two.

Think of life in survival mode by picturing an animal, such as a deer contentedly grazing in the forest. Let's assume that it is in homeostasis, in perfect balance. But if it perceives some danger in the outside world—say, a predator—its fight-or-flight nervous system gets turned on. This *sympathetic nervous system* is part of the autonomic nervous system, which maintains the body's automatic functions such as digestion, temperature regulation, blood-sugar levels, and the like. To prepare the animal to deal with the emergency it has detected, the body is chemically altered—the sympathetic nervous system automatically activates the adrenal glands to mobilize enormous amounts of energy. If the deer is chased by a pack of coyotes, it utilizes that energy to flee. If it is nimble enough to get away unharmed, then perhaps after 15 to 20 minutes when the threat is no longer present, the animal resumes grazing, its internal balance restored.

We humans have the same system in place. When we perceive danger, our sympathetic nervous system is turned on, energy is mobilized, and so on, in much the same way as the deer. During early human history, this wonderfully adaptive response helped us confront threats from predators and other risks to our survival. Those animal qualities served us well for our evolution as a species.

Thought Alone Can Trigger the Human Stress Response— and Keep It Going

Unfortunately, there are several differences between *Homo sapiens* and our planetary cohabitants in the animal kingdom that don't serve us as well. Every time we knock the body out of chemical balance, that's called "stress." The *stress response* is how the body innately responds when it's knocked out of balance, and what it does to return back to equilibrium. Whether we see a lion in the Serengeti, bump into our not-so-friendly ex at the grocery store, or freak out in freeway traffic because we're late for a meeting, we turn on the stress response because we are reacting to our external environment.

Unlike animals, we have the ability to turn on the fight-or-flight response by thought alone. And that thought doesn't have to be about anything in our present circumstances. We can turn on that response in anticipation of some future event. Even more disadvantageous, we can produce the same stress response by revisiting an unhappy memory that is stitched in the fabric of our gray matter.

So either we anticipate stress-response-producing experiences or we recollect them; our bodies are either existing in the future or in the past. To our detriment, we turn short-term stressful situations into long-term ones.

On the other hand, as far as we can tell, animals don't have the ability (or should I say *dis*ability) to turn on the stress response so frequently and so easily that they can't turn it off. That deer, back to happily grazing, isn't consumed with thoughts about what just happened a few minutes ago, let alone the time a coyote chased it two months ago. This kind of repetitive stress is harmful to us, because no organism was designed with a mechanism to deal with negative effects on the body when the stress response is turned on with great frequency and for long duration. In other words, no creature can avoid the consequences of living in long-term emergency situations. When we turn on the stress response and can't turn it off, we're headed for some type of breakdown in the body.

Let's say you keep turning on the fight-or-flight system due to some threatening circumstance in your life (real or imagined). As your racing heart pumps enormous amounts of blood to your extremities and your body is knocked out of homeostasis, you're becoming prepared by the nervous system to run or fight. But let's face it: you can't flee to the Bahamas, nor can you throttle your fellow employee—that would be primitive. So as a consequence, you condition your heart to race all the time, and you may be headed for high blood pressure, arrhythmias, and so on.

And what's in store when you keep mobilizing all that energy for some emergency situation? If you're putting the bulk of your energy toward some issue in your external environment, there will be little left for your body's internal environment. Your immune system, which monitors your inner world, can't keep up with the lack of energy for growth and repair. Therefore, you get sick, whether it be from a cold, cancer, or rheumatoid arthritis. (All are immune-mediated conditions.)

When you think about it, the real difference between animals and ourselves is that although we both experience stress, humans reexperience and *"pre*-experience" traumatic situations. What is so harmful about having our stress response triggered by pressures from the past, present, and future? When we get knocked out of chemical balance so often, eventually that out-of-balance state becomes the norm. As a result, we are destined to live out our genetic destiny, and in most cases that means suffering from some illness.

The reason is clear: The domino effect from the cascade of hormones and other chemicals we release in response to stress can dysregulate some of our genes, and that may create disease. In other words, repeated stress pushes the genetic buttons that cause us to begin to head toward our genetic destiny. So what was once very adaptive behavior and a beneficial biochemical response (fight or flight) has become a highly maladaptive and harmful set of circumstances.

For instance, when a lion was chasing your ancestors, the stress response was doing what it was designed to do—protect them from their outer environment. That's adaptive. But if, for days on end, you fret about your promotion, overfocus on your presentation to upper management, or worry about your mother being in the hospital, these situations create the same chemicals *as though* you were being chased by a lion.

Now, that's maladaptive. You're staying too long in emergency mode. Fight-or-flight is using up the energy your internal environment needs. Your body is stealing this vital energy from your immune, digestive, and endocrine systems, among others, and directing it to the muscles that you'd use to fight a predator or run from danger. But in your situation, that's only working against you.

From a psychological perspective, overproduction of stress hormones creates the human emotions of anger, fear, envy, and hatred; incites feelings of aggression, frustration, anxiety, and insecurity; and causes us to experience pain, suffering, sadness, hopelessness, and depression. Most people spend the majority of their time preoccupied with negative thoughts and feelings. Is it likely that most of the things that are happening in our present circumstances are negative? Obviously not. Negativity runs so high because we are either living in anticipation of stress or re-experiencing it through a memory, so most of our thoughts and feelings are driven by those strong hormones of stress and survival.

When our stress response is triggered, we focus on three things, and they are of highest importance:

- The body. (*It must be taken care of.*)

- The environment. (*Where can I go to escape this threat?*)

- Time. (*How much of it do I have to use in order to evade this threat?*)

Living in survival is the reason why we humans are so dominated by the Big Three. The stress response and the hormones that it triggers force us to focus on (and obsess about) the body, the environment, and time. As a result, we begin to define our "self" within the confines of the physical realm; we become less spiritual, less conscious, less aware, and less mindful.

Put another way, we grow to be "materialists"—that is, habitually consumed by thoughts of *things* in the external environment. Our identity becomes wrapped up in our bodies. We are absorbed by the outer world because that is what those chemicals force us to pay attention to—things we own, people we know, places we have to go, problems we face, hairstyles we dislike, our body parts, our weight, our looks in comparison to others, how much time we have or don't have . . . you get the picture. And we remember who we are based primarily on what we know and the things we do.

Living in survival causes us to focus on the .00001 percent instead of the 99.99999 percent of reality.

Survival: Living as a "Somebody"

Most of us embrace the traditional notion of ourselves as a "somebody." But who we really are has nothing to do with the Big Three. Who we are is a consciousness connected to a quantum field of intelligence.

When we become this somebody, this materialistic physical self living in survival, we forget who we truly are. We become disconnected and feel separate from the universal field of intelligence. The more we live impacted by stress hormones, the more their chemical rush becomes our identity.

If we fancy ourselves solely physical beings, we limit ourselves to perceiving only with our physical senses. The more we use our senses to define our reality, the more we allow our senses to *determine* our reality. We slip into that Newtonian mode of thinking, which locks us into trying to predict the future based on some past experience. If you recall, the Newtonian model of reality is all about predicting an outcome. Now we are trying to control our reality instead of surrendering to something greater. All we're doing is trying to survive.

If the quantum model of reality ultimately defines everything as energy, why do we experience ourselves more as physical beings than as beings of energy? We could say that the survival-oriented emotions (emotions are *energy in motion*) are lower-frequency or lower-energy emotions. They vibrate at a slower wavelength and therefore ground us into being physical. We become denser, heavier, and more corporeal, because that energy causes us to vibrate more slowly. The body quite literally becomes composed of more mass and less energy . . . more matter, less mind.[1]

SURVIVAL EMOTIONS VS. ELEVATED EMOTIONS

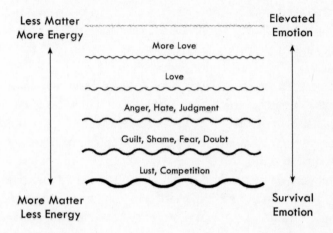

Figure 5A. The higher-frequency waves at the top are vibrating faster and there-fore are closer to the vibratory rate of energy and less to that of matter. Moving down the scale, you can see that the slower the wavelength, the more "material" the energy becomes. Thus, the survival emotions ground us to be more like mat-ter and less like energy. Emotions such as anger, hatred, suffering, shame, guilt, judgment, and lust make us feel more physical, because they carry a frequency that is slower and more like that of physical objects. However, the more elevated emotions such as love, joy, and gratitude are higher in frequency. As a result, they are more energy-like and less physical/material.

So it might make sense that if we inhibit our more primitive survival emotions and begin to break our addiction to them, our energy will be higher in frequency, and less likely to root us to the body. In a way, we can liberate energy from the body, when the body has "become" the mind, into the quantum field. As our emotions become more elevated, we will naturally ascend to a higher level of consciousness, closer to Source . . . and feel more connected to universal intelligence.

Addicted to Being a Somebody

When the stress response is turned on, whether in response to a real or conjured-up threat, a powerful cascade of chemicals rushes into our system and gives us a strong jolt of energy, momentarily "waking up" our bodies and certain parts of the brain to put all of our attention on the Big Three. This is very addictive to us because it's like drinking a triple espresso—we get turned "on" for a few moments.

In time, we unconsciously become addicted to our problems, our unfavorable circumstances, or our unhealthy relationships. We keep these situations in our lives to feed our addiction to survival-oriented emotions, so that we can remember who we think we are as a somebody. We just love the rush of energy we get from our troubles!

Moreover, we also associate this emotional high with every person, thing, place, and experience in our outer world that is known and familiar. We become addicted to these elements in our environment as well; we embrace our environment as our identity.

If you agree that we can turn on the stress response just by thinking, then it stands to reason that we can get the same rush of addictive stress chemicals as if we were being chased by a predator. As a consequence, we become addicted to our very thoughts; they begin to give us an unconscious adrenaline high, and we find it very hard to think differently. To think greater than how we feel or to think outside of the proverbial box becomes just too uncomfortable. The moment we begin to deny ourselves the substance we are addicted to—in this case, the familiar thoughts and feelings associated with our emotional addiction—there are cravings, withdrawal pains, and a host of inner subvocalizations urging us not to change. And so we remain chained to our familiar reality.

Thus, our thoughts and feelings, which are predominantly self-limiting, hook us back to all the problems, conditions, stressors, and bad choices that produced the fight-or-flight effect in the first place. We keep all these negative stimuli around us so that we can produce the stress response, because that addiction reinforces the idea of who we are, only serving to reaffirm our own personal identity. Simply put, most of us are addicted to the problems and conditions of our lives that produce stress. No matter whether we're in a bad job or a bad relationship, we hold our troubles close to us because they help reinforce who we are as a somebody; they feed our addictions to low-frequency emotions.

Most harmful of all, we live in fear that if those problems were taken away, we wouldn't know what to think and how to feel, and we wouldn't get to experience the rush of energy that causes us to remember who we are. For most of us, God forbid we *not* be a somebody. How awful would it be to be a "nobody," to not have an identity?

The Selfish Self

As you can see, what we identify as our self exists within the context of our collective emotional association with our thoughts and feelings, our problems, and all those elements of the Big Three. Is it any wonder that people find it so hard to go within and leave this self-produced reality behind? How would we know who we are if it weren't for our environment, our bodies, and time? That's why we are so dependent upon the external world. We limit ourselves to using our senses to define and cultivate emotions, so that we can receive the physiological feedback that reaffirms our own personal addictions. We do all this to feel human.

When our survival response is way out of proportion to what is happening in our outer world, that excess of stress-response hormones causes us to become fixated within the parameters of self. So we become overly selfish. We obsess about our bodies or a particular aspect of our environment, and we live enslaved to time. We're trapped in this particular reality, and we feel powerless to change, to break the habit of being ourselves.

These excessive survival emotions tip the scales of a healthy *ego* (the self we consciously refer to when we say "I"). When the ego is in check, its natural job is to make sure we are protected and safe in the outer world. As an example, the ego makes sure we stay far away from a bonfire or a few steps away from the cliff's edge.

When the ego is balanced, its natural instinct is self-preservation. There's a healthy balance between its needs and those of others, its attention to itself and to others.

When we're in survival mode in an emergency situation, it makes sense that the self should take priority. But when chronic, long-term stress chemicals push the body and brain out of balance, the ego becomes overfocused on survival and puts the self first, to the exclusion of anything else—we're selfish all the time. Thus, we become self-indulgent, self-centered, and self-important, full of self-pity and self-loathing. When the ego is under constant stress, it's got a "me first" priority.

Under those conditions, the ego is primarily concerned with predicting every outcome of every situation, because it is over-focused on the outer world and feels completely separated from the 99.99999 percent of reality. In fact, the more we define reality through our senses, the more this reality becomes our law. And material reality as law is the very opposite of the quantum law. Whatever we place our awareness on is our reality. Consequently, if our attention is focused on the body and our physical realm, and if we become locked into a particular line of linear time, then this becomes our reality.

To forget about the people we know, the problems we have, the things we own, and the places we go; to lose track of time; to go beyond the body and its need to feed its habituations; to give up the high from emotionally familiar experiences that reaffirm the identity; to detach from trying to predict a future condition or review a past memory; to lay down the selfish ego that is only concerned with its needs; to think or dream greater than how we feel, and crave the unknown—this is the beginning of freedom from our present lives.

If Our Thoughts Can Make Us Sick, Can They Make Us Well?

Let's go one step further. I explained earlier that we can turn on the stress response by thought alone. I also mentioned the scientific fact that the chemicals associated with stress pull the genetic trigger by creating a very harsh environment outside of our cells and thus creating disease. So by pure reason, our thoughts can actually make us sick. If our thoughts can make us sick, might they also make us well?

Let's say that a person had some experiences within a short time frame that caused him to feel resentful. As a result of his unconscious reactions to those occurrences, he held on to his bitterness. Chemicals corresponding to this emotion flooded his cells. Over weeks, his emotion turned into a mood, which continued for months and changed into a temperament, which was sustained for years and formed a strong personality trait called resentment. In fact, he memorized this emotion so well that the body knew resentment better than the conscious mind, because he remained in a cycle of thinking and feeling, feeling and thinking, that way for years.

Based on what you learned about emotions as the chemical signature of an experience, wouldn't you agree that as long as this person clings to resentment, his body will react as though it is still experiencing the long-ago events that first caused him to embrace this emotion? Moreover, if the body's reaction to those chemicals of resentment disrupted the function of certain genes, and this sustained reaction kept signaling the same genes to respond in the same way, might the body eventually develop a physical condition such as cancer?

If so, is it possible that once he unmemorized the emotion of continuous resentment—by no longer thinking the thoughts that created the feelings of resentment, and vice versa—his body (as the unconscious mind) would be free from that emotional enslavement? In time, would he stop signaling the genes the same way?

And finally, let's say he began thinking and feeling in new ways, to such a degree that he invented a new ideal of himself related to a new personality. As he moved into a new state of being, might he signal his genes in beneficial ways and condition the body into an elevated emotional state, ahead of the actual experience of good health? Could he do this to the extent that the body would begin to change by thought alone?

What I just described in simple terms happened to a student in one of my seminars, who overcame cancer.

·@·

Bill, 57, was a roofing contractor. A lesion had appeared on his face, and a dermatologist diagnosed malignant melanoma. Although Bill underwent surgery, radiation, and chemotherapy, the cancer recurred in his neck, then his side, and finally his calf. Each time, he underwent a similar course of treatment.

Naturally, Bill experienced "Why me?" moments. He understood that his excessive sun exposure was a risk factor, but he knew others who had been similarly exposed and didn't develop cancer. He fixated on that unfairness.

After treatment for the same cancer on his left flank, Bill pondered whether his own thoughts, emotions, and behaviors had contributed to his condition. In a moment of self-reflection, he realized that for more than 30 years, he had been stuck in resentment, thinking and feeling that he always had to give up what he wanted for the sake of others.

For example, he had wanted to become a professional musician after high school. But when an injury left his father unable to work, Bill had to join his family's roofing company. He habitually reexperienced his feelings upon being told he had to give up his aspirations, to the extent that his body still lived in that past. This also set up a pattern of dreams deferred. Whenever something didn't go his way, such as the housing market collapsing just after he expanded the business, he always found someone or something to blame.

Bill had so memorized the emotional response pattern of bitterness that it dominated his personality and became an unconscious program. His state of being had signaled the same genes for so long that they had created the disease that now afflicted him.

No longer could Bill allow his environment to control him: the people, places, and influences in his life had always dictated how he thought, felt, and behaved. He sensed that to break the bonds with his old self and reinvent a new one, he would have to leave his familiar environment. So for two weeks in Baja, Mexico, he retreated from his familiar life.

The first five mornings, Bill contemplated how he thought when he felt resentment. He became a quantum observer of his thoughts and feelings; he became conscious of his unconscious mind. Next, he paid attention to his previously unconscious behaviors and actions. He decided to halt any thought, behavior, or emotion that was unloving toward himself.

After the first week of this vigilance, Bill felt free, because he had liberated his body from its emotional addiction to resentment. By inhibiting the familiar thoughts and feelings that had driven his behaviors, in a sense he impeded the signals of the survival emotions from conditioning his body to the same mind. His body then released energy, which was available to use to design a new destiny for himself.

For the next week, Bill became so uplifted that he thought about the new self he wanted to be, and how he would respond to the people, places, and influences that previously controlled him. For instance, he decided that whenever his wife and kids expressed a wish or need, he would respond with kindness and generosity instead of making them feel like a burden. In short, he focused on how he wanted to think, act, and feel when presented with situations that had challenged him in the past. He was creating a new personality, a new mind, and a new state of being.

Bill began to put into practice what he'd placed in his mind while sitting on that Baja beach. Shortly after his return, he noticed that the tumor on his calf had fallen off. In a week or so, when he went to his doctor, he was cancer free. He has remained that way.

By firing his brain in new ways, Bill changed biologically and chemically from his previous self. As a result, he signaled new genes in new ways; and those cancer cells couldn't coexist with his new mind, new internal chemistry, and new self. Once trapped by the emotions of the past, he now lives in a new future.

Creation: Living as a Nobody

At the end of the previous chapter, I briefly described what it is like to live in creative mode. Those are the moments of being fully engaged and in flow so that the environment, the body, and time all seem immaterial and don't invade our conscious thoughts.

Living in creation is living as a nobody. Ever notice that when you're truly in the midst of creating anything, you forget about yourself? You dissociate from your known world. You are no longer a somebody who associates your identity with certain things you own, particular people you know, certain tasks you do, and different places you lived at specific times. You could say that when you are in a creative state, you forget about the habit of being *you*. You lay down your selfish ego and become self-less.

You have moved beyond time and space and become pure, immaterial awareness. Once you're no longer connected to a body; no longer focused on people, places, or things in your external environment; and beyond linear time, you're entering the door of the quantum field. You cannot enter as a somebody, you must do so as a nobody. You have to leave the self-centered ego at the door and enter the realm of consciousness *as* pure consciousness. And as I said in Chapter 1, in order to change your body (to foster better health), something in your external circumstances (a new job or relationship, perhaps), or your timeline (toward a possible future reality), you have to become no body, no thing, no time.

Thus, here is the grand hint: to change any aspect of your life (body, environment, or time), you must transcend it. You must leave behind the Big Three in order to control the Big Three.

The Frontal Lobe: Domain of Creation and Change

When we are in creation, we are activating the brain's creative center, the frontal lobe (part of the forebrain and comprising the prefrontal cortex). This is the newest, most evolved part of our human nervous system and the most adaptable part of the brain. It tends to be the creative center of who we are, and the brain's

CEO or decision-making apparatus. The frontal lobe is the seat of our attention, focused concentration, awareness, observation, and consciousness. It is where we speculate on possibilities, demonstrate firm intention, make conscious decisions, control impulsive and emotional behaviors, and learn new things.

For the sake of our understanding, the frontal lobe performs three essential functions. These will all come into play as you learn and practice the how-to meditative steps for breaking the habit of being yourself in Part III of this book.

1. Metacognition: Becoming Self-Aware to Inhibit Unwanted States of Mind and Body

If you want to create a new self, you first have to stop being the old self. In the process of creation, the first function of the frontal lobe is to become self-aware.

Because we have *metacognitive* capabilities—the power to observe our own thoughts and self—we can decide how we no longer want to *be* . . . to think, act, and feel. This ability to self-reflect allows us to scrutinize ourselves and then make a plan to modify our behaviors so we can produce more enlightened or desirable outcomes.[2]

Your attention is where you place your energy. To use attention to empower your life, you will have to examine what you've already created. This is where you begin to "know thyself." You look at your beliefs about life, yourself, and others. You are *what* you are, you are *where* you are, and you are *who* you are because of what you believe about yourself. Your beliefs are the thoughts you keep consciously or unconsciously accepting as the law in your life. Whether you are aware of them or not, they still affect your reality.

So if you truly want a new personal reality, start observing all aspects of your present personality. Since they primarily operate below the level of conscious awareness, much like automatic software programs, you'll have to go within and look at these elements you probably haven't been aware of before. Given that your personality comprises how you think, act, and feel, you must pay attention to your unconscious thoughts, reflexive behaviors, and automatic emotional reactions—put them under observation to determine if they are true and whether you want to continue to endorse them with your energy.

To become familiar with your unconscious states of mind and body takes an act of will, intention, and heightened awareness. If you become more aware, you will become more attentive. If you become more attentive, you will be more conscious. If you grow to be more conscious, you will notice more. If you notice more, you have a greater ability to observe self and others, both inner and outer elements of your reality. Ultimately, the more you observe, the more you awaken from the state of the unconscious mind into conscious awareness.

The purpose of becoming self-aware is so that you no longer allow any thought, action, or emotion you don't want to experience to pass by your awareness. Thus, in time, your ability to consciously inhibit those states of being will stop the same firing and wiring of the old neural networks that are related to the old personality. And as a result of no longer re-creating the same mind on a daily basis, you prune away the hardware that is related to the old self. In addition, by interrupting the feelings that are associated with those thoughts, you are no longer signaling genes in the same way. You are stopping the body from reaffirming itself as the same mind. This process is whereby you quite simply begin to "lose your mind."

So as you develop the skill of becoming familiar with all aspects of your old self, you will ultimately become more conscious. Your goal here is to unlearn who you used to be, so that you can free up energy to create a new life, a new personality. *You can't create a new personal reality as the same personality.* You have to become someone else. Metacognition is your first task in moving from your past to creating a new future.

2. Creating a New Mind to Think about New Ways of Being

The second function of the frontal lobe is to create a new mind—to break out of the neural networks produced by the ways that your brain has been firing for years on end, and influence it to rewire in new ways.

When we set aside time and private space to think about a new way of being, that is when the frontal lobe engages in creation. We can imagine fresh possibilities and ask ourselves important questions about what we really want, how and who we want to be, and what we want to change about ourselves and our circumstances.

Because the frontal lobe has connections to all other parts of the brain, it is able to scan across all the neural circuits to seamlessly piece together stored bits of information in the form of networks of knowledge and experience. Then it picks and chooses among those neural circuits, combining them in a variety of ways to create a new mind. In doing that, it creates a model or internal representation that we see as a picture of our intended result. It makes sense, then, that the more knowledge we have, the greater the variety of neural networks we've wired, and the more capable we are of dreaming of more complex and detailed models.

To initiate this step of creation, it is always good to move into a state of wonder, contemplation, possibility, reflection, or speculation by asking yourself some important questions. Open-ended inquiries are the most provocative approach to producing a fluent stream of consciousness:

- What would it be like to . . . ?

- What is a better way to be . . . ?

- What if I was this person, living in this reality?

- Who in history do I admire, and what were his/her admirable traits?

The answers that come will naturally form a new mind, because as you sincerely respond to them, your brain will begin to work in new ways. By beginning to mentally rehearse new ways of being, you start rewiring yourself neurologically to a new mind— and the more you can "re-mind" yourself, the more you'll change your brain and your life.

Whether you want to be wealthy or a better parent—or a great wizard, for that matter—it might not be a bad idea to fill your brain with knowledge on your chosen subject, so you have more building blocks to make a new model of the reality you want to embrace. Every time you acquire information, you're adding new synaptic connections that will serve as the raw materials to break the pattern of your brain firing the same way. The more you learn, the more ammo you have to unseat the old personality.

THE FRONTAL LOBE as CREATOR

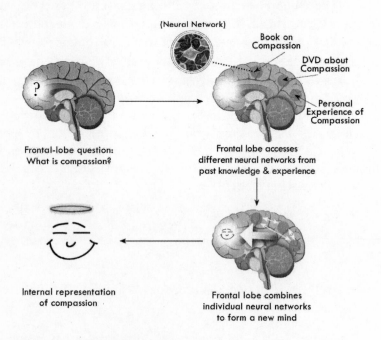

Figure 5B. When the frontal lobe is working in creative mode, it looks out over the landscape of the entire brain and gathers all of the brain's information to create a new mind. If compassion is the new state of being that you want to create, then once you ask yourself what it would be like to be compassionate, the frontal lobe would naturally combine different neural networks together in new ways to create a new model or vision. It might take stored information from books you read, DVDs you saw, personal experiences, and so forth to make the brain work in new ways. Once the new mind is in place, you see a picture, hologram, or vision of what compassion means to you.

3. Making Thought More Real Than Anything Else

During the creative process, the frontal lobe's third vital role is to make thought more real than anything else. (Stay tuned for the how-to in Part III.)

When we're in a creative state, the frontal lobe becomes highly activated and lowers the volume on the circuits in the rest of the brain so that little else is being processed but a single-minded thought.[3] Since the frontal lobe is the executive that mediates the rest of the brain, it can monitor all of the "geography." So it lowers the volume on the sensory centers (responsible for "feeling" the body), motor centers (responsible for moving the body), association centers (where our identity exists), and the circuits that process time . . . in order to quiet them all down. With very little neural activity, we could say that there is no mind to process sensory input (remember that *mind* is the brain in action), no mind to activate movement within the environment, and no mind to associate activities with time; then we have no body, we have become "no thing," we are no time. We are, in that moment, pure consciousness. With the noise shut off in those areas of the brain, the state of creativity is one in which there is no ego or self as we have known it.

When you are in creation mode, the frontal lobe is in control. It becomes so engaged that your thoughts become your reality and your experience. Whatever you're thinking about in those moments is all there is for the frontal lobe to process. As it "lowers the volume" from other areas of the brain, it shuts out distractions. The inner world of thought becomes as real as the outer world of reality. Your thoughts are captured neurologically and branded into your brain's architecture as an experience.

If you effectively execute the creative process, this experience produces an emotion, as you know, and you begin to feel like that event is actually happening to you in the present. You are one with the thoughts and feelings associated with your desired reality. You are now in a new state of being. You could say that in that moment, you are now rewriting the subconscious programs by reconditioning the body to a new mind.

THE FRONTAL LOBE
as the VOLUME CONTROL

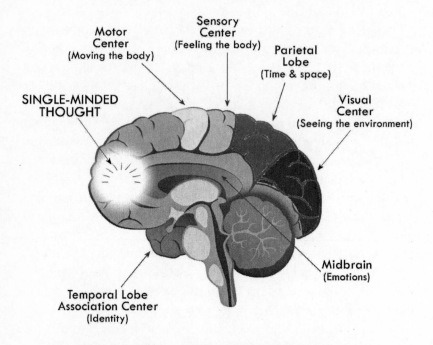

Motor Center
(Moving the body)

Sensory Center
(Feeling the body)

Parietal Lobe
(Time & space)

SINGLE-MINDED THOUGHT

Visual Center
(Seeing the environment)

Midbrain
(Emotions)

Temporal Lobe Association Center
(Identity)

Figure 5C. When the thought that you are attending to becomes the experience, the frontal lobe quiets down the rest of the brain so that nothing else is being processed but that single-minded thought. You become still, you no longer feel your body, you no longer perceive time and space, and you forget about yourself.

Lose Your Mind, Liberate Your Energy

In the act of creation, when we become that nobody or no thing in no time, we no longer create our customary chemical signature, because we are not the same identity; we don't think and feel in the same way. Those neural networks our survival thinking had wired are turned off, and the personality that was addicted to continually signaling the body to produce stress hormones is . . . gone.

In short, the emotional self that lived in survival mode is no longer functioning. The moment that happens, our former identity, the "state of being" bound by survival-based thinking and feeling, is no more. Since we are no longer "being" the same being, emotional energy that had been bound to the body is now free to move.

So where does the energy go that once fed that emotional self? It has to go somewhere, so it moves to a new place. That energy in the form of emotion moves up the body from the hormonal centers to the heart area (on its way to the brain) . . . and all of a sudden we feel great, joyful, expanded. We fall in love with our creation. That's when we experience our natural state of being. Once we stop energizing that emotional self powered by the stress response, we have moved from being selfish to selfless.[4]

With that old energy transmuted into a higher-frequency emotion, the body is liberated from its emotional bondage. We are lifted above the horizon to behold a whole new landscape. No longer perceiving reality through the lenses of those past survival emotions, we see new possibilities. We are now quantum observers of a new destiny. And that release heals the body and frees the mind.

Let's revisit the chart of energy and frequencies from the survival emotions to the elevated emotions (see Figure 5A). When anger or shame or lust are released from the body, they will be transmuted into joy, love, or gratitude. On this journey to broadcasting higher energy, the body (which we conditioned to be the mind) becomes less "of the mind" and becomes more coherent energy; the matter that makes up the body expresses a higher vibratory rate, and we feel more connected to something greater. In short, we are demonstrating more of our divine nature.

When you're living in survival, you're trying to control or force an outcome; that's what the ego does. When you're living in the elevated emotion of creation, you feel so lifted that you would never try to analyze how or when a chosen destiny will arrive. You trust that it will happen because you have already experienced it in mind and body—in thought and feeling. You know that it will, because you feel connected to something greater. You are in a state of gratitude because you feel like it's already happened.

You may not know all the specifics of your desired outcome—when it will take place, where, and under what circumstances—but you trust in a future that you can't see or otherwise perceive with your senses. To you it has already occurred in no space, no time, no place, from which all things material spring forth. You are in a state of knowingness; you can relax into the present and no longer live in survival.

To anticipate or analyze when, where, or how the event will occur would only cause you to return to your old identity. You are in such joy that it's impossible to try to figure it out; that's only what human beings do when they are living in limited states of survival.

As you linger in this creative state where you are no longer your identity, the nerve cells that once fired together to form that old self are no longer wiring together. That's when the old personality is being biologically dismantled. Those feelings connected to that identity, which conditioned the body to the same mind, are no longer signaling the same genes in the same ways. And the more you overcome your ego, the more the physical evidence of the old personality is changed. The old you is gone.

THE TWO STATES
of the MIND & BODY

SURVIVAL	VS.	CREATION
Stress		Homeostasis
Contraction		Expansion
Catabolism		Anabolism
Dis-ease		Health
Imbalance		Order
Breakdown		Repair
Degeneration		Regeneration
Fear/Anger/Sadness		Love/Joy/Trust
Selfish		Selfless
Environment/Body/Time		No Thing/No Body/No Time
Energy Loss		Energy Created
Emergency		Growth/Repair
Narrow Focused		Open Focused
Separate		Connected
Reality Determined by Senses		Reality Beyond Senses
Cause & Effect		Causing an Effect
Limited Possibilities		All Possibilities
Incoherence		Coherence
Known		Unknown

Figure 5D. Survival mode versus creation mode.

By completing Part I of this book, you have intentionally acquired a knowledge base that will help you create your new self. Now let's build on that base.

We've covered a lot of possibilities: the concept that your subjective mind can affect your objective world; your potential to change your brain and body by becoming greater than your environment, your body, and time; and the prospect that you can move out of the reactive, stressful mode of living in survival, as though only the outer world is real, and enter the inner world of the creator. It is my hope that you can now view these possibilities as possible *realities*.

If you can, then I invite you to continue on to Part II, where you will gain specific information about the role of your brain and the meditative process that will prepare you to create real and lasting change in your life.

PART II

YOUR BRAIN
AND
MEDITATION

CHAPTER SIX

THREE BRAINS: THINKING TO DOING TO BEING

It's often useful to compare one's brain to a computer, and it's true that yours already has all the hardware you'll need to change your "self" and your life. But do you know how best to use that hardware to install new software?

Picture two computers with identical hardware and software—one in the hands of a tech novice, and the other being used by an experienced computer operator. The beginner knows little about what kinds of things a computer can do, let alone how to do them.

The intention behind Part II, simply put, is to provide pertinent information about the brain so that when you, as its operator, begin to use the meditative process to change your life, you will know what needs to happen in your brain and in your meditations, and why.

Change Entails New Ways of Thinking, Doing, and Being

If you know how to drive a car, then you've already experienced probably the most elementary example of thinking, doing, and being. At first, you had to *think* about every action you took, and about all those rules of the road. Later, you became fairly proficient at driving, as long as you paid conscious attention to what you were *doing*. Eventually, you were *being* a driver; your conscious mind slid over and became a passenger, and ever since, your subconscious mind has probably occupied the driver's seat most of the time; driving has become automatic and second nature to you. Much of what you learn is via this progression from thinking to doing to being, and three areas of the brain facilitate this mode of learning.

But did you know that you can also go directly from thinking to being—and it's likely that you've already experienced this in your life? Through the meditation that is at the heart of this book (this chapter will give you a prelude), you can go from thinking about the ideal self you want to become, straight to being that new self. That is the key to quantum creating.

Change all begins with thinking: we can immediately form new neurological connections and circuits that reflect our new thoughts. And nothing gets the brain more excited than when it's learning—assimilating knowledge and experiences. These are aphrodisiacs for the brain; it "fondles" every signal it receives from our five senses. Every second, it processes billions of bits of data; it analyzes, examines, identifies, extrapolates, classifies, and files information, which it can retrieve for us on an "as needed" basis. Truly, the human brain is this planet's ultimate supercomputer.

As you'll recall, the basis for understanding how you can actually change your mind is the concept of hardwiring—how neurons engage in long-term, habitual relationships. I've talked about Hebbian learning, which states: "Nerve cells that fire together, wire together." (Neuroscientists used to think that after childhood, brain structure was relatively immutable. But new findings reveal that many aspects of the brain and nervous system can change structurally and functionally—including learning, memory, and recovery from brain damage—throughout adulthood.)

But the opposite is also true: "Nerve cells that no longer fire together, no longer wire together." If you don't use it, you lose it. You can even focus conscious thought to disconnect or unwire unwanted connections. Thus, it is possible to let go of some of the "stuff" you've been holding on to that colors the way you think, act, and feel. The rewired brain will no longer fire according to the circuitry of the past.

The gift of *neuroplasticity* (the brain's ability to rewire and create new circuits at any age as a result of input from the environment and our conscious intentions) is that we can create a new level of mind. There's a sort of neurological "out with the old, in with the new," a process that neuroscientists call *pruning* and *sprouting*. It's what I call unlearning and learning, and it creates the opportunity for us to rise above our current limitations and to be greater than our conditioning or circumstances.

In creating a new habit of being ourselves, we are essentially taking conscious control over what had become an unconscious process of being. Instead of the mind working toward one goal (*I'm not going to be an angry person*) and the body working toward another (*Let's stay angry and keep bathing in those familiar chemicals*), we want to unify the mind's intent with the body's responses. To do this, we must create a new way of thinking, doing, and being.

Given that to change our lives, we first have to change our thoughts and feelings, then *do* something (change our actions or behaviors) to have a new experience, which in turn produces a new feeling, and then we must memorize that feeling until we move into a state of being (when mind and body are one), at least we've got a few things going for us. Along with the brain being neuroplastic, we could say that we have more than one brain to work with. In effect, we have three of them.

(For our purposes, this chapter will limit its focus to those functions of the "three brains" that relate specifically to breaking the habit of being ourselves. On a personal note, I find that studying what the brain and the other components of the nervous system do for us is an endlessly fascinating exploration. My first book, *Evolve Your Brain*, covered this topic in more detail than would serve our purposes here; there are additional resources for study on my website, **www.drjoedispenza.com**; and of course, many other excellent publications and websites are available for those who want to learn more about the brain, the mind, and the body.)

THE THREE BRAINS

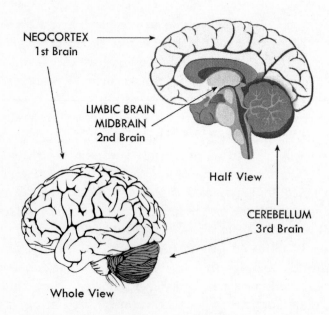

Figure 6A. The "first brain," the neocortex or thinking brain (in white). The "second brain" is the limbic or emotional brain, responsible for creating, maintaining, and organizing chemicals in the body (in gray). The "third brain," the cerebellum, is the seat of the subconscious mind (in charcoal).

From Thinking to Doing: The <u>Neocortex</u> Processes Knowledge, Then Prompts Us to Live What We Learned

Our "thinking brain" is the *neocortex,* the brain's walnut-like outer covering. Humanity's newest, most advanced neurological hardware, the neocortex is the seat of the conscious mind, our identity, and other higher brain functions. (The frontal lobe, discussed in earlier chapters, is one of four parts of the neocortex.)

Essentially, the neocortex is the brain's architect or designer. It allows you to learn, remember, reason, analyze, plan, create, speculate on possibilities, invent, and communicate. Since this area is where you log sensory data such as what you see and hear, the neocortex plugs you into external reality.

In general, the neocortex processes knowledge and experience. First, you gather knowledge in the form of facts or *semantic* information (philosophical or theoretical concepts or ideas that you learn intellectually), prompting the neocortex to add new synaptic connections and circuits.

Second, once you decide to personalize or apply knowledge you have acquired—to demonstrate what you learned—you will invariably create a new experience. This causes patterns of neurons called *neural networks* to form in the neocortex. These networks reinforce the circuitry of what you learned intellectually.

If the neocortex had a motto, it might be: *Knowledge is for the mind.*

Simply put, knowledge is the *precursor* to experience: Your neocortex is responsible for processing ideas that you have not yet experienced, which exist as a potential for you to embrace at some future time. As you entertain new thoughts, you begin to think about modifying your behavior so that you can do something differently when the opportunity presents itself, in order to have a new outcome. As you then alter your routine actions and typical behaviors, something different from the norm should happen, which will produce a new event for you to experience.

From New Events to New Emotions: The <u>Limbic Brain</u> Produces Chemicals to Help Us Remember Experiences

The *limbic brain* (also known as the *mammalian brain*), located under the neocortex, is the most highly developed and specialized area of the brain in mammals other than humans, dolphins, and higher primates. Just think of the limbic brain as the "chemical brain" or the "emotional brain."

When you're in the midst of that new experience, and your senses send a rush of corresponding information from the external world to your neocortex, its neural networks organize themselves to reflect the event. Thus, experience enriches the brain even further than new knowledge.

The moment those networks of neurons fire with a pattern specific to that new experience, the emotional brain manufactures and releases chemicals in the form of peptides. This chemical cocktail has a specific signature that reflects the emotions you are experiencing in the moment. As you now know, emotions are the end products of experience; a new experience creates a new emotion (which signals new genes in new ways). Thus, emotions signal the body to record the event chemically, and you begin to *embody* what you are learning.

In the process, the limbic brain assists in forming long-term memories: you can remember any experience better because you can recall how you felt emotionally while the event was occurring. (The neocortex and limbic brain together enable us to form *declarative memories,* meaning that we can declare what we've learned or experienced.[1] See Figure 6B[1] for more information on declarative and nondeclarative memories.)

You can see, then, how we are marked emotionally by highly charged experiences. All people who have been married can tell you where they were and what they were doing when they or their beloved proposed. Perhaps they were eating a great meal on the patio of their favorite restaurant, feeling the balmy breezes of that summer night and enjoying the sunset while the strains of Mozart played softly in the background, when their dinner partner got down on one knee and held out a little black box.

The combination of everything they were experiencing in that moment made them feel very different from their normal self. The typical internal chemical balance that their identity self had memorized got knocked out of order by what they saw, heard, and felt. In a sense, they woke up from the familiar, routine environmental stimuli that typically bombard the brain and cause us to think and feel in predictable ways. Novel events surprise us to the point that we become more aware in the present moment.

If the limbic brain had a motto, it might be: *Experience is for the body.*

If knowledge is for the mind, and experience is for the body, then when you apply knowledge and create a new experience, you teach the body what the mind has intellectually learned. Knowledge without experience is merely philosophy; experience without knowledge is ignorance. There's a progression that has to take place. You have to take knowledge and live it—embrace it emotionally.

If you're still with me as I've been discussing how to change your life, you've learned about gaining knowledge, and then taking action to have a new experience, which produces a new feeling. Next, you have to memorize that feeling and move what you've learned from the conscious mind to the subconscious mind. You've already got the hardware to do that in the third brain area we'll discuss.

From Thinking and Doing to Being: The <u>Cerebellum</u> Stores Habitual Thoughts, Attitudes, and Behaviors

Do you remember my talking about the common experience when we can't consciously remember a phone number, ATM PIN, or lock combination, but we've practiced it so often that the body knows better than the brain, and our fingers automatically get the job done? That may seem like a small thing. But when the body knows equal to or better than the conscious mind, when you can repeat an experience at will without much conscious effort, then you have memorized the action, behavior, attitude, or emotional reaction until it has become a skill or a habit.

When you reach this level of ability, you have moved into a state of being. In the process, you've activated the third brain area that plays a major role in changing your life—the *cerebellum,* seat of the subconscious.

The most active part of the brain, the cerebellum is located at the back of the skull. Think of it as the brain's microprocessor and memory center. Every neuron in the cerebellum has the potential to connect with at least 200,000—and up to a million—other cells, to process balance, coordination, awareness of the spatial relation of body parts, and execution of controlled movements. The cerebellum stores certain types of simple actions and skills, along with hardwired attitudes, emotional reactions, repeated actions, habits, conditioned behaviors, and unconscious reflexes and skills that we have mastered and memorized. Possessing amazing memory storage, it easily downloads various forms of learned information into programmed states of mind and body.

When you are in a state of being, you begin to memorize a new neurochemical self. That's when the cerebellum takes over, making that new state an implicit part of your subconscious programming. The cerebellum is the site of *nondeclarative memories,* meaning that you've done or practiced something so many times that it becomes second nature and you don't have to think about it; it's become so automatic that it's hard to declare or describe how you do it. When that happens, you will arrive at a point when happiness (or whatever attitude, behavior, skill, or trait you've been focusing on and rehearsing mentally or physically) will become an innately memorized program of the new self.

Let's use a true-to-life example to take a practical look at how these three brains take us from thinking to doing to being. First, we'll see how through conscious mental rehearsal, the thinking brain (neocortex) uses knowledge to activate new circuits in new ways to make a new mind. Then, our thought creates an experience, and via the emotional (limbic) brain, that produces a new emotion. Our thinking and feeling brains condition the body to a new mind. Finally, if we reach the point where mind and body are working as one, the cerebellum enables us to memorize a new neurochemical self, and our new state of being is now an innate program in our subconscious.

A Real-Life Example of the Three Brains in Action

As a practical look into these ideas, suppose that you recently read a few thought-provoking books about compassion, including one written by the Dalai Lama, a biography of Mother Teresa, and an account of the work of Saint Francis of Assisi.

This knowledge allowed you to think outside the box. Reading this material would have forged new synaptic connections in your thinking brain. Essentially, you learned about the philosophy of compassion (through other people's experiences, not yours). Moreover, you've sustained those neural connections by reviewing what you learned on a daily basis: You're so enthusiastic that you are solving all of your friends' problems by offering advice and holding court. You have become the great philosopher. Intellectually, you know your stuff.

As you're driving home from work, your spouse calls to say that you've been invited to dinner with your mother-in-law in three days. You pull off the road, and already you're thinking about how you have disliked your MIL intensely ever since she hurt your feelings ten years ago. Soon you've got a mental laundry list: you never liked her opinionated way of talking; how she interrupts others; how she smells; even how she cooks. Whenever you're around her, your heart races, your jaw tightens, your face and body are tense, you feel jittery, and you just want to jump up and leave.

Still sitting in your car, you remember those books on the philosophy of compassion, and you think about what you learned theoretically. It occurs to you, *Maybe if I try to apply what I read in those books, I might have a new experience of my mother-in-law. What did I learn that I can personalize to change the outcome of this dinner?*

When you contemplate applying that understanding with your MIL, something wonderful begins to happen. You decide not to react to her with your typical set of automatic programs. Instead, you begin to think about who you no longer want to be, and who you want to be instead. You ask yourself, *How do I not want to feel, and how am I not going to act, when I see her?* Your frontal lobe begins to "cool off" the neural circuits that are connected to the old you; you're starting to unwire or prune away that old you from functioning as an identity. You could say that because your brain isn't firing in the same way, you're no longer creating the same mind.

Then you review what those books said to help you plan how you want to think, feel, and act toward your MIL. You ask yourself, *How can I modify my behavior—my actions—and my reactions so my new experience leads to a new feeling?* So you picture yourself greeting and hugging her, asking her questions about things you know she is interested in, and complimenting her on her new hairdo or glasses. Over the next few days, as you mentally rehearse your new ideal of self, you continue to install more neurological hardware so you'll have the proper circuits in place (in effect, a new software program) when you actually interact with your MIL.

For most of us, to go from thinking to doing is like inspiring snails to pick up the pace. We want to stay in the intellectual, philosophical realm of our reality; we like to identify with the memorized, recognizable feeling of our familiar self.

Instead, by surrendering old thought patterns, interrupting habitual emotional reactions, and forgoing knee-jerk behaviors, then planning and rehearsing new ways of being, you are putting *yourself* into the equation of that knowledge you learned, and beginning to create a new mind—you are reminding yourself who you want to be.

But there is another step that we must address here.

What happened as you began to observe your "old-personality self" related to the familiar thoughts, habitual behaviors, and memorized emotions that you previously connected with your mother-in-law? In a way, you were going into the operating system of the subconscious mind, where those programs exist, and you were the *observer* of those programs. When you can become aware of or notice who you are being, you are becoming conscious of your unconscious self.

As you began to psychologically project yourself into a potential situation ahead of the actual experience (the impending dinner), you began to rewire your neural circuitry to look as though the event (being compassionate toward your MIL) had already taken place. Once those new neural networks began to fire in unison, your brain created a picture, vision, model, or what I will call a *hologram* (a multidimensional image) representing the ideal self that you were focused on being. The instant this happened, you made what you were thinking about more real than anything else. Your brain captured the thought as the experience, and "upscaled" its gray matter to look as though the experience had already occurred.

Embodying Knowledge Through Experience: Teaching the Body What the Mind Has Learned

Soon it's game time, and you find yourself sitting at dinner, face-to-face with "good ol' Mom." Instead of knee-jerking when her typical behaviors manifest, you stay conscious, remember what you learned, and decide to try it out. Rather than judging, attacking, or feeling animosity toward her, you do something completely different for you. Like the books encouraged, you stay in the present moment, open your heart, and really listen to what she's saying. You no longer hold her to her past.

Lo and behold, you modify your behavior and restrain your impulsive emotional reactions, thereby creating a new experience with your MIL. That activates the limbic brain to cook up a new blend of chemicals, which generates a new emotion, and all of a sudden, you truly start to feel compassion for her. You see her for who she is; you even see aspects of yourself in her. Your muscles relax, you feel your heart opening, and you breathe deeply and freely.

You had such a great feeling that day that it lingers. Now you're inspired and open-minded, and you find that you truly love your mother-in-law. As you couple your new, internal feeling of goodwill and love with this person in your external reality, you connect compassion with your mother-in-law. You form an *associative memory*.

Once you began to feel the emotion of compassion, in a sense you (chemically) instructed your body what your mind (philosophically) knew, and that activated and modified some of your genes. Now you've gone from thinking to doing: your behaviors match your conscious intentions; your actions are equal to your thought; mind and body are aligned and working together. You did exactly what those people did in those books. So by intellectually learning compassion with your brain and mind, then demonstrating this ideal in your environment through experience, you embodied this elevated feeling. You just conditioned your body to a new mind of compassion. Your mind and body were working together. *You embodied compassion.* In a sense, the word has become flesh.

Two Brains Have Taken You from Thinking to Doing, but Can You Create a State of Being?

From your efforts to embody compassion, you now have your neocortex and limbic brain working together. You're out of the box of the familiar, habitual memorized self, which operates within a set of automatic programs, and you're in a new thinking and feeling cycle. You have experienced how compassion feels; and you like it better than covert hostility, rejection, and suppressed anger.

Hold on, though, you are not yet ready for sainthood! It's not enough to have mind and body working together *one time.* That got you from thinking to doing, but can you reproduce that feeling of compassion at will? Can you repeatedly embody compassion independent of conditions in your environment, so that no person or situation could ever create that old state of being in you again?

If not, you haven't yet mastered compassion. *My definition of mastery is that our internal chemical state is greater than anything in our external world.* You are a master when you've conditioned yourself with chosen thoughts and feelings, you've memorized desired emotional/chemical states, and nothing in your external life deters you from your aims. No person, no thing, and no experience at any time or place should disrupt your internal chemical coherence. You can think, act, and feel differently whenever you choose.

If You Can Master Suffering,
You Can Just as Easily Master Joy

You probably know someone who has mastered suffering, right? So you call her and ask, "How are you?"

So-so.

"Listen, I'm going to go out with some friends to a new art gallery, and then eat at this restaurant that has really healthy desserts. Afterward, we're going to listen to some live music. Would you like to come with us?"

No. I don't feel like it.

But if she said what she actually meant, she'd say, *I've memorized this emotional state, and nothing in my environment—no person, no experience, no condition, no thing—is going to move me from my internal chemical state of suffering. It feels better to be in pain than to let go and be happy. I am enjoying my addiction for now, and all these things that you want to do might distract me from my emotional dependency.*

But guess what? We can just as easily master an internal chemical state such as joy or compassion.

In the preceding example with your mother-in-law, if you practiced your thoughts, behaviors, and feelings enough times, "being" compassionate would become rather natural. You would evolve from just *thinking* about it, to *doing* something about it, to *being* it. "Being" means that it's easy, natural, second nature, routine, and unconscious. Compassion and love would be as automatic and familiar to you as those self-limiting emotions you just changed.

So now you need to replicate this experience of thinking, feeling, and acting out of compassion. If you do, you will break the addiction of your past emotional state and neurochemically condition your body and mind to memorize the internal chemical state called compassion better than your conscious mind. Ultimately, if you repeatedly re-create the experience of compassion at will, practicing it independent of any circumstance in your life, your body would become the mind of compassion. You would memorize compassion so well that nothing from your outside world could move you from this state of being.

Now all three brains are working together; and you are biologically, neurochemically, and genetically in a state of compassion. When compassion becomes unconditionally ordinary and familiar for you, you have progressed from knowledge to experience to wisdom.

Progressing to a State of Being:
The Role of Our Two Memory Systems

We have three brains that allow us to evolve from thinking to doing to being. Take a look at this chart:

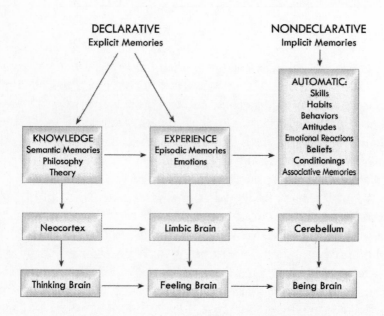

Figure 6B(1). Declarative and nondeclarative memories.

There are two memory systems in the brain:

— The first system is called **declarative** or **explicit memories.** When we remember and can declare what we have learned or experienced, those are declarative memories. There are two types of declarative memories: knowledge (semantic memories derived from philosophical knowledge) and experience (episodic memories derived from sensory experiences, identified as events in our lives with particular people, animals, or objects, while we were doing or witnessing a certain thing at a particular time and place). Episodic memories tend to imprint longer in the brain and body than semantic memories.

— The second memory system is called **nondeclarative** or **implicit memories.** When we practice something so many times that it's become second nature—we no longer have to think about it; it's like we almost can't declare how we do it—the body and mind are one. This is the seat of our skills, habits, automatic behaviors, associative memories, unconscious attitudes, and emotional reactions.

KNOWLEDGE + EXPERIENCE = WISDOM

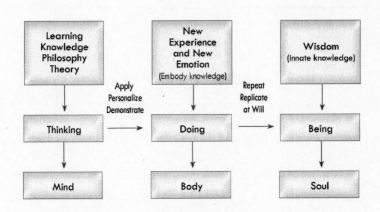

Figure 6B(2). Three brains: thinking to doing to being.

Thus, when we take what we learn intellectually (neocortex), and apply it, personalize it, or demonstrate it, we will modify our behavior in some way. When we do, we will create a new experience, which will produce a new emotion (limbic brain). If we can repeat, replicate, or experience that action at will, we will move into a state of being (cerebellum).

Wisdom is accumulated knowledge that has been gained through repeated experience. And when "being" compassionate is as natural as suffering; judging; blaming; or being frustrated, negative, or insecure, now we are wise. We are liberated to seize new opportunities, because somehow life seems to organize itself equal to how or who we are being.

EVOLVING YOUR BEING

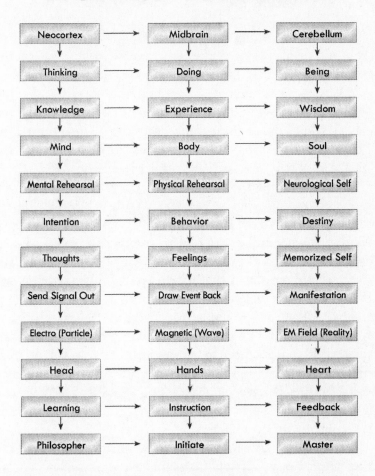

Figure 6C. This chart shows the progression of how the three brains align to correlate different avenues of personal evolution.

Going from Thinking Straight to Being:
A Prelude to Meditation

Going from thinking to doing to being is a progression that we've all experienced many times, whether it was when we learned to be a driver, a skier, a knitter, or a person to whom speaking a second language has become second nature.

Now, let's talk about one of evolution's great gifts to us as humans: the ability to go from thinking to being—without taking any physical action. Said another way, we can create a new state of being ahead of having an actual material experience.

We do this all the time, and it's not a case of "Fake it till you make it." For example, you have a sexual fantasy in which you inwardly experience all the thoughts, feelings, and actions you look forward to when your partner returns from a trip. You're so present with your internal experience that your body is chemically altered and responds as if that future event is already upon you in that exact moment. You have moved into a new state of being. Similarly, whether you're mentally rehearsing the speech you're going to give, reminding yourself how you're going to handle the confrontation that you need to have with your co-worker, or imagining what you want to eat when you're really hungry but stuck in traffic—and in each case you're thinking about that to the exclusion of everything else—your body will begin to move into a state of being just by thought alone.

Okay, but how far can you take this? Through thinking and feeling alone, can you finally be the person you want to be? Can you create and live a chosen reality, as my daughter did when she experienced the summer job of her dreams?

That's where meditation comes in. People use meditative techniques for a lot of reasons, as you know. In this book, you will learn a special meditation designed for a specific purpose—to help you overcome the habit of being yourself and become that ideal self you desire. Through the remainder of this chapter, we'll connect some of the knowledge we've covered up to now with the meditation you will soon learn. (Whenever I discuss meditation or the meditative process, I will be referring to the process that will be our focus in Part III.)

Meditation allows us to change our brains, bodies, and state of being. Most important, we can make these changes without having to take any physical action or have any interaction with the external environment. Through meditation, we can install the necessary neurological hardware, just as those piano players and finger exercisers made changes through mental rehearsal. (Those research subjects used mental rehearsal alone, but for our purposes, it is one component of the meditative process, albeit a very important one.)

If I asked you to think about the qualities that your ideal self would possess, or if I suggested that you contemplate what it would feel like to be a person of greatness such as Mother Teresa or Nelson Mandela, then just by contemplating a new way of being, you would begin firing your brain in new ways and making a new mind. That's mental rehearsal in action. I'm now asking you to reflect on what it would feel like to be happy, content, satisfied, and at peace. What would you envision for yourself if you were to create a new ideal of *you?*

Essentially, the meditative process allows you to answer this question by bringing together all of the information, learned and wired synaptically into your brain, about what it means to be happy, content, satisfied, and at peace. In meditation, you take that knowledge and then place yourself in the equation. Instead of merely asking what it would mean to be happy, you put yourself in the position of practicing, and thus living in, a state of happiness. After all, you know what happiness looks and feels like. You've had past experiences with it yourself; you've seen other people's versions of it. Now, you get to pick and choose from that knowledge and experience to create a new ideal of yourself.

I've talked about how, through the frontal lobe, you activate new circuits in new ways to create a new mind. Once you experience that new mind, your brain creates a kind of holographic image that gives you a model to follow in creating your future reality. Because you have installed new neural circuits ahead of any real experience, you don't have to carry out a nonviolent revolution, as Gandhi did; you don't have to lead your people and be burned at the stake, as Joan of Arc was. You simply have to use your knowledge and experience of those qualities of courage and conviction to produce an emotional effect within you. The result will be a state of mind. By repeatedly producing that state of mind, it will become familiar to you, and you will be wiring new circuits. The more often you produce that state of mind, the more those thoughts will become the experience.

Once that thought-experience transformation takes place, the end product of that experience will be a feeling, an emotion. When this occurs, your body (as the unconscious mind) does not know the difference between an event that takes place in physical reality and the emotions you created by thought alone.

As someone who is conditioning the body to a new mind, you'll find that your thinking brain and the emotional brain are now working in concert. Remember that thoughts are for the brain, and feelings are for the body. When you are both thinking and feeling in a specific way as a part of the meditative process, you are different from when you started out. The newly installed circuits, the neurological and chemical changes that have been produced by those thoughts and emotions, have altered you in such a way that there is physical evidence in the brain and body that shows those changes.

At that point, you've moved into a state of being. You're no longer just *practicing* happiness or gratitude or whatever; you are *being* grateful or happy. You can produce that state of mind and body every day; you can continually reexperience an event and produce the emotional response to that experience of how you would feel if you were that new, ideal self.

If you can get up from your meditative session and be in that new state of being—altered neurologically, biologically, chemically, and genetically—you have activated those changes ahead of any experience, and you will be more prone to acting and thinking in ways equal to who you are being. You have broken the habit of being yourself!

THINKING TO BEING

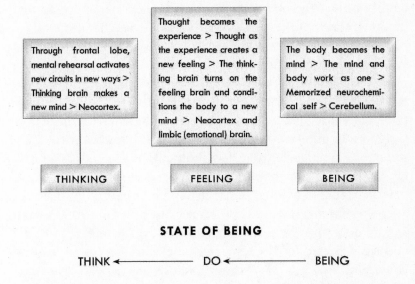

| Through frontal lobe, mental rehearsal activates new circuits in new ways > Thinking brain makes a new mind > Neocortex. | Thought becomes the experience > Thought as the experience creates a new feeling > The thinking brain turns on the feeling brain and conditions the body to a new mind > Neocortex and limbic (emotional) brain. | The body becomes the mind > The mind and body work as one > Memorized neurochemical self > Cerebellum. |

THINKING   **FEELING**   **BEING**

STATE OF BEING

THINK ⟵——————— DO ⟵——————— BEING

Figure 6D. You can go from thinking to being without having to do anything. If you are mentally rehearsing a new mind, there will come a moment that the thought you are thinking about will become the experience. When this occurs, the end product of that inward experience is an emotion or feeling. Once you can feel what it would feel like to be that person, your body (as the unconscious mind) begins to believe it is in that reality. Now your mind and body begin to work as one, and you are "being" that person without having to do anything yet. As you move into a new state of being by thought alone, you will be more prone to do things and think things equal to how you are being.

As a reminder, when you are in a new state of being—a new personality—you also create a new personal reality. Let me repeat that. *A new state of being creates a new personality . . . a new personality produces a new personal reality.*

How will you know whether this meditative practice has activated your three brains to produce the intended effect? Simple: you will feel different as a result of investing in the process. If you feel exactly as you did before, if the same catalysts produce the same reactions in you, then nothing has happened in the quantum field. Your same thoughts and feelings are reproducing the same electromagnetic signal in the field. You haven't changed chemically, neurologically, genetically, or in any other way. But if you eventually get up after your meditation sessions and feel different from when you began them, and if you can maintain that modified state of mind and body, then you *have* changed.

What you've changed inside of you—the new state of being that you created—should now produce an effect outside of you. You've moved beyond the cause-and-effect model of the universe, that old Newtonian concept of something external to you controlling your thoughts, actions, and emotions. I'll return to this point in a bit.

You will also know that your meditation has been fruitful if something unexpected and new shows up in your life as a result of your efforts. Remember: the quantum model tells us that if you have created a new mind and a new state of being, you have an altered electromagnetic signature. Because you are thinking and feeling differently, you are changing reality. Together, thoughts and feelings can do this; separately they cannot. Let me remind you again: *You can't think one way and feel another and expect anything in your life to change.* The combination of your thoughts and feelings is your state of being. Change your state of being . . . and change your reality.

Here's where coherent signals really come into play. If you can send into the quantum field a signal coherent in thought and feeling (state of being), independent of the external world, then something different will show up in your life. When it does, you'll no doubt experience a powerful emotional response, which will inspire you to create a new reality once again—and you can use that emotion to generate an even more wonderful experience.

Let me get back to Newton. We are all conditioned by the Newtonian notion that life is dominated by cause and effect. When something good happens to us, we express gratitude or joy. So we go through life waiting for someone or something outside ourselves to regulate our feelings.

Instead, I'm asking you to take control and to invert the process. Rather than waiting for an occasion to cause you to feel a certain way, create the feeling ahead of any experience in the physical realm; convince your body emotionally that a "gratitude-generating" experience has already taken place.

To do this, you can pick a potential in the quantum field and get in touch with how it would feel if you were experiencing it. I'm asking you to use thought and feeling to put yourself in the shoes of that future self, that possible you, so vividly that you begin to emotionally condition your body to believe that you are that person *now*. When you open your eyes after your meditative session, who do you want to be? What would it feel like to be this ideal self, or to have this desired experience?

To fully break the habit of being yourself, say good-bye to cause and effect and embrace the quantum model of reality. Choose a potential reality that you want, live it in your thoughts and feelings, and give thanks ahead of the actual event. Can you accept the notion that once you change your internal state, you don't need the external world to provide you with a reason to feel joy, gratitude, appreciation, or any other elevated emotion?

When your body experiences that the event is occurring in that moment and it feels real to you, based solely on what you're focused on mentally and are feeling emotionally, then you are experiencing the future now. The moment you are in that state of being, in that *now* moment and present in that experience, that's when you are connected to all possible realities that exist in the quantum field. Remember that if you are in the past or the future, based on your familiar emotions or anticipation of some effect, you don't have access to all possibilities the quantum field holds. The only way to access the quantum field is by being in the now.

Keep in mind that this cannot be just an intellectual process. Thoughts and feelings must be coherent. In other words, this meditation requires that you drop down about ten inches out of your head and move into your heart. Open your heart and think about how it would feel if you embodied a combination of all the traits that you admire and that make up your ideal self.

You may object that you can't know how it would feel, because you've never experienced what it's like to have those traits and to be that ideal self. My response is that your body can experience this before you have any physical evidence, ahead of your senses: If a future desire that you've never experienced actually does manifest in your life, you'd have to agree that you would experience an elevated emotion such as joy, excitement, or gratitude . . . so those emotions are what you can naturally focus on. Instead of being enslaved to emotions that are only the residue of the past, you are now using elevated emotions to create the future.

The elevated emotions of gratitude, love, and so forth all have a higher frequency that will help you move into a state of being where you can feel as though the desired events have actually occurred. If you are in a state of greatness, then the signal you send into the quantum field is that the events have already come to pass. Giving thanks allows you to emotionally condition your body to believe that what is producing your gratitude has already happened. By activating and coordinating your three brains, meditation allows you to move from thinking to being—and once you are in a new state of being, you are more prone to act and think equal to who you are being.

Perhaps you've wondered why it may be hard to move into a state of gratitude or to give thanks ahead of the actual experience. Is it possible that you've been living by a memorized emotion that has become so much a part of your identity, on a subconscious level, that now you cannot feel any other way than you're accustomed to? If so, maybe your identity has become a matter of how you appear to the world on the outside, to distract you and change how you feel on the inside.

In the next chapter, we're going to examine how to close that gap and bring about true liberation. When you can readily feel gratitude or joy, or fall in love with the future—without needing any person, thing, or experience to cause you to feel that way—then these elevated emotions will be available to fuel your creations.

CHAPTER SEVEN

THE GAP

I was sitting on my couch one day, thinking about what it means to be happy. As I contemplated my utter lack of joy, I thought about how most people who were important to me would have given me a pep talk right on the spot. I imagined it verbatim: *You're so incredibly lucky. You have a wonderful family, which includes beautiful kids. You are a successful chiropractor. You lecture to thousands of people, you travel the world going to unusual places, you were featured in <u>What the BLEEP Do We Know!?</u>, and many people loved your message. You even wrote a book, and it is doing well.* They would have hit all of the right emotional and logical notes. But to me, something wasn't right.

I was at a point in my life where I was traveling from city to city every weekend doing lectures; sometimes I was in two cities within three days. It occurred to me that I was so busy that I had no time to actually practice what I was teaching.

This was an unnerving moment, because I began to see that all of my happiness was created from outside of me, and that the joy I experienced when I was traveling and lecturing had nothing to do with *real* joy. It appeared to me that I *needed* everyone, everything, and everyplace outside of me in order to feel good. This image that I was projecting to the world was dependent on external factors.

And when I was not out lecturing or doing interviews or treating patients, and I was home, I felt empty.

Don't get me wrong; in some ways those things outside of me were great. If you had asked anyone who saw me lecturing, deeply engrossed in working on a presentation during a flight, or answering dozens of e-mails while in an airport or hotel lounge, such an observer would have said that I appeared to be pretty happy.

The sad truth is that if you had asked *me* at one of those moments, I would have probably responded in much the same way: *Yes, things are great. I'm doing well. I'm a lucky guy.*

But if you had caught me in a quiet moment, when all those other stimuli weren't bombarding me, I would have responded in a completely different manner: *Something's not right. I feel unsettled. Everything feels like the same old, same old. Something is missing.*

On the day I recognized the core reason for my unhappiness, I also realized that I needed the external world to remember who I was. My identity had become the people I talked to, the cities I visited, the things I did while I was traveling, and the experiences I needed in order to reaffirm myself as this person called Joe Dispenza. And when I wasn't around anyone who could help me recall this personality that the world might know as me, I wasn't sure who *I* was anymore. In fact, I saw that all of my perceived happiness was really just a reaction to stimuli in the external world that made me feel certain ways. I then understood that I was totally addicted to my environment, and I was dependent on external cues to reinforce my emotional addiction. What a moment for me. I had heard a million times that happiness comes from within, but it never hit me like this before.

As I sat on the couch in my house that day, I looked out the window and an image came to me. I envisioned my two hands, one above the other, separated by a gap.

THE IDENTITY GAP

HOW WE APPEAR
- The identity I project to the outer environment
- Who I want you to think I am
- The facade
- Ideal for the world

WHO WE REALLY ARE
- How I feel
- Who I really am
- How I am on the inside
- Ideal for self

Figure 7A. The gap between "who we really are" and "how we appear."

The top hand represented how I appeared on the outside, and the bottom was how I knew myself to be on the inside. In my self-reflection, it dawned on me that we human beings live in a duality, as two separate entities—"how we appear" and "who we really are."

How we appear is the image or the façade that we project to the world. That self is everything we do in order to show up looking a certain way and to present to others a consistent exterior reality. This first aspect of the self is a veneer of how we want everyone to see us.

How we really are, represented by that bottom hand, is how we feel, especially when we are not distracted by the external environment. It is our familiar emotions when we are not preoccupied by "life." It's what we hide about ourselves.

When we memorize addictive emotional states such as guilt, shame, anger, fear, anxiety, judgment, depression, self-importance, or hatred, we develop a gap between *the way we appear* and *the way we really are*. The former is how we want other people to see us. The latter is our state of being when we are not interacting with all of the different experiences, diverse things, and assorted people at various times and places in our lives. If we sit long enough without doing anything, we begin to feel *something*. That something is who we really are.

THE LAYERS of EMOTION
WE MEMORIZE that
CREATE the GAP

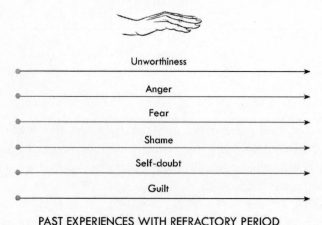

Unworthiness

Anger

Fear

Shame

Self-doubt

Guilt

PAST EXPERIENCES WITH REFRACTORY PERIOD

Figure 7B. The size of the gap varies from person to person. "Who we really are" and "how we appear" are separated by the feelings we memorize throughout different points in our lives (based on past experiences). The bigger the gap, the greater the addiction to the emotions we memorize.

Layer by layer, we wear various emotions, which form our identity. In order to remember who we think we are, we have to re-create the same experiences to reaffirm our personality and the corresponding emotions. As an identity, we become attached to our external world by identifying with everyone and everything, in order to remind us of how we want to project ourselves to the world.

How we appear becomes the façade of the personality, which relies on the external world to remember who it is as a "somebody." Its identity is completely attached to the environment. The personality does everything it can to hide how it really feels or to make that feeling of emptiness go away: *I own these cars, I know these people, I've been to these places, I can do these things, I've had these experiences, I work for this company, I am successful. . . .* It is who we think we are in relation to everything around us.

But that is different from who we are—how we feel—without the stimulation of our outer reality: Feelings of shame and anger about a failed marriage. Fear of death and uncertainty about the afterlife, related to the loss of a loved one or even a pet. A sense of inadequacy due to a parent's insistence on perfectionism and achievement at all costs. A sense of stifled entitlement from having grown up in circumstances barely above poverty. A preoccupation with thoughts of not having the right body type in order to look a certain way to the world. These kinds of feelings are what we want to conceal.

This is who we truly are, the real self hiding behind the image we are projecting. We can't face exposing that self to the world, so we pretend to be someone else. We create a set of memorized automatic programs that work to cover the vulnerable parts of us. Essentially, we lie about who we are because we know that societal mores do not have room for that person. That is the "nobody." That is the person whom we doubt others will like and accept.

Particularly when we are younger and are forming our identity, we are more likely to engage in this kind of masquerade. We see young people trying on identities like they try on clothes. And in truth, what teens wear is often a reflection of who they want to be, more than it reflects who they really are. Ask any mental-health professional who specializes in working with young people, and she will tell you that one word defines what it is like to be an adolescent: *insecurity.* As a result, teens and preteens seek comfort in conformity and in numbers.

Rather than let the world know what you are really like, adopt and adapt (because everyone knows what happens to those who are perceived to be different). The world is complex and scary, but make it less frightening and much simpler by lumping everyone into groups. Pick your group. Pick your poison.

Eventually, that identity fits. You grow into it. Or at least that's what you tell yourself. Along with the insecurity comes a great deal of self-consciousness. Questions abound: *Is this who I really am? Is this who I really want to be?* But it's so much easier to ignore those questions than to answer them.

Life Experiences Define Our Identity . . .
Staying Busy Keeps Unwanted Emotions at Bay

All of us have been emotionally scarred from traumatic or difficult experiences as young people. Early in life, we experienced defining events, the emotions of which contributed, layer by layer, to who we became. Let's face it: we all have been branded by emotionally charged events. As we mentally reviewed the experience repeatedly, the body began to relive the event over and over, just by thought alone. We kept the refractory period of emotion running for so long that we journeyed from a mere emotional reaction to a mood, to a temperament, and ultimately, to a personality trait.

While we are young, we keep busy doing things that, for a while, stave off those old, deep emotions, sweeping them under the rug. It is intoxicating to make new friends, travel to unknown places, work hard and achieve a promotion, learn a new skill, or take up a new sport. We seldom suspect that many of these actions are motivated by feelings left over from certain earlier events in life.

Then we really get busy. We go to school, then possibly college; we buy a car; we move to a new town, state, or country; we begin a career; we meet new people; we get married; we buy a house; we have kids; we adopt pets; we may get divorced; we work out; we start a new relationship; we practice a skill or a hobby. . . . We use everything that we know in the external world to define our identity, and to distract us from how we really feel inside. And since all of these unique experiences produce myriad emotions, we notice that those emotions seem to take away any feelings that we are hiding. And it works for a while.

Don't get me wrong. We all reach greater heights from applying ourselves throughout different periods in our growing years. In order to accomplish many things in our lifetimes, we have to push ourselves outside our comfort zones and go beyond familiar feelings that once defined us. I am certainly aware of this dynamic in life. But when we never overcome our limitations and continue carrying the baggage from our past, it will always catch up with us. And this usually happens starting around our mid-30s (this can vary greatly from one person to another).

Midlife: A Series of Strategies to Make Buried Feelings Stay Buried

By our mid-30s or 40s, when the personality is complete, we have experienced much of what life has to offer. And as a result, we can pretty much anticipate the outcome of most experiences; we already know how they're going to feel before we engage in them. Because we've had several good and bad relationships, we've competed in business or settled into our career, we've suffered loss and encountered success, or we know what we like and dislike, we know the nuances of life. Since we can predict the likely emotions ahead of an actual experience, we determine whether we want to experience that "known" event before it actually occurs. Of course, all of this is happening *behind the scenes of our awareness*.

Here is where it gets sticky. Because we can predict the feelings that most events will bring, we already know what will make our feelings about who we really are go away. However, when we reach midlife, nothing can completely take away that feeling of emptiness.

You wake up every morning and you feel like the same person. Your environment, which you relied on so heavily to remove your pain or guilt or suffering, is no longer taking away those feelings. How could it? You already know that when the emotions derived from the external world wear off, you will return to being the same leopard who hasn't changed its spots.

This is the midlife crisis that most people know about. Some try really hard to make buried feelings stay buried by diving further into their external world. They buy the new sports car (thing); others lease the boat (another thing). Some go on a long vacation (place). Yet others join the new social club to meet new contacts or make new friends (people). Some get plastic surgery (body). Many completely redecorate or remodel their homes (acquire things and experience a new environment).

All of these are futile efforts to do or try something new so that they can feel better or different. But emotionally, when the novelty wears off, they are still stuck with the same identity. They return to who they really are (that is, the bottom hand). They are drawn back to the same reality they have been living for years, just to keep the feeling of who they think they are as an identity. The truth is, the more they do—the more they buy and then consume—the more noticeable the feeling of who they "really are" becomes.

When we're trying to escape this emptiness, or when we're running from any emotion whatsoever that is painful, it is because to look at it is too uncomfortable. So when the feeling starts to get a bit out of control, most people turn on the TV, surf the Internet, or call or text someone. In a matter of moments we can alter our emotions so many times . . . we can view a sitcom or a YouTube video and laugh hysterically, then watch a football game and feel competitive, then watch the news and be angered or fearful. All of these outer stimuli can easily distract us from those unwanted feelings inside.

Technology is a great distraction and a powerful addiction. Think about it: You can immediately change your internal chemistry and make a feeling go away by changing something outside of you. And whatever it was outside of you that made you feel better inside of you, you will rely on that thing in order to sidetrack yourself over and over again. But this strategy doesn't have to involve technology; anything momentarily thrilling will do the trick.

When we keep that diversion up, guess what eventually happens? We grow more dependent on something outside of us to change us internally. Some people unconsciously delve deeper and deeper into this bottomless pit, using different aspects of their world to keep themselves preoccupied—in an effort to re-create the original feeling from the very first experience that helped them escape. They become overstimulated so that they can feel different from how they really are. But sooner or later, everyone realizes that they need more and more of the same to make them feel better. This becomes an all-consuming search for pleasure and ways to avoid pain at all costs—a hedonistic life unconsciously driven by some feeling that won't seem to go away.

A Different Midlife: A Time for Facing Feelings and Letting Go of Illusions

At this time of life, other people who *don't* strive to keep their feelings buried ask some big questions: *Who am I? What is my purpose in life? Where am I going? Who am I doing all of this for? What is God? Where do I go when I die? Is there more to life than "success"? What is happiness? What does all this mean? What is love? Do I love myself? Do I love anyone else?* And the soul begins to wake up. . . .

These types of questions begin to occupy the mind because we see through the illusion and suspect that nothing outside of us can ever make us happy. Some of us ultimately realize that nothing in our environment is going to "fix" the way we feel. We also recognize the enormous amount of energy it takes to keep up this projection of self as an image to the world, and how exhausting it is to keep the mind and body constantly preoccupied. Eventually we come to see that our futile attempt to maintain an ideal for others is really a strategy to make sure that those impending feelings we've been running from never capture us. How long can we juggle, keeping so many balls in the air, just so our lives don't come crashing down?

Instead of buying a bigger TV or the latest smart phone, these people stop running from the feeling that they've been trying to make go away for so long, face it head-on, and intently look at it. When this happens, the individual begins to wake up. After some self-reflection, she discovers who she really is, what she has been hiding, and what no longer is working for her. So she lets go of the façade, the games, and the illusions. She is honest about who she really is, at all costs, and she is not afraid to lose it all. This person stops expending the energy she had been putting into keeping an illusory image intact.

She gets in touch with her feelings and then turns to people in her life and says: *You know what? It doesn't matter if I don't make you happy any longer. I'm through obsessing about how I look or what other people think about me. I am finished living for everyone else. I want to be free from these chains.*

This is a profound moment in a person's life. The soul is waking up and nudging her to tell the truth about who she really is! The lie is over.

Change and Our Relationships: Breaking the Ties That Bind

Most relationships are based on what you have in common with others. Think about this: You meet a person, and immediately the two of you compare your experiences, as if you both are checking to see whether your neural networks and emotional memories are aligned. You say something like this: "I know these 'people.' I am from this 'place,' and I lived in these places at these different 'times' in my life. I went to this school and studied this subject. I own and do these 'things.' And most important, I've had these 'experiences.'"

Then the other person responds: "I know those 'people.' I've lived in those 'places' during those 'times.' I do these 'things,' too. I had those same 'experiences.'"

Thus, you can relate to each other. A relationship is then formed based on neurochemical states of being, because if you share the same experiences, you share the same emotions.

Think of emotions as "energy in motion." If you share the same emotions, you share the same energy. And just like two atoms of oxygen that share an invisible field of energy beyond space and time in order to bond together in a relationship to form air, you are bonded in an invisible field of energy to every thing, person, and place in your external life. Bonds between people are the strongest, though, because emotions hold the strongest energy. As long as either party doesn't change, things will be just fine.

EMOTIONAL BONDS

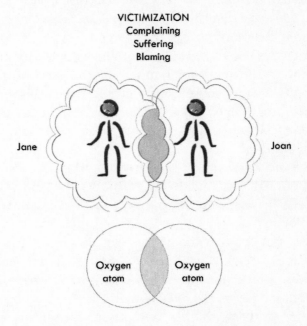

Figure 7C. If we share the same experiences, we share the same emotions and the same energy. Just like two atoms of oxygen bond to form the air we breathe, an invisible field of energy (beyond space and time) bonds us emotionally.

So when our friend in the example in the last section begins to tell the truth about how she really feels, things begin to get very uncomfortable. If her friendships have been based upon complaining about life, then she is bonded energetically in her relationships by the emotions of victimization. If, in a moment of enlightenment, she now decides to break from that habit of being herself, she is no longer showing up as that familiar person to whom everyone could relate. People in her life are using her to remind themselves of who *they* are emotionally as well. Friends and family respond: "What is wrong with you today? You've hurt my feelings!" Which translates to: *I thought we had a good thing going here! I used you to reaffirm my emotional addiction in order to remember who I think I am as a "somebody." I liked you better the other way.*

When it comes to change, our energy is connected to everything that we've had an experience with in our outer world. When we break the addiction of emotion we've memorized, or when we tell the truth about who we really are, doing that takes some real energy. Just as it takes energy to separate two atoms of oxygen that are bonded together, it takes energy to break the bonds with the people in our lives.

So the individuals in this person's life who have shared the same emotional bonds with her rally together and say, "She hasn't been herself lately. Maybe she's lost her mind. Let's get her to a doctor!"

Now remember that they have been people she shared the same experiences with; hence, they shared the same emotions. But now she's breaking the energetic bonds with everyone and everything—and even every *place*—familiar. This is a threatening moment for everyone who has been playing the same game with her for years. She's getting off the train.

So they bring her to the doctor, who gives her Prozac or some other drug, and in a short time, the person's former personality returns. And there she is, projecting her old image to the world, right back to shaking hands on others' emotional agreements. Once more she's numb and smiling—anything to take the feeling away. The lesson goes unlearned.

Yes, the person wasn't being herself—not the "top-hand" self that everyone had grown accustomed to. Instead, briefly, she was the "bottom-hand" self—the one with the past and the pain. And who can blame those loved ones who insisted on the return to her former numbed self that "went along to get along"? That new self emerged as unpredictable, even radical. Who wants to be around *that* person? Who wants to be around the truth?

What Really Matters in the End

If you need the environment in order to remember who you are as a somebody, what happens when you die and the environment rolls up and disappears? Do you know what goes with it? The somebody, the identity, the image, the personality (top hand) that has identified with all of the known and predictable elements in life, who was addicted to the environment. You could have been the most successful, popular, or beautiful person, and you could have had all the wealth you ever needed . . . but when your life ends and your external reality is taken away, everything outside of you can no longer define you. It all goes.

What you're left with is *who you really are* (bottom hand), not how you appear. When your life is over and you cannot rely on your external world to define you, you will be left with that feeling you never addressed. You would not have evolved as a soul in that lifetime.

For instance, if you had certain experiences 50 years prior that marked you as insecure or weak and you felt that way about yourself ever since, then you stopped growing emotionally 50 years ago. If the soul's purpose is to learn from experience and gain wisdom, but you stayed stuck in that particular emotion, you never turned your experience into a lesson; you didn't transcend that emotion and exchange it for any understanding. While that feeling still anchors your mind and body to those past events, you are never free to move into the future. And if a similar experience shows up in your present life, that event will trigger the same emotion and you will act as that person you were 50 years ago.

So your soul says: *Pay attention! I'm letting you know that nothing is bringing you joy. I'm sending you urges. If you keep playing this game, I'm going to stop trying to get your attention, and you will go back to sleep. Then I'll see you when your life is over. . . .*

It Always Takes More and More

Most people who do not know how to change think, *How can I make this feeling go away?* And if the novelty of accumulating new things wears off and stops working, what do they do? They look to *bigger* things, a whole other layer above where they were, and their avoidance strategies become addictions: *If I take a drug or drink enough alcohol, that's going to make this feeling go away. This external thing will produce an internal chemical change and make me feel great. I'll shop a lot, because shopping—even if I don't have the money—makes that emptiness go away. I'll watch pornography . . . I'll play video games . . . I'll gamble . . . I'll overeat. . . .*

THE MIDLIFE CRISIS:
An attempt to create a
NEW IDENTITY from the OUTSIDE

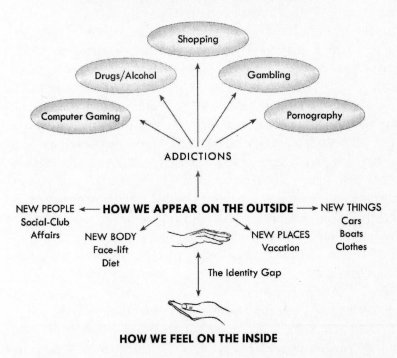

Figure 7D. When the same people and things in our lives create the same emotions, and the feeling we are trying to make go away no longer changes, we look for new people and things, or try going to new places, in an attempt to change how we feel emotionally. If that doesn't work, we go to the next level—addictions.

Whatever the addiction, people are still thinking that some external thing is going to take that internal feeling away. And remember: we have this natural propensity to associate an external thing that's making that feeling go away with our internal chemical change. And we like that external thing if it makes us feel good. So we run away from what feels bad or painful, and we move toward what feels good and comfortable or brings us pleasure.

As the excitement people get from their addiction continually stimulates the pleasure centers in the brain, they get a flood of chemicals from the thrill of the experience. The problem is that each time they gamble, binge, or stay up late playing online games, they need a little bit more the next time.

The reason why people need more drugs or more shopping or more affairs is that the chemical rush that's created from those activities activates the receptor sites on the outside of their cells, which "turns on" the cells. But if receptor sites are continually stimulated, they get desensitized and shut off. So they need a stronger signal, a bit more stimulation, to turn them on the next time—it takes a bigger chemical high to produce the same effects.

So now you've got to bet $25,000 instead of $10,000 because otherwise, there's no thrill. Once a $5,000 shopping spree does nothing for you, you've got to max out two credit cards so you can feel that same rush again. All of this is to make the feeling of who you really are go away. Everything you do to get the same high, you have to keep doing more of, with increasing intensity. More drugs, more alcohol, more sex, more gambling, more shopping, more TV. You get the idea.

Over time, we become addicted to something in order to ease the pain or anxiety or depression we live by on a daily basis. Is this wrong? Not really. Most people do these things because they just don't know how to change from the inside. They are only following the innate drive to get relief from their feelings, and unconsciously they think their salvation comes from the outside world. It has never been explained to them that using the outer world to change the inner world makes things worse . . . it only widens the gap.

And let's say that our ambition in life is to become successful and to accumulate more things. When we do, we reinforce who we are, without ever addressing how we really feel. I call this *being possessed by our possessions*. We become possessed by material objects, and those things reinforce the ego, which needs the environment to remind itself of who it is.

If we wait for anything outside us to make us happy, then we are not following the quantum law. We are relying on the outer to change the inner. If we are thinking that once we have the wealth to buy more things, then we will be overjoyed, we've got it backward. We have to become happy *before* our abundance shows up.

And what happens if addicts can't get more? They feel even angrier, more frustrated, more bitter, more empty. They may try other methods—add gambling to drinking, add shopping to TV and movie escapism. Eventually, though, nothing is ever enough. The pleasure centers have recalibrated to such a high level that when there is no chemical change from the outer world, it seems the addict now cannot find joy in the simplest things.

The point is, true happiness has nothing to do with pleasure, because the reliance on feeling good from such intensely stimulating things only moves us further from real joy.

The Bigger Gap—Emotional Addiction

I don't intend to diminish the severity of the damage caused by what I'll loosely refer to here as material addictions—to drugs, alcohol, sex, gambling, consumerism, and so forth. Those problems cause great harm to the numerous people who suffer from them and to those who love and work with such "addicts." While many people who experience these and other addictions can use the steps in these pages to overcome them—since they are a part of the Big Three—it's beyond the scope of this book to deal with these kinds of addictions specifically. But it is imperative to realize that behind every addiction, there is some memorized emotion that is driving the behavior.

What is not beyond the scope of this book and is, in fact, its central purpose is helping people break the habit of being themselves, whether they view that self as being an alcoholic; a sexaholic; a gambler; a shopaholic; or someone who is chronically lonely, depressed, angry, bitter, or physically unwell.

In thinking about the gap, possibly you said to yourself: *Well, of course we hide from other people our fears, insecurities, weaknesses, and dark side. If we gave those things free rein to be fully expressed, we'd likely be beyond anyone else's caring about us, let alone our caring about ourselves.* In a sense, that's true. But if we are to break free, it means we have to confront that true self and bring out into the light that shadow side of our personality.

The advantage of the system I employ is that you can confront those darker aspects of yourself without bringing them into the light of your everyday reality. You don't have to walk into your place of work or a family gathering and announce: "Hey, listen up, everyone! I'm a bad person because for a long time I resented my parents for having to spend a lot of time with my younger sibling, while I felt my needs were being neglected. So now I'm a really selfish person who craves attention and needs instant gratification in order to stop feeling unloved and inadequate."

Instead, in the privacy of your own home and your own mind, you can work on extinguishing negative aspects of self and replacing those characteristics (or at least, metaphorically, cutting way back on the role they play and allowing them only an occasional, brief appearance) with more positive and productive ones.

I want you to forget about past events validating the emotions you've memorized that have become part of your personality. Your problems will never be resolved by analyzing them while you are still caught up in the emotions of the past. Looking at the experience or reliving the event that created the problem in the first place will only bring up the old emotions and a reason to feel the same way. When you try to figure out your life within the same consciousness that created it, you will analyze your life away and excuse yourself from ever changing.

Instead, let's just unmemorize our self-limiting emotions. A memory without the emotional charge is called *wisdom*. Then we can look back objectively upon the event and see it and who we were being, without the filter of that emotion. If we take care of unmemorizing the emotional state (or eliminating it to the best of our ability), then we gain the freedom to live and think and act independent of the restraints or constraints of that feeling.

So if a person relinquished unhappiness and got on with his life—entered into a new relationship, got a new job, moved to a new place, and made new friends—and then he looked at that past event, he would see that it provided the adversity he needed in order to overcome who he was and become a new person. His perspective would change, just by seeing that he could actually overcome the problem.

Closing and even eliminating the gap between who we are and who we present to the world is likely the greatest challenge we all face in life. Whether we term this living authentically, conquering ourselves, or having people "get" us or accept us for who we are, this is something that most of us desire. Changing—closing the gap—must begin from within.

Yet far too often, most of us change only when we are faced with a crisis, trauma, or discouraging diagnosis of some sort. That crisis commonly comes in the form of a challenge, which may be *physical* (an accident, say, or an illness), *emotional* (the loss of someone we love, for example), *spiritual* (for instance, an accumulation of setbacks that has us questioning our worth and how the universe operates), or *financial* (a job loss, perhaps). Note that all of the above are about *losing* something.

Why wait for trauma or loss to occur and have your ego get knocked off balance due to that negative emotional state? Clearly, when a calamity befalls you, you have to act—you can't take care of business as usual when you've been knocked, as the expression goes, to your knees.

At those critical moments when we've really, really grown tired of being beaten down by circumstances, we'll say: *This can't go on. I don't care what it takes or how I feel* [body]. *I don't care how long it takes* [time]. *No matter what's going on in my life* [environment], *I'm going to change. I have to.*

We can learn and change in a state of pain and suffering, or we can do so in a state of joy and inspiration. We don't have to wait until we are so uncomfortable that we feel forced to move out of our resting state.

Side Effects of Closing the Gap

As you know, one of the key skills you need to develop is self-awareness/self-observation. That's a shortcut definition of what I mean when I talk about meditation in the next chapter. In meditation, you're going to look at the negative emotional state that has had such an impact on your life. You're going to recognize the primary state of your personality that drives your thoughts and behaviors so that you become intimately familiar with every nuance of them. Over time, you're going to use those powers of observation to help you unmemorize that negative emotional state. By doing so, you will surrender that emotion to a greater mind, closing the gap between who you are and who you have presented to the world in the past.

Picture yourself standing in a room with arms outstretched, pushing the opposite walls apart. Do you have any idea how much energy you would consume if you were trying to keep those walls from crushing you? Instead of doing that, what if you released those two walls, took a couple of steps forward (after all, that gap is kind of like a door, isn't it?), and walked out of that room and into a completely new one. What about that other room you left behind? Well, the walls have come together in such a way that you can't ever get back inside it. That gap has closed, and the separate parts of you have become unified. And what's going to happen to all that energy you were expending? Physics states that energy can't be created or destroyed; it can only be transferred or transformed. That's exactly what's going to happen to you when you get to the point that no thought, no emotion, no subconscious behavior goes unnoticed.

You can think of this another way: You'll be going into the operating system of the subconscious and bringing all that data and those instructions into your conscious awareness, to truly see where those urges and proclivities that have taken control of your life are located. You become conscious of your unconscious self.

When we break the chains of that bond, we liberate the body. It is no longer the mind, living in the same past day after day. When we liberate the body emotionally, we close the gap. When we close the gap, we release the energy that was once used to produce it. With that energy, we now have the raw material we can use to create a new life.

CLOSING THE GAP

Layer by layer, when you unmemorize emotions, you liberate energy.

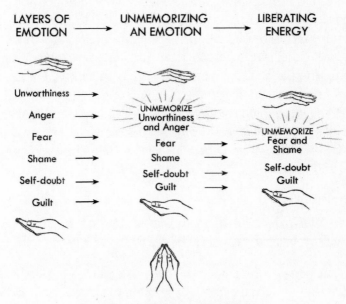

The ultimate goal: TRANSPARENCY.
When how you appear is who you really are.

Figure 7E. As you unmemorize any emotion that has become part of your identity, you close the gap between how you appear and who you really are. The side effect of this phenomenon is a release of energy in the form of a stored emotion in the body. Once the mind of that emotion is liberated from the body, energy is freed up into the quantum field for you to use as a creator.

Another side effect of breaking the bonds of your emotional addictions is that this release of energy is like a healthy shot of some wonderful elixir. Not only are you energized, but you feel something you likely haven't felt in quite a while—joy. When you liberate the body from the chains of an emotional dependency, you will feel up-lifted and inspired. Have you ever taken a long car trip? When you get out of your vehicle and finally stretch a bit and breathe fresh air, and the sound of the car's tires on the pavement or the heater's fan or the air conditioner's whir falls silent, that's a great feeling. Imag-ine how much better those new sensations would feel if you'd been locked in the trunk for 2,000 miles! For a lot of us, that's exactly how we've been feeling for a significant stretch of time.

Keep in mind that it's not enough merely to notice how you've been thinking, feeling, and behaving. Meditation requires you to be more active than that. You also have to tell the truth about yourself. You have to come clean and reveal what you've been hiding in that shadow part of the gap. You have to drag those things out into the bright light of day. And when you really see what you've been doing to yourself, you have to look at that mess and say, *This is no longer serving my best interests. This is no longer serving me. This has never been loving to myself.* Then you can make a decision to be free.

From Victimization to Unexpected Abundance: How One Woman Closed the Gap

One person who reaped the rewards of facing her life with the courage of a quantum observer is Pamela, a participant in one of my seminars. Pamela struggled financially because for two years, her unemployed ex-husband hadn't paid the mandated child sup-port. Frustrated, angry, and feeling victimized, she even reacted negatively to unrelated situations.

The meditation we did that day was about how the end product of any experience is an emotion. Because so many of our experi-ences involve family and friends, we share the resultant emotions with them. That's usually a good thing: bonds related to places we've been, things we've done—even objects we've shared—can strengthen our connection with people. But the flip side is that we also share the emotions associated with negative experiences.

We bond energetically with one another in a place beyond time and space. Because we are entangled with others (to use quantum terms) and frequently bond through survival-oriented emotions, it is almost impossible for us to change when we are still connected by negative experiences and emotions. Thus, reality stays the same.

In Pamela's case, her ex-husband's anxiety, guilt, and feelings of inferiority about not being able to support his children were interwoven into the fabric of her state of being, along with her own emotions of victimization, resentment, and lack. Whenever opportunity knocked, her victimhood reared its ugly head and produced an undesirable outcome. Her destructive emotions and the energy associated with them had virtually frozen her in a stagnant state of thinking, doing, and being. No matter what she did to try to change this situation, she and her ex-husband were bonded together by their mutual negative experiences, emotions, and energies; and thus none of her efforts ever changed her circumstances with him.

The workshop helped Pamela realize that she had to break this bond. She had to let go of the emotions that defined her in her present reality. She also learned how a cycle of thinking, feeling, and acting in the same way for years could produce a cascade effect that might trigger genes for disease—and she didn't want that to happen. *Something had to give.*

I like that phrase, because as Pamela told me afterward, during the meditation she recognized the injurious emotions that her victimization had set in motion—impatience with her kids, complaining and blaming, and feelings of desperation and lack. She let go of those emotions associated with past experiences, simultaneously releasing her self-involved state of being, and gave them up to the greater mind.

In so doing, Pamela released all of that frozen energy into the quantum field, closing the gap between who she thought she was and who she presented to the world. She did this so well— she started to feel so overjoyed and grateful—that she wanted abundance for everyone, not just herself. She moved from *selfish* emotions to *selfless* emotions. She got up from that meditation a different person from who she was before it.

Pamela's energy release signaled the field to begin organizing outcomes that were just right for the new self she was in the process of becoming. Almost immediately, she received evidence of this in two forms.

The first involved her Internet business. When she had previously tried a promotion, she fretted about the response to it, constantly checking her website, and saw only mediocre results. She initiated her second promotion the morning of the workshop, but was too busy to think about the results during the day. That evening, she was feeling the positive effects of having let go of the past. She felt even better when she discovered that she had earned nearly $10,000 that day from the promotion she'd run!

Pamela received the second piece of evidence three days later when her caseworker called to report that her ex had sent a check not just for that month, but for the full $12,000 in back support payments that he owed. She was beyond pleased to have "made" nearly $22,000 after doing that meditation. She did nothing in the physical realm to bring about those results, and couldn't have predicted how that money would find its way to her, but she was enormously grateful that it had.

What Pamela's story illustrates is the power of letting go of negative emotions. When we are mired in our timeworn mind-set and habitual behaviors and perceptions, there's no way for us to find solutions to problems rooted in the past. And those problems (experiences, really) produce powerful energetic emotions. Once we relinquish those, we experience an enormous release of energy, and reality magically rearranges itself.

By Moving Out of the Past, We Can Set Our Sights on the Future

Think about how much of your creative energy is tied up in guilt, judgment, fear, or anxiety related to people and experiences from your past. Imagine how much good you could do by converting any destructive energy to *productive* energy. Contemplate what you could accomplish if you weren't focused on survival (a selfish emotion), but instead worked to create out of positive intentions (a selfless emotion).

Ask yourself: *What energy from past experiences (in the form of limited emotions) am I holding on to that reinforces my past identity and emotionally attaches me to my current circumstances? Could I use this same energy and transform it into an elevated state from which to create a new and different outcome?*

Meditating will help you peel away some of the layers, remove some of the masks you've worn. Both of those things have blocked the flow of that grand intelligence within you. As a result of shedding those layers, you will become *transparent.* You are transparent when how you appear is *who you are.* And when you live your life that way, you will experience a state of gratitude, of elevated joy, which I believe is our natural state of being. As you do this, you begin to move out of the past so that you can set your sights on the future.

As you remove the veils that block the flow of this intelligence within you, you become more *like* it. You become more loving, more giving, more conscious, more willful—because that is *its* mind. The gap closes.

At that stage, you feel happy and whole. You no longer rely on the external world to define you. The elevated emotions you are feeling are unconditional. Nobody else and no event can make you feel that way. You are happy and feel inspired just because of who you are.

You no longer live in a state of lack or want. And do you know the funny thing about not wanting or lacking for anything? That's when you can really begin to manifest things naturally. Most people try to create in a state of lack, unworthiness, separation, or some other limited emotion rather than from a state of gratitude, enthusiasm, or wholeness. That's when the field responds most favorably to you.

All this starts with recognizing that the gap exists, and meditating on the negative emotional states that have produced that gap and dominated your personality. Unless you are prepared to look closely at yourself, and assess your propensities with tender honesty (not beating yourself up for your failings), you will forever be mired in some past event and the negative emotions it produced. See it. Understand it. Release it. Create with the energy available to you by taking the mind out of the body and releasing it into the field.

The Advertising Connection

Please understand that advertising agencies and their corporate clients fully understand the notion of lack and how it plays a commanding role in our behavior. They want us to believe that they have the answers to take away that emptiness, by our identifying with their product.

Advertisers even put famous faces in their ads to subconsciously plant the seed that the consumer can surely relate to this person as the "new you." *Feeling bad about yourself? Buy something! Don't fit in socially? Buy something! Feeling a negative emotion because of some sense of loss, separation, or longing? This microwave/big-screen TV/ car/cell phone . . . whatever . . . is just the ticket. You'll feel better about yourself, be accepted by society, and have 40 percent fewer cavities as well!* We are all controlled emotionally by this notion of lack.

How My Transformation Began . . .
and Perhaps Some Inspiration for Your Own

I started this chapter by telling you of that moment when I was sitting on my couch and realized that there was quite a gap between who I really was and the identity I presented to the world. So I'd like to close this chapter by telling you the rest of the story. . . .

Around the time this happened, I was traveling frequently, lecturing to people who had seen me in the movie *What the BLEEP Do We Know!?* When I was speaking in front of groups, I felt really alive, and I'm sure I came across as happy. But in that moment, I was feeling numb. That's when it hit me. I had to show up being how everybody expected me to be, based on how I appeared in the movie. I'd started believing I was somebody else, and I needed the world to remind me of who I thought I was. I was actually living two different lives. No longer did I want to be trapped by that.

As I sat alone that morning, I felt my heart beating, and I started thinking about who was beating my heart. I realized in one instant that I had distanced myself from this innate intelligence. I closed my eyes and put all of my attention on it. I started to admit who I'd been, what I'd been hiding, and how unhappy I was. I began to surrender some aspects of myself to a greater mind.

I then reminded myself of who I no longer wanted to be. I decided how I no longer wanted to live based on that same personality. Next, I observed my unconscious behaviors, thoughts, and feelings that reinforced my old self and reviewed them until they became familiar to me.

Then I thought about who I did want to be as a new personality . . . until I *became* it. Suddenly I began to feel different—joyful. This had nothing to do with all of those things outside of me; it was part of an identity that was independent of any of that external stuff. I knew that I was on to something.

I had an immediate reaction after that first meditation on the couch, and it caught my attention, because I didn't get up as the same person who had sat down. I stood up and I felt so aware and so alive. It was like I was seeing so many things for the first time. Some mask was removed from me, and I wanted more of that.

So I retreated from my life for about six months. I kept up my clinical practice to some degree, but I canceled all my lectures. My friends thought I was losing my mind (I was), because *What the BLEEP* was at its height, and they reminded me about how much money I could have been making. But I said I would never walk onstage again until I was no longer living an ideal for the world, but one for *myself.* I didn't want to lecture again until I was the living example of everything that I was talking about. I needed to take time for my meditations and to make true change in my life, and I wanted to have joy from within me and not from outside of me. And I wanted that to come across when I lectured.

My transformation wasn't immediate. I meditated every day, looking at my unwanted emotions, and one by one, I began to unmemorize them. I started my meditative processes of unlearning and relearning, and I worked for months to change myself. In the process, I was intentionally dismantling my old identity and breaking the habit of being myself.

That's when I began to feel joyful for no reason. I became happier and happier, and it had nothing to do with anything outside me. Today, I make time to meditate every morning because I want more of that state of being.

※☀※

Whatever has drawn you to this book, when you make up your mind to change, you have to move to a new consciousness. You must become very clear about what you're doing, how you're thinking, how you're living, how you're feeling, and how you're *being* . . . to the point that it isn't you, and you don't want to be it any longer. And that shift has to reach you on a gut level.

What you're about to learn is what *I* did, the steps I took in making my own personal changes. But take heart—*you very well may have done something similar in your life already.* There is just a little more knowledge to come, related to the meditative process, in order for you to make this method of change a skill. So let's get to it.

※☀☀☀※

CHAPTER EIGHT

MEDITATION, DEMYSTIFYING THE MYSTICAL, AND WAVES OF YOUR FUTURE

In the previous chapter, I wrote about the need to bridge the space between who we really are and the image we present to the world. When we're able to do that, we can take steps toward freeing up the necessary energy to become that ideal self, modeled after some of the great people in the history of the world, such as Gandhi and Joan of Arc.

And as I've said, one of the keys to breaking the habit of being yourself is working toward being more observant—whether that entails being more metacognitive (monitoring your thoughts), embracing stillness, or focusing more attention on your behaviors and how elements in your environment might trigger emotional responses. So the big question here is: *How do you do all this?*

In other words, how do you become more observant; break your emotional bonds with the body, the environment, and time; and close the gap?

The answer is simple: *meditation.* You may have noticed that up to this point in the book, I have teased you with brief allusions to meditation as the way to break the habit of being yourself and begin to create a new life as your ideal self. I told you that the information in Parts I and II of this book would prepare you to understand what you will be doing when you apply the meditative steps you will practice in Part III. Now it's time to explain the inner workings of the process that I refer to as meditation.

When I use the term *meditation,* an image of a person seated cross-legged in front of a shrine at home, a bearded and gowned yogi sitting in a secluded cave in the Himalayas, or some other visual may come to mind. That individual may be a representation of what you understand is the way to "go quiet," empty the mind, focus all of one's attention on a thought, or engage in any of the other variations of the practice of meditation.

There are a lot of meditative techniques, but in this book, my wish is to help you produce the most desirable benefit of meditation—being able to access and enter the operating system of the subconscious mind so that you move away from simply *being* yourself and your thoughts, beliefs, actions, and emotions, to *observing* those things . . . and then once you're there, to subconsciously reprogramming your brain and body to a new mind. When you move from *unconsciously* producing thoughts, beliefs, actions, and emotions and take control of them through the *conscious* application of your will, you can unlock the chains of being your old self to become a new self. How you get to the point at which you are able to access that operating system and bring the unconscious into your consciousness is the subject we'll cover through the rest of this book.

One Definition of Meditation: Becoming Familiar with Self

In the Tibetan language, to *meditate* means "to become familiar with." Accordingly, I use the term *meditation* as a synonym for self-observation as well as self-development. After all, to become familiar with anything, we have to spend some time observing it.

Again, the key moment in making any change is going from being it to observing it.

Another way to think of this transition is when you go from being a doer to a doer/watcher. An easy analogy I can use is that when athletes or performers—golfers, skiers, swimmers, dancers, singers, or actors—want to change something about their technique, most coaches have them watch videotape of themselves. How can you change from an old mode of operation to a new one unless you can see what old and new look like?

It's the same with your old and your new self. How can you stop doing things one way without knowing what that way looks like? I frequently use the term *unlearning* to describe this phase of changing.

This process of becoming familiar with the self works both ways—you need to "see" the old and the new self. You have to observe yourself so precisely and vigilantly, as I've described, that you won't allow any unconscious thought, emotion, or behavior to go unnoticed. Since you have the equipment to do this because of the size of your frontal lobe, you can look at yourself and decide what you want to change in order to do a better job in life.

Decide to Stop Being the Old You

When you can become conscious of those unconscious aspects of the old, habituated self, rooted in the operating system of the subconscious, you are beginning the process of changing anything about yourself.

What steps do you normally take when you get serious about doing something differently? You separate yourself from your external world long enough to think about what to do and not do. You start becoming aware of many aspects of the old self, and you begin to plan a course of action related to a new self.

For example, if you want to become happy, the first step is to stop being unhappy—that is, stop *thinking* the thoughts that make you unhappy; and stop *feeling* the emotions of pain, sorrow, and bitterness. If you desire to become wealthy, you'll probably decide to stop *doing* the things that make you poor. If you want to be healthy, you'll have to stop living an *un*healthy lifestyle. These examples are to show you that first, you have to make the decision to stop being the old you, to such a degree that you make room for a new personality—thinking, acting, and doing.

Therefore, if you eliminated stimuli from your external world by closing your eyes and becoming quiet (decreasing your sensory input), putting your body in a state of stillness, and no longer focusing on linear time, you could become aware solely of how you are thinking and feeling. And if you began to pay attention to your unconscious states of mind and body and became "familiar with" your automatic, unconscious programs until they became conscious, would you be meditating?

The answer is yes. To "know thyself" is to meditate.

If you are no longer being that old personality but, instead, are noticing different aspects of it, wouldn't you agree that you are the consciousness observing the programs of that past identity? In other words, if you consciously observe the old self, you are no longer *being* it. As you go from being unaware to being aware, you are beginning to objectify your subjective mind. That is, by your paying attention to the old habit of being you, your conscious participation begins to separate you from those unconscious programs and give you more control over them.

By the way, if you are successful in consciously restraining those routine states of mind and body, then "nerve cells that no longer fire together, no longer wire together." As you prune away the neurological hardware of the old self, you also no longer signal the same genes in identical ways. You are breaking the habit of being *you*.

Contemplate a New, Greater Expression of Self

Now let's take it one step further. Once you have become familiar with the old self to the extent that no thought, no behavior, and no feeling will cause you to fall unconsciously into previous patterns, you might agree that it would be a good idea to begin to become familiar with a *new* self. Accordingly, you may ask yourself, *What is a greater expression of myself that I would like to be?*

If you turn on your frontal lobe and contemplate those aspects of self, you will begin to make your brain work differently than your past self. As your frontal lobe (the CEO) entertains that new question, it looks out over the landscape of the rest of the brain and seamlessly combines all of your stored knowledge and experiences into a new model of thought. It helps create an internal representation for you to begin to focus on.

This contemplation process builds new neurological networks. As you ponder the fundamental question above, your neurons will begin to fire and wire in new sequences, patterns, and combinations because you are thinking differently. And whenever you make your brain work differently, you're changing your mind. As you plan your actions, speculate on novel possibilities, conjure up innovative ways of being, and dream of new states of mind and body, there will be a moment that the frontal lobe will turn on and lower the volume to the Big Three. When this happens, the thought(s) you are thinking will become an internal experience; you will install new software and hardware programs into your nervous system, and it will appear that the experience of being your new self has already been realized in your brain. And if you repeat this process every day, your ideal will become a familiar state of mind.

One more point here. If you attend so well to the thought you are focusing on that it literally becomes an experience, then the end product of that is an emotion. Once that emotion is created, you begin to feel like your new ideal, and that new feeling will start to become familiar. Remember that when your body begins to respond as if the experience is already a present reality, you will signal your genes in new ways . . . and your body will commence to change now, ahead of the physical event in your life. Now you are ahead of time, and most important, you move into a state of being—mind and body working together. And if you repeat this process consistently, this state of being will become familiar to you as well.

If you can maintain that modified state of mind and body, independent of the external environment and the body's emotional needs and greater than time, something should show up differently in your world. That's the quantum law.

Let's summarize here. According to our working model of meditation, all you have to do is remind yourself who you no longer want to "be" until this becomes so familiar that you know your old self—the thoughts, behaviors, and emotions connected to the old you that you want to change—to the extent that you "unfire" and "unwire" the old mind away and no longer signal the same genes in the same ways. Then, you repeatedly contemplate who you do want to "be." As a result, you will fire and wire new levels of mind, to which you will emotionally condition the body until they become familiar and second nature to you. That's change.

A Second Definition of Meditation: Cultivating Self

Besides its meaning in Tibetan, to *meditate* in Sanskrit means "to cultivate self." I especially like this definition because of the metaphorical possibilities it offers—for example, gardening or agriculture. When you cultivate the soil, you take the packed-down earth that has been lying fallow for a while and you churn it up with a spade or other implement. You expose "new" dirt and nutrients, making it easier for seeds to germinate and for tender shoots to take root. Cultivation may also require you to remove plants from the previous season, attend to weeds that went unnoticed, and remove any rocks that rose to the surface by natural sifting.

Thus, last season's plants might represent your past creations derived from the thoughts, actions, and emotions that define the old, familiar you. Weeds could signify long-standing attitudes, beliefs, or perceptions about yourself that are subconsciously undermining your efforts, which you hadn't noticed because you were too distracted by other things. And the rocks can symbolize your many layers of personal blocks and limitations (which naturally rise to the surface over time and block your growth). All these need tending to so you can make room to plant a new garden in your mind. Otherwise, if you planted a new garden or crop without proper preparation, it would yield little fruit.

My hope is that you understand by now that it is impossible to create any new future when you are rooted in your past. You have to clear away the old vestiges of the garden (of the mind) before you can cultivate a new self by planting the seeds of new thoughts, behaviors, and emotions that create a new life.

The other key thing is to ensure that this doesn't happen haphazardly: we're not talking about plants in the wild, which scatter seeds roughshod over the ground, with some tiny percentage of them eventually coming to fruition. Instead, to cultivate requires making conscious decisions—when to till the soil, when to plant, *what* to plant, how each of the items planted will work in harmony with the others, how much water and fertilizer to mix in, and so forth. Planning and preparation are essential to the success of the endeavor. This requires our daily "mindful attention."

Similarly, when we talk about someone cultivating an interest in a particular subject, we mean that he has thoughtfully researched that area of interest. Also, a cultivated person is someone who has carefully chosen what to expose herself to and who has amassed a breadth of knowledge and experience. Again, none of this is done on a whim, and little is left to chance.

When you cultivate anything, you are seeking to be in control. And that's what is required when you change any part of your *self*. Instead of allowing things to develop "naturally," you intervene and consciously take steps to reduce the likelihood of failure. The purpose behind all of this effort is to reap a harvest. When you cultivate a new personality in meditation, the abundant yield you seek to create is *a new reality*.

Creating a new mind is like cultivating a garden. The manifestations you produce from the garden of your mind will be just like crops from the earth's soil. Tend well.

The Meditative Process for Change:
Move from the Unconscious to the Conscious

To sum up the meditative process, you have to break the habit of being yourself and reinvent a new self; lose your mind and create a new one; prune synaptic connections and nurture new ones; unmemorize past emotions and recondition the body to a new mind and emotions; and let go of the past and create a new future.

THE BIOLOGICAL MODEL of CHANGE

FAMILIAR PAST	NEW FUTURE
Unlearning	Relearning
Breaking the habit of being yourself	Reinventing a new self
Pruning synaptic connections	Sprouting new connections
Unfiring & unwiring	Firing & wiring
Unmemorizing an emotion in the body	Reconditioning the body to a new mind/emotion
Losing your mind	Creating a new one
Becoming familiar with the old self	Becoming familiar with the new self
Deprogramming	Reprogramming
Living in the past	Creating a new future
Old energy	New energy

Figure 8A. The biological model of change involves transforming the familiar past to a new future.

Let's look a bit more closely at a few elements of this process.

Obviously, to avoid letting any thought or feeling you don't want to experience get past you unchecked, you have to develop powerful skills of observation and focus. We humans have a limited ability to focus and to absorb input—but we can be much better at it than we normally are in our more unconscious state.

To break the habit of being yourself, you would be wise to select one trait, propensity, or characteristic and focus your attention on that single aspect of your old self that you want to change. For example, you might begin by asking yourself: *When I feel angry, what are my thought patterns? What do I say to others and myself? How do I act? What other emotions spring forth from my being angry? What does anger feel like in my body? How can I become conscious of what triggers my anger, and how can I change my reaction?*

The process of change requires *un*learning first, then learning. The latter is a function of firing and wiring in the brain; the former means that circuits are trimmed. When you stop thinking the same way, when you inhibit your habituations and interrupt those emotional addictions, the old self begins to be neurologically pruned away.

And if every connection between nerve cells constitutes a memory, then as those circuits are dismantled, memories of your old self will go with them. When you think about your former life and who you used to be, it will be like another lifetime. Where are those memories now stored? They will be given to the soul as wisdom.

When those thoughts and feelings that used to signal the body are stopped by your conscious efforts, the liberated energy from those limited emotions is released into the field. You now have energy with which to design and create a new destiny.

When we use meditation as a means to change, when we become conscious and aware, familiar with and willing to do what is necessary to eradicate an undesirable trait and cultivate a desired one, we're doing what mystics have been doing for centuries.

Although I take a clearly biological approach to change, so did the mystics. They just used different terminology to describe the process. The end result is the same—breaking the addiction to the body, the environment, and time. Only when we make that separation can we change. Only when we think greater than the Big Three can we truly live independent of them, and reestablish dominion over how we think and feel on a daily basis.

For too long, we've been running unconscious programs that have been controlling us. Meditation allows us to reassert control.

Awareness comes first—recognizing when and how those programmed responses take over is essential. When you move from the unconscious to the conscious, you begin to close the gap between how you appear and who you are.

The Waves of Your Future

Since knowledge is, as we've seen, the precursor to experience, having a basic understanding of what happens in the brain during meditation will serve you well when you begin to learn and experience the meditative process coming up shortly in Part III.

You probably know that the brain is electrochemical in nature. When nerve cells fire, they exchange charged elements that then produce electromagnetic fields. Because the brain's diverse electrical activity can be measured, these effects can provide important information about what we're thinking, feeling, learning, dreaming, and creating and how we are processing information. The most common technology scientists use to record the brain's changing electrical activity is an electroencephalograph (EEG).

Research has discovered a wide scope of brain-wave frequencies in humans, ranging from the very low levels of activity found in deep sleep (*Delta* waves); to a twilight state between deep sleep and wakefulness (*Theta*); to the creative, imaginative state (*Alpha*); to higher frequencies seen during conscious thought (*Beta* waves); to the highest frequencies recorded (*Gamma* waves), seen in elevated states of consciousness.[1]

To help you better understand your journey into meditation, I'm going to give you an overview of how each of these states relates to you. Once you know what all of these domains are, you will be more adept at knowing when you are in the brain-wave state where the ego tries in vain to change the ego (God knows, I've been there), and when you are in the brain-wave state that is the fertile ground of true change.

As children grow, the frequencies that predominate in their brains progress from Delta to Theta to Alpha and then to Beta. Our job in meditation is to become like a child, moving from Beta to Alpha to Theta to (for the adept or mystic) Delta. So understanding the progression of brain-wave changes during human development can help demystify the process of how we experience meditation.

Brain-Wave Development in Children: From Subconscious to Conscious Mind

Delta. Between birth and two years old, the human brain functions primarily in the lowest brain-wave levels, from 0.5 to 4 cycles per second. This range of electromagnetic activity is known as Delta waves. Adults in deep sleep are in Delta; this explains why a newborn usually can't remain awake for more than a few minutes at a time (and why even with their eyes open, young babies can be asleep). When one-year-olds are awake, they're still primarily in Delta, because they function principally from their subconscious. Information from the outside world enters their brains with little editing, critical thinking, or judgment taking place. The thinking brain—the neocortex, or conscious mind—is operating at very low levels at this point.

Theta. From about ages two to five or six, a child begins to demonstrate slightly higher EEG patterns. These Theta-wave frequencies measure 4 to 8 cycles per second. Children functioning in Theta tend to be trancelike and primarily connected to their internal world. They live in the abstract and in the realm of imagination, and exhibit few of the nuances of critical, rational thinking. Thus, young children are likely to accept what you tell them. (P.S. Santa is real.) At this stage, phrases such as the following have a huge impact: *Big boys don't cry. Girls should be seen and not heard. Your sister is smarter than you. If you get cold, you'll catch a cold.* These types of statements go straight to the subconscious mind, because these slow brain-wave states are the realm of the subconscious (*hint, hint*).

Alpha. Between ages five and eight, brain waves change again, to an Alpha frequency: 8 to 13 cycles per second. The analytical mind begins to form at this point in childhood development; children start to interpret and draw conclusions about the laws of external life. At the same time, the inner world of imagination tends to be as real as the outer world of reality. Children in this age-group typically have a foot in both worlds. That's why they pretend so well. For instance, you may ask a child to pretend that he is a dolphin in the sea, a snowflake in the wind, or a superhero coming to the rescue, and hours later, he is still in character. Ask an adult to do the same, and well . . . you already know the answer.

Beta. From ages 8 to 12 and onward, brain activity increases to even higher frequencies. Anything above 13 cycles per second in children is the frontier for Beta waves. Beta goes on and up to varying degrees from there throughout adulthood, and is representative of conscious, analytical thinking.

After age 12, the door between the conscious mind and the subconscious mind usually closes. Beta is actually divided into low-, mid-, and high-range Beta waves. As children progress into their teens, they tend to move from low-range Beta up into mid- and high-range Beta waves, as seen in most adults.

BRAIN–WAVE DEVELOPMENT

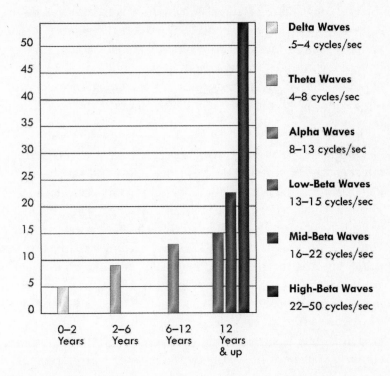

Figure 8B. The progression of brain-wave development from Delta in infancy to Beta in adulthood. Look at the difference in the three ranges of Beta: high-range Beta can be twice as high as mid-range Beta.

Brain-Wave States in Adults: An Overview

Beta. As you're reading this chapter, most likely you are in the everyday waking state of Beta brain-wave activity. Your brain is processing sensory data and trying to create meaning between your outer and inner worlds. While you are engaged in this book's material, you may feel the weight of your body on your seat, you may hear music in the background, you may glance up and see out a window. All of this data is being processed by your thinking neocortex.

Alpha. Now, let's say that you close your eyes (80 percent of our sensory information derives from sight) and purposefully go inward. Since you are greatly reducing sensory data from the environment, less information is entering your nervous system. Your brain waves naturally slow down into the Alpha state. You relax. You become less preoccupied with the elements in your outer world, and the internal world begins to consume your attention. You tend to think and analyze less. In Alpha, the brain is in a light meditative state (when you practice the meditation in Part III, you'll go into an even deeper Alpha state).

On a daily basis, your brain moves into Alpha without much effort on your part. For example, when you're learning something new in a lecture, generally your brain is functioning in low- to mid-range Beta. You're listening to the message and analyzing the concepts being presented. Then when you've heard enough or you particularly like something interesting that applies to you, you naturally pause and your brain slips into Alpha. You do this because that information is being consolidated in your gray matter. And as you stare into space, you are attending to your thoughts and making them more real than the external world. The moment that happens, your frontal lobe is now wiring that information into your cerebral architecture . . . and like magic, you can remember what you just learned.

Theta. In adults, Theta waves emerge in the *twilight state* or *lucid state,* during which some people find themselves half-awake and half-asleep (the conscious mind is awake, while the body is somewhat asleep). This is the state when a hypnotherapist can access the subconscious mind. In Theta, we are more programmable because there is no veil between the conscious and subconscious minds.

Delta. For most of us, Delta waves are representative of deep sleep. In this realm there is very little conscious awareness, and the body is restoring itself.

As this overview demonstrates, when we move into slower brain-wave states, we move deeper into the inner world of the subconscious mind. The reverse is also true: as we move into higher brain-wave states, the more we become conscious and attend to the external world.

With repeated practice, these terrains of the mind will begin to become familiar to you. Just like anything else you persist at, you will come to notice what each brain-wave pattern feels like. You'll know when you are analyzing or thinking too much in Beta; you'll observe when you are not present because you are swinging from the emotions of the past to trying to anticipate a known future. You'll also sense when you are in Alpha or Theta, since you'll feel its coherence. In time, you will know when you are there and when you are not.

BRAIN WAVES

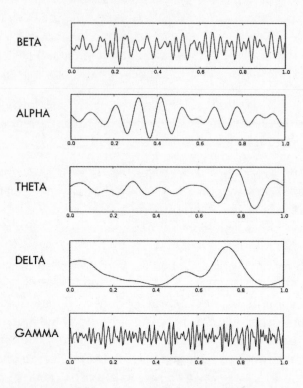

Figure 8C. A comparison of different brain-wave patterns in adults.

Gamma: The Fastest Brain Waves of All

The fastest documented brain-wave frequencies are *Gamma* waves, from 40 to 100 hertz. (Gamma waves are more compressed and have a smaller amplitude compared to the other four types of brain waves I have discussed, so although their cycles per second are similar to high-range Beta, there is not an exact correlation between them.) Having high amounts of coherent Gamma activity in the brain is usually linked to elevated states of mind such as happiness, compassion, and even increased awareness, which usually entails better memory formation This is a heightened level of consciousness that people tend to describe as "having a transcendent or peak experience." For our purposes, think of Gamma as the side effect of a shift in consciousness.

Three Levels of Beta Waves Govern Our Waking Hours

Since we spend most of our conscious waking day with our attention on the external environment and functioning in Beta, let's talk about the three levels of these brain-wave patterns.[2] This understanding will facilitate moving from Beta to Alpha and ultimately to Theta in the meditative state.

1. Low-range Beta is defined as relaxed, interested attention ranging from 13 to 15 hertz (cycles per second). If you are enjoying reading a book and are familiar with the material, your brain would probably be firing in low Beta, because you are paying a certain degree of attention without any vigilance.

2. Mid-range Beta is produced during focused attention on sustained external stimuli. Learning is a good example: if I were to test you on what you read while enjoying that book in low Beta, you would have to perk up a bit, and thus there would be more neocortical activity such as analytical thinking. Mid-Beta operates between 16 and 22 hertz.

With mid-range Beta and even low-range Beta to some extent, these frequencies reflect our conscious or rational thinking and our alertness. They are a result of the neocortex taking in stimuli from the environment through all of our senses and assembling the information into a package to create a level of mind. As you can imagine, with this focus on what we're seeing, hearing, tasting, feeling, and smelling comes a great deal of complexity and activity within the brain to produce that level of stimulation.

3. High-range Beta is characterized by any brain-wave pattern from 22 to 50 hertz. High-Beta patterns are observed during stressful situations where those nasty survival chemicals are produced in the body. Maintaining this sustained focus in such a high-arousal state is not the type of focused attention we use to learn, create, dream, problem solve, or even heal. In truth, we could say that the brain in high Beta is functioning with *too much* focused concentration. The mind is too amped up and the body is too stimulated to be in any semblance of order. (When you're in high Beta, just know for now that you are probably focusing on something too much and it's hard to stop.)

High Beta: A Short-Term Survival Mechanism, a Long-Term Source of Stress and Imbalance

Emergencies always create a considerable need for increased electrical activity in the brain. Nature has gifted us with the fight-or-flight response, to help us quickly focus in potentially dangerous situations. The strong physiological arousal of the heart, lungs, and sympathetic nervous system leads to a dramatic change in psychological states. Our perception, behaviors, attitudes, and emotions are all altered. This type of attention is very different from what we normally use. It causes us to act like a revved-up animal with a big memory bank. The scales of attention become tipped toward the external environment, causing an overfocused state of mind. Anxiety, worry, anger, pain, suffering, frustration, fear, and even competitive states of mind induce high-range Beta waves to predominate during the crisis.

In the short term, this serves all organisms well. There is nothing wrong with this narrow, overfocused range of attention. We "get the job done" because it affords us the ability to accomplish so many things.

However, if we remain in "emergency mode" for a long time, high Beta knocks us far out of balance, because maintaining it requires an immense amount of energy—and because this is the most reactive, unstable, and volatile of all brain patterns. When high Beta becomes chronic and uncontrolled, the brain gets juiced up beyond the healthy range.

Unfortunately, high Beta is terribly overutilized by the majority of the population. We are obsessive or compulsive, insomniac or chronically fatigued, anxious or depressed, forcibly pushing in all directions to be all-powerful or hopelessly holding on to our pain to feel utterly powerless, competing to get ahead or victimized by our circumstances.

Sustained High Beta Sends the Brain into Disorder

To put this into perspective, think about the normal functioning of the brain as part of the central nervous system, which controls and coordinates all other systems of the body: it keeps your heart beating, digests your food, regulates your immune system, maintains your respiratory rate, balances your hormones, controls your metabolism, and eliminates wastes, to name a few. As long as the mind is coherent and orderly, messages that travel from the brain to the body through the spinal cord will produce synchronized signals for a balanced, healthy body.

However, many people spend their waking days in a sustained high-frequency Beta state. To them, everything is an emergency. The brain stays constantly on a very fast cycle, which taxes the entire system. Living in this thin margin of brain waves is like driving a car in first gear while simultaneously stepping on the gas. These people "drive through" their lives without ever stopping to consider shifting gears into other brain states.

Their continual repetition of survival-based thoughts creates feelings of anger, fear, sadness, anxiety, depression, competition, aggression, insecurity, and frustration, among others. People become so caught up in these intoxicating emotions that they try to analyze their problems from *within* these familiar feelings, which only perpetuates more thoughts overfocused on survival. Also, recall that we can turn on the stress response by thought alone—the way we are thinking reinforces the very state of the brain and body, which then causes us to think the same way . . . and the loop goes on. It's the serpent eating its tail.

Long-term high Beta produces an unhealthy cocktail of stress chemicals, which can tip the brain out of balance like a symphony orchestra out of tune. Parts of the brain may stop coordinating effectively with other areas; entire regions work separately and in opposition. Like a house divided against itself, the brain no longer communicates in an organized, holistic fashion. As stress chemicals force the thinking brain/neocortex to become more segregated, we may function like someone with multiple personality disorder, only we're experiencing it all at once instead of one personality at a time.

Of course, when disorderly, incoherent signals from the brain relay erratic, mixed electrochemical messages through the central nervous system to the rest of the physiological systems, this puts the body out of balance, upsetting its homeostasis or equilibrium, and setting the stage for disease.

If we live in this high-stress mode of chaotic brain function for extended periods, the heart is impacted (leading to arrhythmias or high blood pressure), digestion begins to fail (causing indigestion, reflux, and related symptoms), and immune function weakens (resulting in colds, allergies, cancer, rheumatoid arthritis, and more).

All of these consequences stem from an unbalanced nervous system that is operating incoherently, due to the action of stress chemicals and high-range Beta brain waves reaffirming the outer world as the only reality.

Sustained High Beta Makes It Hard to Focus on Our Inner Self

The stress I've been discussing is a product of our addiction to the Big Three. The problem isn't that we are conscious and aware, but that our focus in high Beta is almost exclusively on our environment (people, things, places), our bodies' parts and functions (*I'm hungry . . . I'm too weak . . . I want a better nose . . . I'm fat compared to her . . .*), and time (*Hurry up! The clock is winding down!*).

In high Beta, the outer world appears to be more real than the inner world. Our attention and conscious awareness primarily focus on everything that makes up the external environment. Thus, we identify more readily with those material elements: we criticize everyone we know, we judge the way our bodies look, we're overfocused on our problems, we cling to things we own out of fear that we might lose them, we busy ourselves with places we have to go, and we're preoccupied with time. That leaves us little processing power to pay attention to the changes that we truly want to make—to go inward . . . to observe and monitor our thoughts, behavior, and emotions.

It's difficult for us to focus on our inner reality when we are overfixating on our outer world. In general, we can't concentrate on anything other than the Big Three, we can't open our minds beyond the boundaries of our narrow focus, and we obsess about problems rather than thinking about solutions. Why does it take such effort to let go of the external and go within? The brain in high Beta can't easily shift gears into the imaginary realm of Alpha. Our brain-wave patterns keep us locked into all those elements of our outer world as if they are real.

When you are stuck in high Beta, it's hard to learn: very little new information can enter into your nervous system that is not equal to the emotion you are experiencing. The truth is, the problems you're so busy analyzing can't be resolved *within* the emotion you are analyzing them in. Why not? Well, your analysis is creating higher and higher frequencies of Beta. Thinking in this mode causes your brain to overreact; you reason poorly and think without clarity.

In view of the emotions that grip you, you're thinking in the past—and trying to predict the next moment based on the past—and your brain can't process the present moment. There's no room for the unknown to show up in your world. You're feeling separate from the quantum field, and can't even entertain new possibilities for your circumstances. Your brain isn't in creative mode; it's fixated on survival, preoccupied with possible worst-case scenarios. Again, not much information will be encoded into the system that is not equal to that emergency state. When everything feels like a crisis, your brain makes survival the priority, not learning.

The answer lies outside the emotions you're wrestling with and the thoughts you're overanalyzing, because they keep you connected to your past—the familiar and the known. Solving your problems begins with getting beyond those familiar feelings and replacing your scattered focus on the Big Three with a more orderly mode of thinking.

High Beta's Incoherent Signals
Produce Scattered Thoughts

As you can imagine, when the brain is in high Beta and you're processing sensory information—involving the environment, your body, and time—that activity can create a bit of chaos. Along with understanding that the electrical impulses in your brain occur in a certain quantity (cycles per second), it's also important to be aware of the *quality* of the signal. Just as the discussion of quantum creating showed how vital it is to send a coherent signal into the field to indicate your intended future outcome, the same coherence is essential to your thinking and your brain waves.

At any one time when you're in the Beta range of frequencies, one of the Big Three will have more of your attention. If you're thinking about being late, your emphasis is on time—that thought is sending a higher-frequency wave through your neocortex. Of course, you're also aware of, and therefore sending electromagnetic impulses related to, your body and the environment. It's just that in the case of the latter two, you're sending different wave patterns with a lower frequency through the neocortex.

Your time-focused brain waves might look like this:

Your environment-focused brain waves might look like this:

Your body-focused brain waves might look like this:

Your fractured attention, caused by trying to focus simultaneously on all of the Big Three, would then produce a brain-wave pattern that might look like this:

As you can see, those three different patterns together during stress produce an incoherent signal in high-Beta mode. If you're anything like me, you've had experiences when that last drawing represents how your thoughts felt: scattered.

When we are plugged into all three dimensions—the environment, the body, *and* time—the brain tries to integrate their varied frequencies and wave patterns. That takes up an enormous amount of processor time and space. If we can eliminate our focus on any one of those, the patterns that emerge will be more coherent, and we'll be better able to process them.

THE DIFFERENCE BETWEEN a COHERENT
and an INCOHERENT SIGNAL

Coherent Waves

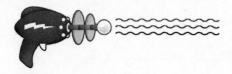

Incoherent Waves

Figure 8D. In the first picture, the energy is orderly, organized, and rhythmic. When energy is highly synchronous and patterned, it is profoundly more powerful. The light emitted by a laser is an example of coherent waves of energy all moving together in unison. In the second picture, the energy patterns are chaotic, disintegrated, and out of phase. An example of an incoherent, less powerful signal is the light from an incandescent lightbulb.

Awareness, Not Analysis, Permits Entry into the Subconscious

Here is a way for you to know if you're in Beta state: if you're constantly analyzing (I call this "being in analytical mind"), you are in Beta and you're not able to enter into the subconscious mind.

The expression "paralysis by analysis" is an apt one here. Well, that's what is happening to us when we live most of our lives in that Beta range. The only time we aren't there is when we're sleeping (then we're in the Delta range of brain-wave activity).

Now you might be thinking, *But you said that we needed to be aware. We need to become familiar with our thoughts, feelings, patterns of responses, and so forth. Doesn't that require analysis?*

Actually, awareness can exist outside of analysis. When you are aware, you may think, *I'm feeling angry.* When you are analyzing, you go beyond that simple observation to add: *Why is this page taking so long to load? Who designed this stupid website? Why is it that whenever I'm in a hurry, like now when I'm trying to get a movie listing, the Internet connection is so slow!* Awareness, as I mean it to be practiced here, is simply noting (watching) a thought or feeling and moving on.

A Working Model of Meditation

Now that we've covered some basics about brain waves in children and adults, this foundation will provide a working model (see the next five figures) to help you understand the meditative process.[3]

Let's start with Figure 8E on the next page. Thanks to the research into children's brain-wave patterns, we know that when we are born, we are completely in the realm of the subconscious.

THE EARLY MIND

Figure 8E. Let this circle represent the mind. When we are born, we are totally subconscious mind.

Next, take a look at Figure 8F. Those plus and minus signs represent how the developing child's mind learns from positive and negative identifications and associations that give rise to habits and behaviors.

Here's an example of a positive identification: When an infant is hungry or uncomfortable, she cries out, making an effort to communicate in order to get her mother's attention. As the nurturing parent responds by feeding the child or changing her diaper, the infant makes an important connection between her inner and outer worlds. It only takes a few repetitions before she learns to associate crying out with being fed or becoming comfortable. It becomes a behavior.

A good example of a negative association is when a two-year-old puts his finger on a hot stove. He learns very quickly to identify the object he sees externally—the stove—with the pain he is feeling internally, and after a few tries, he learns a valuable lesson.

THE DEVELOPING MIND

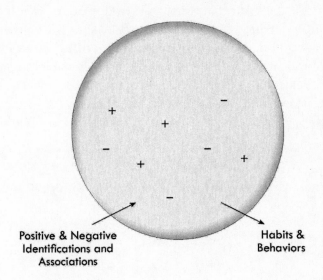

Positive & Negative
Identifications and
Associations

Habits &
Behaviors

Figure 8F. In time, we begin to learn by association through different interactions between our inner world and our outer world, through our senses.

In both examples, we could say that the moment the child notices an internal chemical change in the body, the brain perks up and pays attention to whatever it was in the outer environment that caused this alteration, be it pleasure or pain. These types of identifications and associations begin to slowly develop many habits, skills, and behaviors.

As you learned, somewhere around the age of six or seven, as brain waves change into Alpha, the child begins to develop the *analytical* or *critical mind*. For most children, the analytical mind usually finishes developing between ages 7 and 12.

Meditation Takes Us Beyond Analytical Mind and into the Subconscious

In Figure 8G, the line that runs across the top of the circle is the analytical mind, which acts as a barrier to separate the conscious from the subconscious mind. In adults, this critical mind loves to reason, evaluate, anticipate, forecast, compare what it knows to what it's learning, or contrast knowns and unknowns. For the most part, when adults are conscious, their analytical minds are always working, and thus they are functioning in some realm of Beta waves.

ANALYTICAL MIND

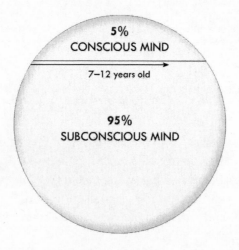

Figure 8G. Between the ages of six and seven, the analytical mind begins to form. It acts as a barrier to separate the conscious mind from the subconscious mind, and it usually finishes developing somewhere between 7 and 12 years old.

Now take a look at Figure 8H. Above that line representing the analytical mind is the conscious mind, which is 5 percent of the total mind. This is the seat of logic and reasoning, which contributes to our will, our faith, our intentions, and our creative abilities.

The subconscious mind, which makes up about 95 percent of who we are, consists of those positive and negative identifications and associations that give rise to habits and behaviors.

THE CONSCIOUS MIND
and THE SUBCONSCIOUS MIND

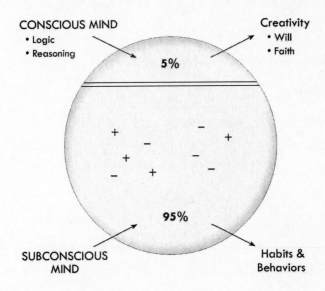

Figure 8H. The total mind is made up of 5 percent conscious mind and 95 percent subconscious mind. The conscious mind primarily operates using logic and reasoning, which gives rise to our will, faith, creative abilities, and intentions. The subconscious mind comprises our myriad positive and negative identifications, which give rise to habits, behaviors, skills, beliefs, and perceptions.

Figure 8I illustrates the most fundamental purpose of meditation (represented by the arrow): to get beyond the analytical mind. When we are in this mind, we cannot truly change. We can analyze our old self, but we cannot uninstall the old programs and install new ones.

Meditation opens the door between the conscious and subconscious minds. We meditate to enter the operating system of the subconscious, where all of those unwanted habits and behaviors reside, and change them to more productive modes to support us in our lives.

MEDITATION—GETTING BEYOND the ANALYTICAL MIND

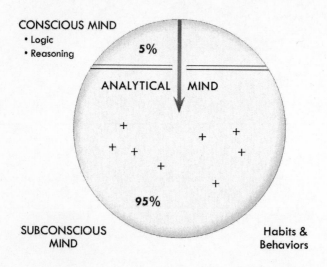

Figure 8I. One of the main purposes of meditation is to go beyond the conscious mind and enter the subconscious mind, in order to change self-destructive habits, behaviors, beliefs, emotional reactions, attitudes, and unconscious states of being.

Meditation Takes Us from Beta into Alpha and Theta Brain-Wave States

Let's examine how you can learn to change gears and access other brain-wave states so you can go beyond your association with the body, the environment, and time. You can naturally slow down the high-speed vigilance of the brain and body into a more relaxed, orderly, systemized pattern of brain waves.

Thus, it is quite possible to consciously alter your brain waves from that high-frequency Beta state into Alpha and Theta (you can train yourself to move up and down the scale of brain waves). As you do, you will open doors to true personal change. You trespass beyond the common type of thinking that is fueled by reactions to being in survival mode; you are entering the realm of the subconscious mind.

During meditation, you transcend the feelings of the body, are no longer at the mercy of the environment, and lose track of time. You forget about *you* as an identity. As you close your eyes, the input from the outside world is reduced, and your neocortex has less to think about and analyze. As a result, the analytical mind begins to become subdued, and electrical activity in the neocortex quiets down.

Then when you restfully pay attention, concentrate, and focus in a relaxed manner, you automatically activate the frontal lobe, which reduces synaptic firing in the rest of the neocortex. Therefore, you lower the volume to the circuits in the brain that process time and space. This allows your brain waves to naturally slow down to Alpha. Now you are moving from a state of survival into a more creative state, and your brain naturally recalibrates itself to a more orderly, coherent brain-wave pattern.

One of the later steps of meditation, if you keep practicing, is to move into the Theta-wave frequency, when your body is asleep but your mind is awake. This is a magical land. You are now in a deeper system of the subconscious and able to immediately change those negative associations to more positive ones.

It's important to remember that if you have conditioned the body to become the mind and your body is somewhat asleep while your mind is awake, you could say that there is no more resistance from the body-mind. In Theta, the body is no longer in control, and you are free to dream, change subconscious programs, and finally create from a totally unobstructed place.

Once the body is no longer running the mind, the servant is no longer the master and you are working in a realm of true power. You are like a child again, entering the kingdom of heaven.

To Sleep, Perchance to Go Down,
Then Up, the Ladder . . . Naturally

When you go to sleep, you pass though the spectrum of brain-wave states, from Beta to Alpha to Theta to Delta. Likewise, when you wake up in the morning, you naturally rise from Delta to Theta to Alpha to Beta, returning to conscious awareness. When you "come to your senses" from the netherworld, you remember who you are, the problems in your life, the person sleeping next to you, the house you own, where you live . . . and *presto!* By association, you're back in Beta as the same you.

Some people fall very quickly through these levels like a steel ball dropping from the top of a building. Their bodies are so fatigued that the natural progression down the ladder to the subconscious states happens too rapidly.

Others cannot shift gears to naturally progress down the ladder into sleep; they are hyperfocused on the cues in their lives that reinforce their addictive mental and emotional states. They become insomniacs, and may take drugs to chemically alter the brain and sedate the body.

Either way, sleep problems may indicate that the brain and the mind are out of sync.

The Best Times to Meditate: Morning and Evening, When the Door to the Subconscious Opens

As a result of normal daily changes in brain chemistry (alternately, the brain produces *serotonin,* primarily a daytime neurotransmitter that makes you alert; and *melatonin,* the nighttime neurotransmitter that begins to relax you for sleep), there are two times when the door to the subconscious mind opens—when you go to bed at night and when you wake up in the morning. So it is a good idea to meditate in the morning or evening, because it will be easier to slip into a state of Alpha or Theta.

I like to wake up early to begin the process, because while I'm still a bit dreamy, I'm still in Alpha. I personally like to create from a clean slate.

Others prefer the late evening. They know that the body (which was in control during the day) is now too tired to "be" the mind.

They can create without any effort by drawing out the Alpha phase, and even entering into Theta, while they are still awake.

Meditation during the middle of the day might be difficult, especially if you work in a busy office, manage a houseful of kids who demand your undivided attention, or are involved in activities that require heightened concentration. At such times you might be in middle to high Beta, and it may take more effort to slip through the door.

BRAIN–WAVE FUNCTION

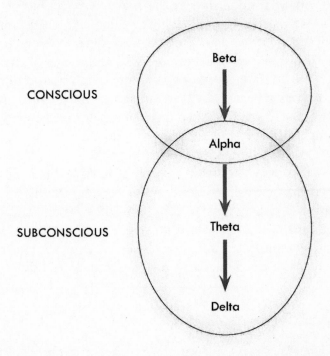

Figure 8J. This diagram shows how our brain-wave functions move from the highest and fastest state of activity (Beta) to the lowest and slowest (Delta). Please take note that Alpha serves as the bridge between the conscious mind and the subconscious mind. The lower/slower the brain waves, the more we are in the subconscious mind; the higher/faster the brain waves, the more we are in the conscious mind.

Taking Control of the Progression into Meditation

Inward contemplative practices retrain the mind, body, and brain to become present, instead of being stressed in anticipation of some future event you are obsessing about. Meditation also lifts the anchor of the body-mind out of the past and frees you from the emotions that keep you hooked to the same familiar life.

The object in meditation is to fall like a feather down from the top of a building, slowly and steadily. You first train yourself to let your body initially relax, but keep your mind focused. Once you begin to master the skill, the ultimate goal is to let your body fall asleep while your mind stays awake or active.

Here is the progression. If waking consciousness is Beta (from low to high, depending on your levels of stress), once you sit up straight to keep your spine erect, close your eyes, take a series of conscious breaths, and go inward, you will naturally switch from the sympathetic nervous system to the parasympathetic nervous system. You will change your physiology from the emergency protection system (fight/fright/flight) to the internal protection system for long-term building projects (growth and repair). As the body relaxes, your brain-wave patterns will naturally begin to move to Alpha.

If done properly, meditation will shift your brain to a more coherent and orderly wave pattern. You will go from focusing on the Big Three to becoming *no body, no thing,* and *no time.* Now you begin to feel connected, whole, and balanced; and you experience healthier, elevated emotions of trust, joy, and inspiration.

Orchestrating for Coherence

If our definition of *mind* is the brain in action or the brain's activity when it processes different streams of consciousness, then meditation naturally produces more synchronized, coherent states of mind.[4]

On the other hand, when the brain is stressed, its electrical activity will be like an entire orchestra of musical instruments playing badly. The mind will be out of rhythm, out of balance, and out of tune.

Your job is to play a masterpiece. If you persist with this band of disorderly, egocentric, self-important members who think that their individual musical instruments need to be heard above all others—and if you insist that they work together and follow your lead—there will come a moment when they will surrender to you as their leader and will act as a team.

This is the moment when brain waves become more synchronized, moving from Beta into Alpha and Theta. More individual circuits start communicating in an orderly fashion and process a more coherent mind. Your awareness shifts from narrow-minded, overfocused, obsessive, compartmentalized, survival thinking to thoughts that are more open, relaxed, holistic, present, orderly, creative, and simple. This is the natural state of being we are supposed to live by.

Take a look at coherence or what is also called *synchrony*, the state when the brain is working in harmony.

THE DIFFERENCE BETWEEN COHERENT and INCOHERENT BRAIN WAVES

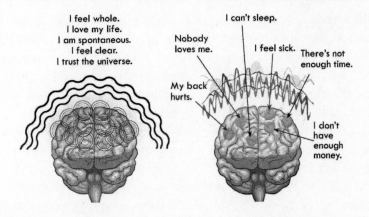

Figure 8K. In the first picture, the brain is balanced and highly integrated. Several different areas are synchronized, forming a more orderly, holistic community of neural networks working together. In the second picture, this brain is disorderly and imbalanced. Many diverse compartments are no longer working as a team, and thus the brain is "dis-eased" and disintegrated.

The Coherent Brain Sets the Stage for Healing

This orderly, new, *synchronized* signal to the body from the brain organizes all of the diverse systems into homeostasis—the cardiovascular system, digestive system, immune system, and so on all move into coherence as well. As the nervous system recalibrates itself, all of the enormous energy that was needed for survival can now be used for creation. The body begins to heal.

For example, Jose, a man at one of my lectures, told me about one of his first times doing a meditation back in his 20s. In those days, he'd had ten olive-sized warts on his left hand. He was so embarrassed by them that he often hid that hand in his pocket.

One day someone gave Jose a book on meditation. The book instructed him to simply focus on his breath and allow his mind to expand beyond the barriers of his body. One night before bed, he decided to try the process. In a matter of moments he went from an overfocused, contracted state to a more expanded, open, focused state. As he vacated his familiar personality and became something other than his typical thoughts and feelings, he went from the habitual random thought patterns driven by the familiar ego to a more expanded sense of self. When this occurred, something shifted.

The next morning when Jose woke up, all ten warts had completely vanished. Shocked and overjoyed, he looked under the sheets for evidence of them, but found nothing. He explained that he didn't know where the warts went. I told him that they returned to the quantum field where they came from. I suggested to him that the universal intelligence that keeps order in his body naturally had done what it always does—create more order to reflect a more coherent mind. When his new subjective, coherent mind matched the objective, coherent higher mind, that greater power within did the healing for him.

All of this happened because when he got out of the way and became no body, no thing, outside time—when he forgot about himself—his focus went from sustained disorder to sustained order . . . survival to creation . . . contraction to expansion . . . incoherence to coherence. Then the unlimited consciousness restored order in his body, and he was healed.

Meditation Plus Action: One Woman's Path Out of Lack

At my workshops, I frequently ask participants to share their surprising stories of life changes. Monique, a therapist from Montreal, Quebec, recently described her own remarkable experience.

For most of her adult life, Monique had lived unconsciously in a near-constant state of lack. Not enough money. Not enough energy. Not enough time to do the things she wanted. Now she was going through a particularly rough patch: her office rent had risen considerably (her house couldn't accommodate an office), she and her husband couldn't afford to send their son to the college of his choice, their washer needed replacing, and the shaky economy had forced several clients to stop seeing her.

One day, while doing the meditation you will learn in this book and pondering her life choices, Monique realized that she couldn't keep doing what she normally did—hunker down and weather the storm with a pseudopositive, woe-is-me-but-things-could-be-worse mentality. She recognized that she'd always made decisions or sought solutions to problems from a perspective of lack—lack of time, of money, and of energy. She had memorized that state of being; *lack* became her personality. The epitome of inertia, she tended to "let the chips fall where they may." Ironically, Monique had worked with her clients to overcome these very traits, and to be more proactive and less reactive.

With great resolve, she decided to change her personality. No longer would she let life trample her and allow things to just happen to her.

Next, Monique created a template of who she wanted to be, how she wanted to think, and what she wanted to feel. She imagined herself as a woman who made all of her choices with an abundance of energy, time, and money. Most important, her goal to become this person was as firm as her vision was precise.

She knew who she no longer wanted to be; and she had definitive plans for how her new self would think, feel, and behave.

When we make a decision that strongly and have a clear intention for what our new reality will be like, the clarity and coherence of those thoughts produces corresponding emotions. As a result, our internal chemistry changes, our neurological makeup is altered (we prune old synaptic connections and sprout new ones), and we even express our genetic code differently.

Monique began to live her life from the perspective of someone who had plenty of money, who had abundant energy, and whose every need was met. She felt wonderful. Certainly, not all the problems from her catalog of worries went away, but she was becoming better at living from a different mind-set.

Several weeks after making that firm decision, Monique was working with her last client of the day. This woman, who had grown up in France, reminisced how every month, her parents had purchased a ticket in the French lottery, a tradition that she had continued.

As Monique drove home that evening, she wasn't thinking about the lottery. She'd never played it, believing that with her limited financial resources, such an expenditure was frivolous. Stopping for gas, she went inside to pay, and there on the counter were lottery cards for various games. On impulse, recognizing that the new Monique who lived in abundance could afford to take a chance on winning, she purchased a ticket.

By the time Monique had stopped at a local pizzeria for a carryout dinner and arrived home, the lottery had slipped her mind. Grabbing the pizza, she discovered that some grease had soaked through the box, stuck to the lottery card, and stained the passenger seat. She set the box on the dining table, with the ticket alongside it. She told her family to start eating without her and that she'd be in the garage tending to the grease stain. While she was scrubbing away, her husband came running out.

"You won't believe it! Your lottery ticket was a winner!"

Now, you'll recall that when the quantum field responds, it does so in a way that one couldn't predict. Perhaps you are thinking, *Of course she won millions and lived happily ever after.*

Not exactly.

Monique won $53,000. Was she happy? Astounded is more like it. The couple owed exactly $53,000 in credit-card and auto-loan debt.

Monique relayed her excitement in telling us that story, but she slyly admitted that next time, instead of holding the intention that all her needs were met, she'd choose to imagine they were met—and then some.

⁘

What Monique's story illustrates is the power of creating a new state of being. She couldn't do that just by imagining that she was a new person; she had to put that new self into action. The old Monique wouldn't have bought a lottery ticket; her new personality aligned her behavior to match her objective, and the field responded in an entirely unexpected yet perfectly appropriate way.

Because Monique developed a new personality who seized opportunities and acted differently, she experienced new and better results in her life. New personality, new personal reality.

You don't have to win the lottery to change your life, of course. But you do have to make the decision to stop being your old self, enter into the operating system where those unconscious programs exist, and then formulate a clear design for a new one.

The Coherent Brain: Takin' It to the Streets

Before I wrap up this chapter, I want to bring up a subject I referenced in *Evolve Your Brain*—namely, Buddhist monks who were studied at the University of Wisconsin at Madison. These "super-meditators" could go into a state of coherent brain waves well beyond what most of us are capable of. When they meditated on thoughts of loving-kindness and compassion, the coherence of the signal they were putting out was nearly off the charts.

Every morning during the study, they meditated while researchers monitored their brain-wave activity. After that, they were sent out onto the campus and into the town to do what they wished—visit museums, go to shops, or what have you. After they returned to the research center, they underwent brain scans again *without first going back into meditation.* Amazingly, despite not meditating throughout the day, and being subjected to the incoherent, chaotic signals that the external world exposes us all to, they maintained the same coherent brain pattern they had achieved in meditation.[5]

Most of us, when faced with the profusion and confusion of stimuli that the external world produces, retreat into survival mode and manufacture the chemicals of stress. Those stress reactions are like disruptors that scramble the brain's signals. Instead, our goal is to become more like those monks. If we can produce coherent signal patterns—those synchronous waves—every day, we'll find that this coherence of signal manifests into something tangible.

In time, if you can repeatedly create internal coherence like those monks did, you too may walk into the external environment and no longer suffer the self-limiting effects of its disruptive stimuli. And because of that, you won't experience the knee-jerk reactions that formerly forced you to return to the old, familiar self that you are so eager to change.

By persisting with meditation and creating coherence within, you will not only remove a lot of the negative physical conditions that plague your body, but you can also progress toward that ideal self you've envisioned. Your inner coherence can counteract negative reactionary emotional states and allow you to unmemorize the behaviors, thoughts, and feelings that make them up.

Once you've gotten to a neutral/empty state, it is far easier to engage a heightened one like compassion; it is easier to bring in pure joy or love or gratitude or any of the elevated emotional states. That's true because those emotions are already profoundly coherent. And when you've moved through the meditative process and produce a brain-wave state that reflects this purity, then you will begin to overcome the body, the environment, and time, which once produced your self-limiting emotional states. They will no longer control you; instead, you will control them.

Having Embodied Knowledge,
You Are Prepared for Experience

You have now equipped yourself with the knowledge necessary to move on to the meditation discussed in Part III, with full understanding of what you will be doing and why.

Remember that knowledge is the forerunner to experience. All the information you have read has been put there to prepare you for an experience. Once you learn to meditate and apply this to your life, you should begin to see feedback. In the following section you will learn how to put all of this into practice and begin to make measurable changes in any area of your life.

I'm reminded of the two-stage journey that many climbers make when they ascend Washington State's Mount Rainier, the highest volcano in the contiguous U.S. (14,410 feet). Leaving their car at the Paradise Jackson Visitor Center (5,400 feet), they first trek to Camp Muir (10,080 feet). Stopping at this base camp affords them the opportunity to look back at all the ground they've covered, assess what they learned from the preparation and experience of that hike, receive additional practical training, and rest overnight. This overview can make all the difference when they continue on to undertake the climb to Rainier's majestic peak.

The knowledge you've gained has allowed you to ascend to this point. Now you're ready to apply everything you've learned. And your newfound wisdom should inspire you to forge ahead to Part III, where you can master the skills to change your mind, and thus your life.

So I invite you to pause briefly, take a look back with appreciation for the information you acquired in Parts I and II, and if you need to, review any areas you may feel are important . . . then join me as you make your final preparation for the meditative journey to your own personal summit.

PART III

STEPPING TOWARD YOUR NEW DESTINY

CHAPTER NINE

THE MEDITATIVE PROCESS: INTRODUCTION AND PREPARATION

As I stated earlier, the main purpose of meditating is to remove your attention from the environment, your body, and the passage of time so that what you intend, what you think, becomes your focus instead of these externals. You can then change your internal state independent of the outside world. Meditating is also a means for you to move beyond your analytical mind so that you can access your subconscious mind. That's crucial, since the subconscious is where all your bad habits and behaviors that you want to change reside.

Introduction

All the information you have received up to this point has been intended to help you understand what you will be doing in this section, as you learn how to use the meditative process to create a new reality. And once you comprehend and repeatedly execute the "how-to" steps presented here, you can then work on *anything* that you want to change in your life. Remind yourself often that in taking the steps to change, you are pruning away the habit of being yourself so that you can create a new mind for your new future. When *I* do the process you are about to learn, I want to lose myself in consciousness, dissociate from my known reality, and be devoid of the thoughts and feelings that define me as the old self.

In the beginning, the newness of the task you are undertaking might cause you to feel unsettled or uncomfortable. That's okay. It's just your body, which has become your mind, resisting the new training process. Understand this before you initiate your discipline, and relax—each step is designed to be easy to understand and simple to follow. Personally, I look forward to my meditation practice as much as anything I do. I find such order, peace, clarity, and inspiration that I rarely miss a day. It took some time for me to arrive at this relationship, so please be patient with yourself.

Turning Small Steps into One Easy Habit

Whenever you've learned anything new that required your full attention and committed practice, you probably followed specific steps during your initial instruction. This makes it easier to break down the complexities of the skill or task at hand so that the mind can stay focused without being overwhelmed. In any endeavor, of course, your goal is to memorize what you're learning so that eventually you can do it naturally, effortlessly, and subconsciously. Essentially, you want to make this new skill a habit.

It's easier to comprehend and execute any new skill when by repetition, you master one small task or procedure at a time and then move on to the next. Over time you string each step together as part of one coordinated process. The sign that you're on your way is when all the steps start to look like one easy, fluid motion and you produce the intended result. That's your aim in learning this meditation as a step-by-step process.

For example, in learning to hit a golf ball, there are a host of cues that your mind has to process in order to have your actions match your intention. Imagine that while you're preparing to tee off for the first time, your best friend shouts, "Keep your head down! Bend your knees! Shoulders square and back erect! Keep your front arm straight, but loosen your grip! Shift your weight when you swing! Hit behind the ball, and follow through!" And my favorite: "Relax!"

All these instructions at once could throw you into a state of paralysis. What if, instead, you worked on one thing at a time, following a methodical order? In time, it seems logical that your swing would look like one motion.

Similarly, if you were learning to cook a French recipe, you would start by following its individual steps. Do that enough times, and there would come a moment when you no longer would prepare the recipe as separate steps, but as one continuous process. You would integrate the instructions into your body-mind, merge many steps into just a few, and eventually, cook the meal in half the time. You'd go from thinking to doing—your *body* memorizes what you were doing, as well as your mind. That's what a procedural memory is. This phenomenon occurs when you do anything long enough. You begin to know that you *know how*.

Building a Neural Network for Meditation

Remember that the more knowledge you have, the better prepared you are for a new experience. Every meditation step you practice will have a meaning to you based on what you learned earlier in this book; each one is based on a scientific or philosophical understanding so that nothing is left to conjecture. The steps are presented in a specific order designed to help you memorize this process for personal change.

Although I have mapped out a suggested four-week program for you to learn the entire process, please take as much time as you need to practice each step until it becomes familiar. The best pace to set is one that is comfortable, so you never feel overwhelmed.

You will begin every session by doing the previous steps you learned, then practice the new material for that week. Because it's more effective to learn some steps together, some weeks will call for you to practice two or more new steps. Also, I recommend that you practice each new mindful step, or group of steps, for at least a week before you move on to the next ones. In a few weeks, you'll build quite a neural network for meditation!

Suggested Four-Week Program

Week One (Chapter 10):	Every day, do STEP 1: **Induction.**
Week Two (Chapter 11):	Start every daily session by once again practicing the first step; then add STEP 2: **Recognizing,** STEP 3: **Admitting and Declaring,** and STEP 4: **Surrendering.**
Week Three (Chapter 12):	Start every daily session by practicing STEPS 1 through 4, then add STEP 5: **Observing and Reminding** and STEP 6: **Redirecting.**
Week Four (Chapter 13):	Start every daily session by practicing STEPS 1 through 6, then add STEP 7: **Creating and Rehearsing.**

Please take your time and build a strong foundation. If you are already an experienced meditator and want to do more at once, that's fine, but work at following all the instructions and committing what you will be doing to memory.

When you can concentrate on what you're doing without letting your thoughts wander to any extraneous stimuli, you will come to a point when your body actually aligns with your mind. Now your new skill will become easier and easier to do, thanks to

Hebb's law of firing and wiring. The ingredients of learning, attention, instruction, and practice will develop an associated neural network to reflect your intentions.

Preparation

Preparing Your Tools

The write stuff. Separately from your meditation sessions, you will read some descriptive text about each step, often accompanied by questions and prompts under the heading "Opportunity to Write." I recommend that you keep a notebook handy to write down your answers. Then review your responses before you go into each day's meditation. That way, your written thoughts can serve as a road map to prepare you to navigate through the meditative procedures in which you will access the operating system of your subconscious.

Listen up. When you are first learning the meditation steps, you may want to listen to prerecorded guided sessions. For example, you will learn an induction technique that you will use in every one of your daily sessions, to help you reach the highly coherent Alpha brain-wave state in preparation for the approach that is the focus of Chapters 11 to 13. In addition, the steps you are to learn each week are available for you to follow in a series of guided meditations.

Two Approaches to the Meditation

Meditation Option 1: Wherever you see this headphone icon . . .

. . . a guided induction or meditation is available. To listen to these guided sessions, you can download them from **www.drjoedispenza .com** and either play them in MP3 format or burn them onto a CD.

After you read each chapter, then journal your responses in a notebook, you can download the corresponding meditation. Each week, as you add the next step or steps to those you practiced the previous week, you can find the next related meditation available for download. They will be listed as the "Week One meditation," "Week Two meditation," "Week Three meditation," and "Week Four meditation"— Week Four will include the entire meditation.

For example, when you hear the Week Two meditation, it will lead you through the Week One step—which is an induction technique— then will add the three steps you will practice for Week Two. When you do the Week Three meditation, you will repeat the steps you learned in Weeks One and Two, then add the steps for Week Three.

Meditation Option 2: Alternatively, scripts for these guided sessions are included in the Appendices so that you can read them until you memorize the sequence, or dictate them into a recording device.

Appendices A and B provide two techniques for the induction. Appendix C is the script for the entire meditation, encompassing all of the steps you will learn in Part III. If you decide to use the Appendix C script to guide your meditation, then each week, please start with the steps you learned in previous weeks, then build on them by doing that week's meditation.

Preparing Your Environment

Location, location, location. You have learned that overcoming your environment is a critical step in breaking the habit of being yourself. Finding the right environment in which to meditate, one with a minimum of distractions, will really give you a leg up on defeating the first of the Big Three (we'll cover the other two, the body and time, in a moment). Pick a comfortable place where you can be alone and not be seduced by the addiction of the external world. Make it secluded, private, and easily accessible. Go to this place every day, and make it your special location. You will form a strong connection with this setting. It will represent where you frequent to tame the distracted ego, overcome the old self, create a new self, and forge a new destiny. In time you will truly look forward to being there.

A participant in one event I led told me that she always fell asleep when she meditated. Our conversation went like this:

"Where do you practice your mindfulness training?"

"In bed."

"What does the law of association say about your bed and sleep?"

"I associate my bed with sleep."

"What does the law of repetition demonstrate about sleeping in your bed every night?"

"If I sleep in the same place nightly, I am hardwiring an association of *bed* with *sleep*."

"Given the fact that neural networks are formed by combining the law of association with the law of repetition, might you have formed a neural network to the effect that *bed* means *sleep?* And since neural networks are automatic programs that we unconsciously use every day, does it stand to reason that when you are on your bed, your body (as the mind) will tell you to automatically and unconsciously fall into oblivion?"

"Yep. I guess I need a better place to meditate!"

Not only did I suggest that she stay out of bed when she meditates, but that she find a different place separate from her bedroom. When you want to build a new neural network, it makes good sense to do your mindfulness practices in a setting that represents growth, regeneration, and a new future.

And please, do not see this location as a torture chamber in which you *have to* meditate. This type of attitude will undermine your efforts.

Preventing distractions from your environment. Make sure you won't be interrupted or distracted by people (a Do Not Disturb sign can help) or pets. As much as possible, eliminate sensory stimuli that could force your mind back to your old personality or to awareness of the external world, especially to elements of your familiar environment. Turn off your phone and computer; I know it's hard, but those calls, texts, tweets, IMs, and e-mails can wait. You also don't want the aroma of coffee brewing or food cooking to waft into your meditation setting. Ensure that the room is a comfortable temperature, with no drafts. I usually use a blindfold.

Music. Music can be useful as long as you don't play selections that will bring to mind distracting associations. If I play music, I typically use soft, relaxing, trance-inducing instrumentals or chants without lyrics. When not listening to music, I often put in earplugs.

Preparing Your Body

Position, position, position. I sit up very straight. My back is totally vertical, my neck is erect, my arms and legs are resting poised and still, and my body is relaxed. What about using a recliner? Just as with sitting in bed, many people fall asleep in recliners. Sitting upright in a regular chair, limbs uncrossed, is best. If you prefer to sit on the ground and cross your legs "Indian-style," that's fine, too.

Preventing bodily distractions. In effect, you want to "put the body away" so that you can focus without needing to pay it any attention. For example, use the restroom. Dress in loose clothes, remove your watch, drink a little water, and have more within reach. Take care of any hunger pangs before you begin.

Head nodding vs. nodding off. Since we're talking about the body, let me address an issue that may come up in your own meditation practice. Although you are sitting upright, you may find your head nodding as though you are about to fall asleep. This is a good sign: you are moving into the Alpha and Theta brain-wave states. Your body is used to lying down when your brain waves slow down. When you suddenly "nod" like this, your body wants to doze off. With continued practice, you'll become accustomed to your brain slowing down while you sit upright. The head nodding will eventually stop, and your body won't tend to fall asleep.

Making Time to Meditate

When to meditate. As you know, daily changes in brain chemistry result in easier access to the subconscious mind just after you wake up in the morning and before you go to bed at night. These are the best times to meditate because you can more readily slip into the Alpha or Theta states. I prefer to meditate around the same time every morning. If you are really enthusiastic and would like to meditate at both these times of day, go for it. However, I suggest that folks just starting out do so once daily.

How long to meditate. Take a few minutes before each day's meditation session to review any writing you have done in connection with the steps you are about to practice—as I said, think of these notes as your road map to the journey you are about to take. You may also find it helpful to reread portions of the text—to remind you of what you're about to do—before you go into meditation.

While you're learning the process, every session will start with 10 to 20 minutes for induction. As you add steps, your time frame should lengthen by about 10 to 15 minutes per step. Over time, you will move more rapidly through the steps with which you are already familiar. By the time you learn how to do all those in this process, your daily meditation (including induction) will generally take 40 to 50 minutes.

If you need to finish by a certain time, set a timer to go off ten minutes before you must end your session. That will give you a "heads-up" to complete the session, rather than having to stop abruptly without bringing what you were doing to a close. And set aside enough time to meditate so that the clock doesn't become a concern. After all, if you are meditating and find yourself thinking about your watch, you haven't overcome time. Essentially, you may have to wake up earlier or go to bed later in order to carve out a slot in your day.

Preparing Your State of Mind

Mastering the ego. To be honest, I do have those days where I battle my ego tooth and nail, since it wants to be in control. Some mornings as I begin the process, my analytical mind starts thinking about flights to catch, meetings with staff, injured patients, reports and articles I need to write, my kids and their complexities, phone calls I have to make, and random thoughts from nowhere that pop into my head. I'm obsessing about everything predictable in my external life. Typically, my mind, like most people's, is either anticipating the future or remembering the past. When that occurs, I have to settle down and realize that those are all known associations that have nothing to do with creating something new in the present moment. If this happens to you, it is your job to go beyond the tedium of normal thinking and enter into the creative moment.

Mastering the body. If your body bucks like an unbridled stallion because it wants to *be* the mind—to get up and do some*thing*, think about some*place* it has to go in the future, or remember a past emotional *experience* with some *person* in your life—you must settle it down into the present moment and relax it. Every time you do, you are reconditioning your body to a new mind, and in time, it will acquiesce. It was conditioned by an unconscious mind, and it has to be retrained by you—so love it, work with it, and be kind to it. It will ultimately surrender to you as its master. Remember to be determined, persistent, excited, joyful, flexible, and inspired. When you do so, you are reaching for the hand of the divine.

Now let's begin. . . .

CHAPTER TEN

OPEN THE DOOR TO YOUR CREATIVE STATE

(Week One)

At an early point in my professional career, I learned about and eventually taught hypnosis and self-hypnosis. One of the techniques that hypnosis experts use to get individuals into a so-called trance is called *induction*. Simply put, we teach people how to change their brain waves. All someone has to do in order to be hypnotized or to hypnotize him- or herself is to move down from high- or mid-range Beta waves into a more relaxed Alpha or Theta state. Thus, meditation and self-hypnosis are similar.

I could have included induction with the preparatory information in the last chapter, because induction prepares you to enter a coherent brain-wave state that is conducive to meditation. By mastering induction, you will build a solid foundation for the meditative practices you will learn in upcoming steps. However, unlike those arrangements that you will make *before* you begin each day's meditation, such as turning off your phone and putting your dog or cat in another room, *induction is a step you will include during the session—in fact, it must be the first step you master, and it will lead off every session.*

Just to head off any confusion, after opening each meditative session with induction, you will not be in what the entertainment industry misleadingly depicts as a hypnotic trance. You will be perfectly primed and able to complete all steps in the process that follows over the next three chapters.

STEP 1: INDUCTION

Induction: Open the Door to Your Creative State

I urge you to spend at least a week of daily sessions, or more if needed, devoted to practicing induction. Remember that this process will take up the first 20 minutes of every meditation session. You want this to become a familiar and comfortable habit, so don't rush through it. Your objective is to "stay present."

Preparation for induction. In addition to the aspects of preparation I discussed earlier, here are some further tips: First, sit up straight and close your eyes. As soon as you do so, blocking some sensory/environmental input from coming in, your brain waves lessen in frequency, moving toward that desirable Alpha state. Then surrender, stay present, and love yourself enough to move through this process. You may find that soothing music aids in the progression from high Beta to Alpha, although it isn't necessary to use sounds.

Induction techniques. There are many similar variations on induction techniques. Whether you use either the Body-Part or Water-Rising Induction, alternate them on different days, employ some other method you've used in the past, or devise a different one altogether isn't important. What is important is that you move from that analytical Beta state to the sensory state of Alpha, and focus on the body, which is the subconscious mind and the operating system, where you can then make the changes you want.

Overview: Body-Part Induction

One induction technique may at first seem contradictory—you'll focus attention on your body and environment. Those are two of the Big Three that you have to overcome, but in this case, you're in control of your thoughts about them.

Why is it desirable to focus on the body? Remember, it and the subconscious mind are merged. So when we become acutely aware of the body and sensations related to it, we enter the subconscious mind. We're in that operating system I've mentioned often. Induction is a tool that can be used to get into that system.

The cerebellum plays a role in proprioception (awareness of how our bodies are positioned in space). So in this induction, as you rest your awareness on different parts of your body in space and the space around your body in space, you're using your cerebellum to perform this function. And since the cerebellum is the seat of the subconscious mind, as you place your consciousness on where your body is oriented in space, you access your subconscious mind and bypass your thinking brain.

Moreover, induction shuts down the analytical mind by forcing you into a sensing/feeling mode. Feelings are the language of the body, which in turn is the subconscious mind, so induction allows you to use the body's natural language to interpret and change the language of the operating system. In other words, if you're sensing or putting your awareness on different aspects of your body, you would be thinking less, shifting your analytical thoughts from past to future less, and broadening your focus more to encompass a very different scope—not narrowly obsessive, but rather, creative and open—and you would move from Beta to Alpha.

All of this happens as you move from that narrow-minded range of attention to an expanded focus on the body and the space around it. Buddhists refer to this as an *open focus,* occurring when brain waves naturally become orderly and synchronized.[1] Open focus produces a new, powerfully coherent signal that allows parts of the brain that were not communicating with other parts to now do so. That enables *you* to produce an extremely coherent signal. While you can measure that on a brain scan, more important is that you can feel the difference in the clarity and focus of your thoughts, intentions, and feelings.

Body-Part Induction:
The How-to*

Specifically, you will focus on the location or orientation of your body in space. For example, think about the location of your head, starting at its top and gradually moving down. As the induction progresses from body part to body part, sense and become aware of the space that each occupies. Also sense the density, the weight (or heaviness), or the volume of space that it occupies. By focusing your attention on your scalp, then next on your nose, then your ears, and so on, moving down the body until you've focused on the bottoms of your feet, you will notice some changes. This movement from part to part, and the emphasis on the spaces within the spaces, is the key to this.

Next, become aware of the teardrop-shaped area surrounding your body, and the space it takes up. When you can sense that area of space around your body, your attention now is no longer *on* your body. Now you are not your body, but something grander. This is how you become less body and more mind.

Finally, become aware of the area that the room you are in occupies in space. Sense the volume that it fills. When you reach this point, this is when the brain begins to change its disorderly wave patterns to more balanced and orderly ones.

The Why

We can measure these differences in how you are thinking—we can view your thought patterns on an EEG to see how you've moved from Beta- to Alpha-wave activity. We're not interested in just getting you into an Alpha state of any kind, though; you want to be in a *highly coherent*, organized Alpha. That's why you will concentrate first on your body and its orientation in space, then move from those individual parts to the volume or perimeter of space surrounding the body, and eventually focus your observation on the entire room. If you can sense that density of space, if you can notice it and pay attention to it, you will naturally move

---

* Condensed; see Appendix A for full version.

from a state of thinking to feeling. When that happens, it's impossible to maintain the high-Beta state that characterizes the emergency mode of survival and an overfocused condition.

Water-Rising Induction*

Another similar induction technique you can use is to imagine water moving into the room where you are sitting, then gradually rising. Observe (sense) the space in which the room is situated, and the space that the water occupies. At first, the water would rise to cover your feet; move up the shins to the knees; spill over them and into your lap; move up your abdomen and chest, covering your arms, rising to your neck . . . up past your chin, lips, and head . . . until the water fills the entire room. While some people may not like the idea of being covered completely by water, others find it soothingly warm and inviting.

WEEK ONE
GUIDE TO MEDITATION

As a reminder, during your Week One meditations, your job is to practice the induction technique. If you record this induction yourself, make certain that you repeat the same questions that I have provided in my guided-induction instructions in the Appendices, with their emphasis on words and phrases such as *sense, notice, feel, become aware of, become conscious of,* and *attend to.* Also, words such as *volume, density, perimeter of space, weight of space,* and so forth will help you focus your observation.

---

* Condensed; see Appendix B for full version.

Instead of moving quickly from one part to another, allow some time to pass (a good 20 to 30 seconds or more) for those sensory inputs and the feelings of those parts in space to really settle in. Roughly, allow about 20 minutes to do the Body-Part Induction from head to toe, or in the case of the water immersion, from toe to head. If you have meditated before, you will no doubt understand that eventually you lose any sense of time passing as your brain waves diminish in frequency and you move into that calm and relaxed Alpha state where the inner world is more real than the outer world.

CHAPTER ELEVEN

PRUNE AWAY THE HABIT OF BEING YOURSELF

(*Week Two*)

During Week Two, it's time to add three steps in pruning away the habit of being yourself: *recognizing,* then *admitting and declaring,* followed by *surrendering.* First, read through all these steps and answer the related questions. Then devote at least a week to daily meditation sessions in which you first go into induction, then move through the three steps. Of course, if you need more than one week to feel competent at all this, that's fine.

STEP 2: RECOGNIZING

Recognizing: Identify the Problem

The first move necessary in fixing anything is to understand what is presently not working. You have to know what the problem is and then name it in order to have power over it.

Many people who have had a near-death experience report that they underwent a "life review" in which they saw, as if watching a movie, all of their covert and overt actions, their expressed and suppressed sentiments, their public and private thoughts, and their conscious and unconscious attitudes. They saw who they were and how their thoughts, words, and deeds affected everyone and everything in their lives. Afterward, they typically describe having a greater understanding about themselves and a desire to do a better job of living from then on. And as a result, they perceive new possibilities and better ways "to be" in any opportunity. Having seen themselves from a truly objective point of view, they clearly know what they want to change.

Recognition is like having a life review every day. Since you have all of the equipment in your brain to notice who you are being, why not do this *before* you die, and, in effect, be reborn in the same life? With practice, this type of awareness can help you override what would otherwise be the predetermined destiny of your brain and body—the automatic, enslaving hardwired programs of the mind and the memorized emotions that have chemically conditioned the body.

Only when you are truly conscious and aware do you begin to wake up from the dream. To become still, quiet, patient, and relaxed, and then be attentive to the habits of the old-personality self, disengages your subjective consciousness from overutilized attitudes and extreme emotional states. You no longer are the same mind, because you are now freeing yourself from the chains of the self-centered nature of the ego lost in itself. And when you see who you have been, by means of the observer's watchful eye, you will crave life more, because you will truly desire to make a greater difference the next day.

As you develop the skills of contemplation and self-observation, you are cultivating the ability to separate your consciousness from the subconscious programs that have defined the old self. To move your consciousness from being the old self to being the *observer* of the old self loosens the connection to the old you. And as you recognize who you have been through the skill of metacognition (your ability via the frontal lobe to observe who you are being), for the first time your consciousness is no longer immersed in unconscious programs; you are becoming conscious of what was once unconscious. This is making the first strides toward personal change.

Begin Your Own Life Review

In order to discover and explore aspects of the old self that you want to change, it is necessary to pose some "frontal lobe" questions.

Opportunity to Write

Take some time to ask yourself questions such as these, or any others that occur to you, and write down your answers:

- What kind of person have I been?
- What type of person do I present to the world? (What is one side of my "gap" like?)
- What kind of person am I really like inside? (What is the other side of my "gap" like?)
- Is there a feeling that I experience—even struggle with— over and over again, every day?
- How would my closest friends and family describe me?
- Is there something about myself that I hide from others?
- What part of my personality do I need to work on improving?
- What is one thing I want to change about myself?

Choose an Emotion to Unmemorize

Next, choose one of your afflictive emotional states and limited states of mind (the following examples can help you get started)—one of the habits of being yourself that you want to relinquish. Since memorized feelings condition the body to be the mind, these self-limiting emotions are responsible for your automatic thought processes, which create your attitudes, which influence your limited beliefs (about self in relationship to everyone or everything), which contribute to your personal perceptions. Every one of the emotions listed below originates from the chemicals of survival, which strengthen the ego's control.

Opportunity to Write

Pick one emotion that is a big part of who you are (your chosen emotion may be one that's not listed below) and that you want to unmemorize. Remember that this word has meaning to you because it is a feeling that is familiar to you. It is one aspect of the self that you want to change. I recommend that you write down the emotion you came up with, because you will be working with it throughout this and later steps.

Examples of survival emotions:

Insecurity	Shame	Sadness
Hatred	Anxiety	Disgust
Judgment	Regret	Envy
Victimization	Suffering	Anger
Worry	Frustration	Resentment
Guilt	Fear	Unworthiness
Depression	Greed	Lack

Most people see these examples and say, "Can I pick more than one?" It is important in the beginning to work with one emotion at a time. In any case, they are all linked together neurologically and chemically. For example, have you ever noticed that when you're angry, you're frustrated; when you're frustrated, you hate; when you hate, you judge; when you judge, you're envious; when you're envious, you're insecure; when you're insecure, you're competitive; when you're competitive, you're selfish? All of these emotions are run by the same combined survival chemicals, which then stimulate related states of mind.

On the other hand, the same is true for elevated states of mind and emotion. When you're joyous, you love; when you love, you feel free; when you're free, you're inspired; when you're inspired, you're creative; when you're creative, you're adventurous . . . and so on. All of these feelings are driven by different chemicals that then influence how you think and act.

Let's use anger as an example of a recurring emotion you might choose to work with. As you unmemorize anger, all of the other self-limiting emotions will incrementally decrease within you as well. If you become less angry, you'll be less frustrated, hateful, judgmental, envious, and so on.

The good news is that you are actually taming the body to no longer run unconsciously as the mind. Consequently, as you change one of these destructive emotional states, the body will be less prone to live out of control, and you will change many other personality traits.

Observe How the Unwanted Emotion
Feels in Your Body

Next, close your eyes and think about how you feel when you experience that particular emotion. If you can observe yourself overcome by that emotion, pay attention to how it feels in your body. There are different sensations that correlate to different emotions. I want you to become aware of all of those physical signs. Do you become hot, irritated, jittery, weak, flushed, deflated, tight? Scan your body with your mind and notice in what area you feel that emotion. (If you do not feel anything in your body, that's okay; just remember what you want to change about yourself. Your observation is changing it moment by moment.)

Now, become familiar with your body's present state. Does your breathing change? Do you feel impatient? Are you physically in pain, and if so, if that pain had an emotion, what would it be? Just notice what physiologically is happening in the moment and don't try to run from it. *Be* with it. The host of different feelings in your body becomes an emotion when you name it as anger, fear, sadness, or whatever the case may be. So let's get down to all of those feelings and physical sensations that create the emotion you want to unmemorize.

Allow yourself to feel that emotion without being distracted by anything or anyone. Don't do anything or try to make it go away. Almost everything you have done in your life has been to run from this feeling. You used everything outside of you to try to make it go away. Be present with your emotion and feel it as energy in your body.

This emotion has motivated you to appropriate everything you know in your environment to fashion an identity. Because of this feeling, you created an ideal for the world instead of an ideal for yourself.

This feeling is who you really are. Acknowledge it. It is one of the many masks of your personality that you have memorized. It started from an emotional reaction to an event in your life, which lingered into a mood, which developed into a temperament, which created your personality. This emotion has become the memory of yourself. It speaks nothing about your future. Your attachment to it means that you are mentally and physically bound by your past.

If emotions are the end product of experiences, then by embracing the same emotion every day, the body is being fooled into believing that your external world is staying the same. And if your body is being conditioned to reexperience the same circumstances in your environment, you can never evolve and change. As long as you live by this emotion daily, you can only think in the past.

Define the State of Mind
Associated with the Emotion

Next, ask yourself this simple question: "How do I think when I feel this way?"

Let's say that you want to change anger as one of your personality traits. Ask yourself, "What is my attitude when I feel anger?" The answer might be *controlling* or *hateful,* or it might be *self-important.* By the same means, if you want to overcome fear, you might have to address the state of mind of feeling overwhelmed, anxious, or desperate. Suffering might lead to feeling victimized, depressed, lazy, resentful, or needy.

Now, become aware of or remember your thinking when you feel this way. What is the state of mind that is powered by this emotion? This feeling influences everything you do. States of mind represent an attitude that is driven by the memorized feelings subconsciously anchored in the body. An attitude is a series of thoughts that are connected to a feeling, or vice versa. It is the repetitive cycle of thinking and feeling, feeling and thinking. Therefore, you need to define your neural habit that is influenced by your particular emotional addiction.

Opportunity to Write

Become aware of how you think (your state of mind) when you are feeling the emotion you want to change. You may pick from the list below, or add any that are not listed. Your selection will be based on the unwanted emotion you identified previously, but it's natural to be in one or more limiting states of mind relating to that emotion. So write down one or two that resonate with you, because you will work with these in upcoming steps.

Examples of limiting states of mind:

Competitive	Lacking	Controlling
Overwhelmed	Overly intellectual	Deceptive
Complaining	Self-important	Conceited
Blaming	Shy/timid/introverted	Dramatic
Confused	Needing recognition	Rushing
Distracted	Under-/overconfident	Needy
Self-pitying	Lazy	Self-involved
Desperate	Dishonest	Sensitive/insensitive

Most of your behaviors, choices, and deeds are equal to this feeling. Therefore, you will think and act in predictable, routine ways. There can be no new future, just more of the same past. It's time to remove the colored lenses and no longer see life through a filter of the past. Your job is to be with that emotional attitude without doing anything but observing it.

You've just identified an unwanted emotion and its corresponding state of mind that you want to unmemorize. But remember that you still have a couple of steps to read through before you integrate them all into your daily meditation. . . .

STEP 3: ADMITTING AND DECLARING

Admitting: Acknowledge Your True Self
Rather Than the Self You Show to Other People

Allowing yourself to be vulnerable, you move beyond the realm of your senses and begin to introduce yourself to the universal consciousness that is the giver of your life. You develop a relationship with this greater intelligence, telling it who you have been and what you want to change about yourself, and admitting what you have been hiding.

Owning up to who we really are and what our past mistakes have been and asking to be accepted are among the most challenging things for us to do as humans. Think of how you felt as a child when you had to fess up to your parents, a teacher, or a friend. Have those feelings of guilt, shame, and anger changed now that you're an adult? Most likely you still experience them, but maybe not as strongly.

What makes achieving Step 3 possible is knowing that we are admitting our faults and failures to our higher power and not to another similarly flawed human. As a result, when we admit to ourselves and to that universal power, there is:

No punishment
No judgment
No manipulation
No emotional abandonment
No blame
No scorekeeping
No rejection
No loss of love
No damnation
No separation
No banishment

All of the preceding acts are derived from the old paradigm of God, which has been shrunk to the likeness of an insecure man, completely self-absorbed, steeped in the concepts of good and bad, right and wrong, positive and negative, success and failure, love and hate, heaven and hell, pain and pleasure, and fear and more fear. This traditional model must be addressed, because one must enter this consciousness with a *new* consciousness.

This enigma can be called *innate intelligence, chi, divine mind, spirit, the quantum, the life force, infinite mind, the observer, universal intelligence, the quantum field, invisible power, mother-father life, cosmic energy,* or *higher power.* Regardless of what name you give it, you must see this energy as an unlimited source of power within you and around you, which you utilize and create from throughout your life.

It is the consciousness of intent and the energy of unconditional love. It is impossible for it to judge, punish, threaten, or banish anyone or anything because it would be doing those very things to itself.

It only gives in love, compassion, and understanding. It already knows everything about you (it's *you* who has to make an effort to know and develop a relationship with *it*). It has been observing you from the moment you were created. You are an extension of it.

It only waits in hope, in admiration, and in patience . . . it only wants you to be happy. And if you are happy being unhappy, that's fine, too. That's how much it loves you.

This self-organizing invisible field is wise beyond comprehension because it exists through an interconnected matrix of energy that extends in all dimensions in space and time, past, present, and future. It records the thoughts, desires, dreams, experiences, wisdom, evolution, and knowledge from all of eternity. It is an immense, immaterial, multidimensional field of information. It "knows" much more than you and I do (even though we think we know it all). Its energy can be likened to many levels of frequency; and like radio waves, every frequency carries information. All of life on a molecular level vibrates, breathes, dances, shimmers, and is alive; it is completely receptive and malleable to our willful intentions.

Let's suppose you want joy in your life. So you ask the universe for it every day. However, you've memorized suffering into such a state of being that you whine all day long, you hold everyone responsible for the way you feel, you make excuses for yourself, and you mope around constantly feeling sorry for yourself. Can you see that you can *declare* joy all you want, but you are *demonstrating* being a victim? Your mind and body are in opposition. You are thinking a certain way one moment; then you are being something else the remainder of the day. Hence, can you humbly and sincerely admit who you have been, what you have been hiding, and what you want to change about yourself, so that you eliminate unnecessary pain and suffering before you create the related experiences in your reality? To vacate and lay down your familiar personality for a brief period of time and knock on the door of the infinite in a state of joy and reverence is so much more conducive to change than allowing your personality to be fractured by your insistent course of destiny, created by who you were repeatedly "being." Let's change in joy instead of changing in pain.

Opportunity to Write

Now, close your eyes and become still. Look into the vastness of this mind (and into yourself) and begin to tell it who you have been. Develop a relationship with the greater consciousness that is giving you life, by honestly and inwardly talking to it. Share with it the details of those stories that you have carried around with you. Writing down what comes to you will be useful in later steps.

Examples of what you might admit to your higher power:

- I am afraid of falling in love because it hurts too much.

- I pretend I am happy, but I am really suffering because I am lonely.

- I do not want anyone to know that I feel so guilty, so I lie about myself.

- I lie to people so that they like me and so I won't feel so unloved and unworthy.

- I can't stop feeling self-pity. I think, act, and feel this way all day long because I do not know how *else* I can feel.

- I have felt like a failure most of my life, so I try extra hard to be a success.

Now, take a moment and review what you have written and what you want to admit to this power.

Declaring: Outwardly Acknowledge Your Self-Limiting Emotion

In this part of the meditation process, you actually speak out loud who you have been and what you have been hiding about yourself. You tell the truth about self, put the past to rest, and close the gap between how you appear and who you really are. You give up your façade and the constant effort of being someone else. By declaring the truth about yourself out loud, you are breaking the emotional ties, agreements, dependencies, attachments, bonds, and addictions to all those external cues in your life.

In the workshops that I conduct around the world, this is the most difficult part of the steps. No one really wants anyone to know who they really are. They want to maintain how they appear. However, as you have learned, it takes an enormous amount of energy to keep up this ongoing image. This is the point where you want to release that energy.

And remember: since emotions are energy in motion, everything that you've experienced and interacted with in your external life has an energetic emotion attached to it. Essentially, you are bonded to some person, thing, or place by an energy that exists beyond time and space. This is how you continually remember yourself as an ego with a personality, identifying emotionally with and being tied to everything in your life.

For example, if you hate someone, that hate keeps you emotionally attached to the other person. Your emotional bond is the energy that keeps this individual in your life so that you can feel hate and thus reinforce one aspect of your personality. In other words, you use that person to stay addicted to hatred. By the way, it should be obvious by now that your hatred is primarily hurting you. As you release chemicals from your brain to your body, you truly hate *yourself.* To speak the truth about yourself out loud in this step empowers you to become free from hatred and less connected to the person or thing in your external reality that reminds you of who you have been.

If you recall the gap discussed earlier, you know that most people rely on the environment to remember themselves as a "somebody." Therefore, if you have memorized an emotion as part of your personality and you are addicted to it, then when you declare who you have been emotionally, you are calling energy back (releasing it) to you from your emotional bonds with everything and everyone in your life. This conscious statement by you will free you from the old self.

In addition, by claiming your limitations and consciously revealing what you have been hiding, you are freeing the body from being the mind; and for that reason, you are closing the gap between how you appear and who you really are. When you verbalize who you have been, you also liberate energy stored in your body. This will become "free energy" for you to use later on in the meditation to create a new self and life.

Bear in mind that your body will not want to do this very readily. Your ego automatically hides this emotion because it doesn't want anyone to know the truth about itself. It wants to remain in control. The servant has become the master. But the master now must let the servant know that he or she has been delinquent, unconscious, and absent. So it makes sense that your body will not want to relinquish control, because it does not trust you. But if you just open your mouth and speak out in spite of the body's control, it will begin to feel lighter and relieved, and you will begin to be back in command.

This is how you define who you really are without any associations to your external environment. You are severing your energetic bond to the emotional attachment of all of the elements in the outer world. If admitting is an inner acknowledgment, then declaration is an outward one.

What Is It That You Want to Declare?

It's time to merge this part of Step 3 with the previous part. Remember that you're building this section into one fluid process. Using the example of anger, you might say aloud, "I have been an angry person my whole life."

Remember the general aim of what you want to declare. In this part of your meditation for the week, while you are sitting up with eyes closed, you'll open your mouth and softly say the emotion that you are declaring: *anger.*

While you prepare yourself to do this and while you are engaged in verbalizing your declaration, it probably will not feel good to you. Do it anyway; that's your body talking to you.

Your end result is that you are inspired, uplifted, and energized. Make this step simple, easy, and lighthearted. Do not overanalyze what you have done. Just know that the truth shall set you free.

◦◉◦

Remember that you're not ready to start your Week Two meditations yet. In this section, you've recognized an unwanted emotion and its corresponding state of mind that you want to unmemorize, then you admitted it inwardly and declared it outwardly. There's one more step to read, after which you can put all four together in your Week Two meditation. . . .

STEP 4: SURRENDERING

Surrendering: Yield to a Greater Power and Allow It to Resolve Your Limitations or Blocks

Surrendering is the final step in this section, in which you are pruning away the habit of being yourself.

Most of us struggle with the idea of letting go, of allowing someone or something else to have control. Keeping in mind whom you are surrendering to—the Source, Infinite Wisdom—should make this process go much easier.

Einstein said that no problem could be solved from the same level of consciousness that created it. The limited state of mind of your personality is responsible for creating your limitations, and the answer has not come to you . . . so why not go to a grander, more resourceful consciousness to help you overcome this facet of yourself? Since all potentials exist in this infinite sea of possibilities, you are humbly asking it to take your limitations from you in a different way than the mode in which *you* have been trying to resolve this issue. Since the best way to transform yourself has not occurred to you and what you have been doing up to this point to overcome the problems in your life has not worked out yet, it's time to contact a greater resource.

The consciousness of the ego could never see the solution. It is steeped in the emotional energy of the dilemma; and therefore it only thinks, acts, and feels equal to that mind. It only creates more of the same.

Your change will be executed in a way that is unlimited from the objective mind's perspective. It sees you from the perspective of *not being you.* It perceives potentials that you have not even thought of because you were too busy being lost in the dream by responding to life in predictable ways.

However, if you say that you have surrendered to the objective consciousness's assistance yet still try to do things your own way, can you see that it is impossible for it to assist you in changing anything in your life? By your own free will, you would thwart its efforts.

Most of us obstruct this mind because we go back to trying to resolve our problems by living within the same unconscious, habitual lifestyle. We get in our own way. In fact, most of us wait until the ego is driven into the ground to the point that we can no longer continue "business as usual." This is when we usually surrender and receive some type of aid.

You can't both surrender and try to control the outcome. Surrender requires that you give up what you think you know from your limited mind, especially your belief about how this problem in your life should be taken care of. To truly surrender is to let go of the ego's control; trust in an outcome that you haven't thought of yet; and allow this all-knowing, loving intelligence to take over and provide the best solution for you. You must come to the understanding that this invisible power is real, is fully conscious of you, and can completely take care of any aspect of the personality. When you do, it will organize your life in a way that is just right for you.

When you ask for help by simply releasing to a greater mind the emotion you have admitted and declared, you won't have to:

- Bargain
- Beg
- Make deals or promises
- Commit halfway
- Manipulate
- Weasel
- Ask for forgiveness
- Feel guilty or shameful
- Live with regrets
- Suffer from fear
- Provide excuses

Moreover, you won't have to give your higher mind conditions like "You should . . ." and "It would be better if . . ." You can't tell this unlimited grand essence how to go about anything. If you do, you are back to trying to do things your way, and naturally it will stop helping you so as to allow you your free will. Instead, can your free will be "Thy will be done"?

Just surrender in . . .

- Sincerity
- Humility
- Honesty
- Certainty
- Clarity
- Passion
- Trust

. . . and then get out of the way.

Joyously give up the emotion you want to let go of to a more expanded mind, and *know* that it will do this for you. When your will matches its will, when your mind matches its mind, and when your love of self matches its love for you . . . it answers the call.

The side effects of *surrendering* include:

- Inspiration
- Joy
- Love
- Freedom
- Awe
- Gratitude
- Exuberance

When you feel joy or live in a state of joy, you have already accepted the future outcome that you want as a reality. When you live as if your prayers have already been answered, this greater mind can do what it does best by organizing your life in new and unusual ways.

What if you knew that some issue facing you had been completely taken care of? What if you were certain that something exciting or great was about to happen to you? If you knew it without a doubt, there would be no worry, no sadness, no fear, and no stress. You would be lifted. You would be looking forward to your future.

If I told you that I was taking you to Hawaii in a week and you knew that I was serious, wouldn't you start to get happy in anticipation? Your body would begin to physiologically respond ahead of the actual experience. Well, the quantum mind is like a big mirror—it reflects back to you what you accept and believe as true. So your outer world is a reflection of your inner reality. The most important synaptic connection you can make when it comes to this mind is to know that *it is real.*

Think about how a placebo works. You know by now that we have three brains that allow us to evolve from thinking to doing to being. Often subjects with health issues who are given a sugar pill that they think is medicine accept the *thought* that they are going to get better, begin to *act* as if they are better, begin to *feel* better, and finally are *being* better. And as a result, the subconscious mind within them, which is connected to the universal mind all around them, begins to change their internal chemistry to mirror their new belief about their restored health. The same principle applies here. *Believe* that the quantum mind will answer your call and help you.

If you begin to doubt, become anxious, worry, get discouraged, or overanalyze how this assistance might happen, you have undone everything that you originally accomplished. You got in your own way. You blocked something greater from helping you. Your emotions demonstrated that you disbelieved in quantum possibilities, and therefore you lost your connection to the future that the divine mind was orchestrating for you.

This is when you have to go back and reinstate a more powerful frame of mind. Talk to the quantum mind as if it knows you very well and loves and cares for you . . . because it *does.*

Opportunity to Write

In anticipation of this conversation, write down some things you would like to say in your surrender statement.

Examples of surrender statements:

Universal mind within me, I forgive my worries, my anxieties, and my small-minded concerns, and I give them to you. I trust that you have the mind to resolve them much better than I could. Arrange the players in my world so that doors open for me.

Innate intelligence, I release my suffering and my self-pity to you. I have mismanaged my inner thoughts and actions for long enough. I allow you to intervene and provide a greater life in a way that is just right for me.

Prepare to surrender. Now close your eyes, and begin to become familiar with what you want to say to this greater mind. Review what you have written so that you can take your limitations to it. The more present you are, the more focused you can become. As you begin to inwardly recite your prayer, remember that this invisible consciousness is watchful and aware of you; it notices everything that you think, do, and feel.

Ask for help, and turn over your unwanted state of mind. Next, ask the universal consciousness to take this part of you and reorganize it into something greater. Once you do, then hand it over to this higher mind. Some people mentally open a door and pass it through, others hand it over in a note, while some place it in a beautiful box, then let it dissolve into the higher mind. It doesn't matter what you imagine. I just simply let it go.

What matters is your intention—that you feel connected to a very loving, universal consciousness, and that you begin to become free from your old self with its help. The more purposefully you are able to manage your thoughts and the more you can feel the joy of being free from this condition, the more you are matching a greater will, its mind, and its love.

Give thanks. Once you have completed your prayer, remember to give thanks ahead of the manifestation. When you do, you are sending a signal into the quantum field that your intention has already come to fruition. Thankfulness is the supreme state of receivership.

WEEK TWO
GUIDE TO MEDITATION

Now you're ready to do your Week Two meditation. Here's a suggested way to move through all the steps you've learned. If you feel that you already did any of these actions while you were reading and journaling, just go ahead and repeat them during your meditations. You may be surprised by the results.

- **Step 1:** First, go through your induction technique and continue to become more and more used to this process to enter the subconscious mind.

- **Step 2:** Next, by becoming aware of what you want to change about yourself in mind and body, "recognize" your own limitations. That is, define a specific emotion that you want to unmemorize and look at the associated attitude that is driven by that feeling.

- **Step 3:** Continuing on, inwardly "admit" to a higher power within you who you have been, what you want to change about yourself, and what you have been hiding. Then, outwardly "declare" what emotion you are releasing so as to free the body from the mind and break the bonds to the elements in your environment.

- **Step 4:** Finally, "surrender" this self-limiting state to a greater mind and ask that it be resolved in a way that is right for you.

Practice these individual steps regularly during your sessions, until they begin to become so familiar to you that they merge into one smooth step. Then you will be ready to proceed on.

Keep in mind that as you continue to add steps to your meditation process, you will always start by doing the series of four intentional actions you just learned.

CHAPTER TWELVE

DISMANTLE THE MEMORY OF THE OLD YOU

(Week Three)

Once again, you will read through and perform your writing on Steps 5 and 6 before you do your Week Three meditation sessions.

STEP 5: OBSERVING AND REMINDING

In this step, you observe the old self and remind yourself who you no longer want to be.

Just like our working definition of meditation in Part II of the book, to observe and remember is to become familiar with; to cultivate the "self"; and to make known what is, in some way, unknown. Here you will become completely conscious of (by observing) the specific unconscious or habitual thoughts and actions that make up that state of mind and body that you named earlier, in Step 2: Recognizing. Then you will remind yourself about (by remembering) all of the aspects of the old self that you no longer want to be. You will become familiar with yourself "being" the old personality—the precise thoughts you no longer want to give power to, and the exact behaviors you no longer want to engage in—so you never fall back into being the old self. This frees you from the past.

What you mentally rehearse and what you physically demonstrate is who you are on a neurological level. The "neurological you" is made up of the combination of your thinking and actions on a moment-to-moment basis.

This step is designed to create greater awareness and a better observation of who you have been (metacognition). As you reflect and review your old self, you will get clear on who you no longer want to be.

Observing: Become Conscious of Your Habitual States of Mind

In Step 2: Recognizing, you have already observed the emotion that drives you. Now I want you to become so familiar with your specific thoughts and actions derived from the old sensations that you can catch yourself while you live your life. With repeated practice, you can become so aware of the old patterns that you never allow them to manifest to fruition. The end result is that you stay ahead of the old self so that you have control over it. So when you start to notice the beginnings of the feeling that normally drives your unconscious thoughts and habits unfolding in your day, it has become so familiar to you that the slightest inkling is now brought to your awareness.

As an example, if you are overcoming a dependency on some substance such as sugar or tobacco, the more you are able to sense when the pangs and tugs of the body's chemical addiction begin, the sooner you will be able to do battle against them. Everyone knows when the cravings start to occur. You begin to notice impulses, urges, and sometimes loud screams, which sound like, "Just do it! Submit! Give in! Go ahead—just this one time!" As you continuously forge onward and upward, in time you can notice when these cravings come up, and you will be better equipped to handle them.

The same is true with personal change, except the substance is not something that exists outside of you. In reality, it is *you.* Your feelings and thoughts are actually a part of you. Nevertheless, your real objective here is to be so aware of the self-limiting state of being that you would never let one thought or behavior go unnoticed by you.

Almost all of what we demonstrate starts with a thought. But just because you have a thought doesn't necessarily mean it is true. Most thoughts are just old circuits in your brain that have become hardwired by your repetitive volition. Thus, you have to ask yourself, "Is this thought true, or is it just what I think and believe while I am feeling this way? If I act on this impulse, will it lead me to the same result in my life?" The truth is, these are echoes from your past that are connected to strong feelings, which activate old circuits in your brain and cause you to react in predictable ways.

Opportunity to Write

What automatic thoughts do you think when you feel that emotion you identified in Step 2? It is important to write them down and memorize the list. To help you recognize your own unique set of self-limiting thoughts, you may find the following examples helpful.

Examples of limiting automatic thoughts (your daily, unconscious mental rehearsal):

- *I'll never get a new job.*
- *No one ever listens to me.*
- *He always makes me feel angry.*
- *Everyone uses me.*
- *I want to call it quits.*

- *Today is a bad day for me, so why bother trying to change it.*

- *It's her fault that my life is this way.*

- *I'm really not that smart.*

- *I honestly can't change. Maybe it would be better to start another time.*

- *I don't feel like it.*

- *My life sucks.*

- *I hate my situation with _____.*

- *I'll never make a difference. I can't.*

- *_____ does not like me.*

- *I have to work harder than most people.*

- *It's my genetics. I am just like my mother.*

Just as with habitual thoughts, habitual actions also make up your own unique undesirable states of mind. You are influenced to behave in memorized ways by the very emotion that has conditioned your body to be your mind. This is who you are when you go unconscious. You start off with good intentions, and then you find yourself sitting on the couch eating potato chips with the remote control in one hand and a cigarette in the other. However, just a few hours before, you proclaimed that you were going to get in shape and stop all self-destructive behaviors.

Most unconscious actions are taken to emotionally reinforce the personality and fulfill an addiction, in order to feel more of the same way. For example, people who feel guilty on a daily basis will have to perform certain actions to fulfill their emotional destiny. Most certainly, they will get in trouble in life to feel more guilt. Many unconscious actions match and thus satisfy who we are emotionally.

On the other hand, many people exhibit certain habits in order to temporarily make the feeling they have memorized go away. They look for instant gratification from something outside of them to momentarily free them from their pain and emptiness. Being addicted to computer games, drugs, alcohol, food, gambling, or shopping is used to resolve one's inner pain and emptiness.

Your addictions create your habits. Since nothing that exists outside of you could ever resolve your emptiness on a permanent basis, invariably you will have to do more of the same activity over again. After the thrill or the rush wears off a few hours later, you will have to return to the same addictive tendency once more, but do it longer. However, when you unmemorize the negative emotion of your personality, you eliminate the destructive unconscious behavior.

Opportunity to Write

Think about the unwanted emotion you identified. How do you habitually act when you are feeling this way? You may recognize your own patterns among the examples below, but be sure to add those behaviors that are specific to you. Now, write down the unique ways you behave when you feel that emotion.

Examples of limiting actions/behaviors
(your daily, unconscious physical rehearsal):

- Sulking
- Feeling sorry for yourself by sitting alone
- Eating away depression
- Calling someone to complain about how you feel
- Playing obsessively on the computer
- Picking a fight with someone you love
- Drinking too much and making a fool out of yourself
- Shopping and spending more than you have
- Procrastinating
- Gossiping or spreading rumors

- Lying about yourself

- Throwing a temper tantrum

- Treating fellow employees with disrespect

- Flirting with other people when you are married

- Bragging

- Yelling at everyone

- Gambling too much

- Driving aggressively

- Trying to be the center of attention

- Sleeping in every day

- Talking too much about the past

If you are having difficulty coming up with answers, ask yourself what you think about during various situations in your life, and inwardly "watch" how you think and respond. You can also inwardly "look through the eyes" of other people. How would they say they see you? How do you act?

Reminding: Recall the Aspects of the Old Self You No Longer Want to Be

Now review and memorize your list. This is an essential part of meditation. Your goal is "to become familiar with" how you think and act when this specific emotion is driving you. It is to remind you how you no longer want to be, and how you were making yourself so unhappy. This step helps you become aware of how you unconsciously behave and what you say to yourself while you're thinking and feeling, feeling and thinking, so that you have more conscious control in your waking day.

Executing this step is a work in progress. In other words, if you sit down every day for a week to focus on this, you will probably find that you continue to modify and refine your list. That's good.

When you do this step, you enter the operating system of the "computer" programs in the subconscious mind and throw the spotlight on them for your review. You ultimately want to become so familiar with these cognitions that you inhibit them from firing in the first place. You will prune away the synaptic connections that made up the old self. And if everywhere that a neurological connection is formed constitutes a memory, then you are in fact dismantling the memory of the old you.

Throughout this next week, continue to review the list again so that you know even better who you no longer want to be. If you can memorize all these aspects of the old self, you will separate your consciousness even further from the old self. When your habitual, automatic thoughts and reactions are completely familiar to you, they will never slip by unnoticed or unrecognized. And you will be able to anticipate them before they are initiated. This is when you are free.

In this step, remember: *awareness is your goal.*

⊛⊛⊛

You know the drill by now . . . read Step 6 and do your writing; then you'll be ready to start your Week Three meditations.

Step 6: Redirecting

Here's what happens when you use the tools of redirecting: You prevent yourself from behaving unconsciously. You stop yourself from activating your old programs, and you biologically change, causing unfiring and unwiring of nerve cells. Similarly, you stop the same genes from being signaled in the same ways.

If you've struggled with the idea of surrendering control, this step allows you to more consciously and judiciously take back the reins in order to break the habit of being yourself. When you become masterful at being able to redirect yourself, you're building a solid foundation on which to create your new-and-improved self.

Redirecting: Play the Change Game

During your meditations this week, take some of the situations you came up with in the step just before, and as you picture them or observe yourself in your mind, tell yourself (out loud), "Change!" It's simple:

1. Imagine a situation where you are thinking and feeling in an unconscious way.
    . . . **Say "Change!"**

2. Become aware of a scenario (with a person, for example, or a thing) where you could easily fall into an old behavior pattern.
    . . . **Say "Change!"**

3. Picture yourself in an event in your life where there is a good reason to fall short of your ideal.
    . . . **Say "Change!"**

The Loudest Voice in Your Head

After you remind yourself to stay conscious throughout your day, as you learned in the previous step, you can now use a tool to change right in the moment. Whenever you catch yourself in real life thinking a limiting thought or engaging in a limiting behavior, just say "Change!" out loud. Over time, your own voice will become the new voice in your head—and the *loudest* one. It will become the voice of redirection.

As you repeatedly interrupt the old program, your efforts will begin to further weaken the connections between those neural networks that make up your personality. By the principle of Hebbian learning, you will unhook the circuits connected to the old self during your daily life. At the same time, you are no longer epigenetically signaling the same genes in the same ways. This is another step so that you will become more conscious. It is developing "conscious control" of yourself.

When you can stop a knee-jerk emotional reaction to some thing or person in your life, you are choosing to save yourself from returning to the old you that thinks and acts in such limited ways. By the same idea, as you gain conscious control over your thoughts that may be initiated from some stray memory or association connected with some environmental cue, you will move away from the predictable destiny in which you think the same thoughts and perform the same actions, which will create the same reality. It is a reminder placed by you in your own mind.

As you become aware, redirect your familiar thoughts and feelings, and recognize your unconscious states of being, you are also no longer using up your valuable energy. When you are living in a state of survival, you are signaling your body into emergency status by knocking it out of homeostasis and thus mobilizing a lot of energy. Those emotions and thoughts represent a low frequency of energy that is consumed by the body. So when you are conscious and change them *before* they make it to the body, then every time you notice or redirect them, you are conserving vital energy you may use for creating a new life.

Associative Memories Trigger Automatic Responses

Since staying conscious is crucial to creating that new life, it is important to understand how associative memories have made it so difficult for you to stay conscious in the past, and how practicing redirection can help free you from your old self.

Earlier in this book, we saw that Pavlov's classical-conditioning experiment with dogs beautifully illustrates why it can be so hard for us to change. The dogs' reaction in that experiment—learning to salivate in response to a bell—is an example of a conditioned response based on an *associative memory.*

Your associative memories exist in the subconscious mind. They are formed over time when the repeated exposure to an external condition produces an automatic internal response in the body, which then elicits an automatic behavior. As one or two of the senses respond to the same cue, the body reacts without much of the conscious mind's involvement. It turns on by a thought or a memory alone.

By the same token, we live by numerous similar associative memories in our lives, triggered by so many known identifications derived from our environment. For instance, if you see someone you know well, chances are that you are going to respond in automatic ways without ever consciously knowing it. Seeing that individual will create an associated memory from some past experience that is connected to some emotion, which then triggers an automatic behavior. The chemistry of your body changes the moment you "think" about him or her in the past memory. A program runs from the repeated conditioning that you memorized about that person into your subconscious mind. And just like Pavlov's dogs, in moments you are physiologically responding unconsciously. Your body takes over and begins to run you subconsciously, based on some past memory.

Your body is now predominantly in control. You're out of the driver's seat consciously because your subconscious body-mind is now controlling you. What are the cues that cause this to occur so quickly with you? They can be anything or everything in your external world. Their source is your relationship to your known environment; it is your life, which is connected to all of the people and things you experienced at different times and places.

This is why it is so difficult to stay conscious in the process of change. You see a person, hear a song, visit a place, remember an experience, and your body begins to immediately "turn on" from a past memory. And your associated thought about how to identify with someone or something activates a cascade of reactions below the conscious mind that then returns you back to the same personality self. You think, act, and feel in predictable, automatic, memorized ways. You subconsciously reidentify with your past known environment, which then returns you to your known self living in the past.

When Pavlov continued to ring the bell without the reward of food being present, in time the dogs' automatic response lessened because they no longer maintained the same association. We could say that the dogs' repeated exposure to the bell without the food dwindled their neuroemotional response. They stopped salivating because the bell became a sound without any associative memory.

Catch Yourself Before "Going Unconscious"

As you run through a series of situations in your mind's eye in which you stop yourself from being the old self (emotionally), your repeated exposure to the same stimuli (mentally) will, over time, weaken your emotional response to that condition. And as you consistently present yourself to the same motives of the old identity and notice how you automatically responded, you will become conscious enough in your life that you catch yourself from going unconscious. In time, all of those associations that turned on the old program will become just like the dogs' experience of the bell without the food—you no longer knee-jerk back physiologically to the neurochemical you, connected to familiar people or things.

Thus, your thought about a person who makes you angry or your interaction with the ex-boyfriend can no longer tug on you because you've mindfully stopped yourself enough times. As you break the addiction to the emotion, there can be no autonomic response. It is your conscious awareness in this step that then frees you from the associated emotion or thought process in your daily life. Most of the time, these reflexive reactions go by unchecked by you because you are too busy "being" the old you.

It is important that you rationalize beyond the barometer of your feelings to understand that these survival emotions are affecting your cells in adverse ways by pushing the same genetic buttons and breaking down your body. It raises the question: "Is this feeling, behavior, or attitude loving to myself?"

After I say "Change," I like to say, "This is not loving to me! The rewards of being healthy, happy, and free are so much more important than being stuck in the same self-destructive pattern. I don't want to emotionally signal the same genes in the same way and affect my body so adversely. Nothing is worth it."

WEEK THREE
GUIDE TO MEDITATION

During your Week Three meditations, your aim is to now add Step 5: Observing and Reminding, then Step 6: Redirecting, to the previous steps, so that you are doing all six. Steps 5 and 6 will ultimately merge to become one step. Throughout your day, as limiting thoughts and feelings come up, observe yourself and automatically say "Change!" out loud; or hear this—instead of the old voice(s)—as the loudest voice in your head. When that happens, you will be ready for the creation process.

- **Step 1:** As usual, begin by doing the induction.

- **Steps 2–5:** After you recognize, admit, declare, and surrender, it's time to continue to address the specific thoughts and actions that naturally slip past your awareness. Observe the old you until you become completely familiar with those programs.

- **Step 6:** Then, as you are observing the old you while you are in your meditation, pick a few scenarios in your life and say "Change!" out loud.

CHAPTER THIRTEEN

CREATE A NEW MIND FOR YOUR NEW FUTURE

(Week Four)

Step 7: Creating and Rehearsing

Week Four will be a bit different from previous weeks. First, as you read and write for Step 7, you will receive knowledge about *creating* and instruction on the "how-to" process of using *mental rehearsal*. Then you'll read the Guided Mental-Rehearsal Meditation to follow, to familiarize you with this new process.

Next, it's time to *do* what you have learned. Every day this week, you will practice the Week Four meditation, which includes Steps 1 through 7. As you listen, you will apply the focused attention and repetition you have employed to create the new you and your new destiny.

Overview: Creating and Rehearsing the New You

Before you begin the final series of steps, I want to point out that the preceding steps were all designed to help you break the habit of being yourself so that you could make room both consciously and energetically for reinventing a new self. Up until this point, you've worked at pruning away old synaptic connections. Now it's time to sprout new ones, so that the new mind you create will become the platform of who you will be in your future.

Your previous efforts have facilitated unlearning some things about your old self. You've weeded out many aspects of the old you. You've become familiar with your unconscious states of mind that represent how you thought, behaved, and felt. Through the practice of metacognition, you've consciously observed the routine, habitual ways your brain fired within the box of your former personality. The skill of self-reflection has allowed you to separate your free-willed consciousness from the automatic programs that caused your brain to fire in the exact same sequences, patterns, and combinations. You've examined how your brain has probably been working for years now. And since the working definition of mind is the brain in action, you've objectively looked at your limited mind.

Creating the New You

Now that you are beginning to "lose" your mind, it's time to create a new one. Let's begin to "plant" a new you. Your daily meditations, contemplations, and rehearsals will be like tending to a garden to yield a greater expression of you. Learning new information and reading about great people in history who represent your new ideal is like sowing the seeds. The more creative you are in reinventing a new identity, the more diverse the fruits you will experience in your future. Your firm intention and conscious attention will be like water and sunlight for your dreams in your garden.

As you emotionally rejoice in your new future before it is made manifest, you cast a safety net and fence protecting your vulnerable potential destiny from pests and difficult climatic conditions, because your elevated energy shields your creation. And by falling in love with the vision of who you are becoming, you are nurturing the potential plants and fruit with a miracle fertilizer. Love is a higher-frequency emotion than those survival emotions that allowed the weeds and pests to come in the first place. To eliminate the old and make way for the new is the process of transformation.

Rehearsing the New You

Next, it's time to practice creating a new mind over and over again until it begins to become familiar to you. As you know, the more you fire circuits together, the more you wire them into lasting relationships. And if you fire a series of thoughts related to a particular stream of consciousness, it will be easier to produce that same level of mind the time after that. Therefore, as you repeat the same frame of mind every day by mentally rehearsing a new ideal of self, over time it will become more routine, more familiar, more natural, more automatic, and more subconscious. You will begin to remember *you* as someone else.

In the previous steps, you also unmemorized an emotion that was stored in your body-mind. Now it's time to recondition your body to a *new* mind and signal your genes in new ways.

Your goal in this final step is to master a new mind in the brain as well as the body. Thus, it becomes so familiar to you that you are able to reproduce that same level of being at will and make it look natural and easy. It's important that you memorize this new state of mind by thinking in new ways; equally relevant is to then memorize a new feeling in the body so that nothing in your outer world can move you from it. This is when you are ready to create a new future and then live in it. When you rehearse, you bring the new you out of nothing repeatedly and consistently, so that you "know how" to call it up at will.

Creating: Use Imagination and Invention to Bring Your New Self into Existence

In this step, you'll start by asking yourself some open-ended questions. As you pose questions that cause you to speculate, to think in different ways than you typically think, and to entertain new possibilities, this turns on your frontal lobe.

This entire contemplation process is the building method for making a new mind. You are creating the platform of the new self by forcing the brain to fire in novel ways. You're beginning to change your mind!

Opportunity to Write

Please take time to write down your answers to the following questions. Then review them, reflect on them, analyze them, and think about all the possibilities your answers raise.

Questions to turn on your frontal lobe:

- What is the greatest ideal of myself?
- What would it be like to be _____?
- Who in history do I admire, and how did they act?
- Who in my life do I know who is/feels _____?
- What would it take to think like _____?
- Whom do I want to model?
- How would I be if I were _____?
- What would I say to myself if I were this person?
- How would I talk to others if I were changed?
- How or whom do I want to remind myself to be?

Your personality consists of how you think, act, and feel. So I've grouped some questions to help you determine more specifically how you want your new self to conduct itself. Remember, when you come up with your own answers, then contemplate them, you are installing new hardware in your brain and signaling your genes to activate in new ways in your body. (Feel free to continue to list your answers in your journal if you don't think you can mentally keep track of them.)

How Do I Want to Think?

- How would this new person (my ideal) think?
- What thoughts do I want to put my energy behind?
- What is my new attitude?
- What do I want to believe about *me?*
- How do I want to be perceived?
- What would I say to myself if I was this person?

How Do I Want to Act?

- How would this person act?
- What would he or she do?
- How do I see myself behaving?
- How would I speak as this new expression of self?

How Do I Want to Feel?

- How would this new self *be?*
- What would I feel?
- What would my energy be like as this new ideal?

When you meditate to create the new you, your job is to reproduce the same level of mind every day, to think and feel differently than you usually do. You should be able to repeat that same frame of mind at will and make it commonplace. Furthermore, you have to allow your body to feel that new feeling until you actually *are* that new person. In other words, *you cannot get up as the same person who sat down.* Transformation must occur in the here and now, and your energy should be different from when you started. If you get up as the same person, feeling just as you did when you started, nothing has really happened. You are still the same identity.

Therefore, if you say to yourself, "I didn't feel like it today; I'm too tired; I have too much to do; I am busy; I have a headache; I'm too much like my mother; I can't change; I want to get something to eat; I can start tomorrow; this doesn't feel good; I should turn on the TV and watch the news," and so on; and if you allow those subvocalizations to take the stage of the frontal lobe, you will invariably get up as the same personality.

You must use your will, intention, and sincerity to go beyond these urges of the body. You must recognize this banter and chatter as a fight by the old self for control. You must allow it to rebel, but then bring it back to the present moment, relax it, and then start over again. And over time, it will begin to trust *you* to be the master again.

Rehearsing: Memorize the New You

Now that you've contemplated your answers, it's time to rehearse them. Review how you will think, act, and feel as your new ideal. Let's be clear here. I don't want you to become too mechanistic or rigid. This is a creative process. Allow yourself to be imaginative, free, and spontaneous. Don't force your answers to be one way or another. Don't try to go through your list in the same exact way during each meditative session. There are many different means to arrive at your end.

Just think about the greatest expression of yourself and then remind yourself how you will act. What will you say, how will you walk, how will you breathe, and how will you feel if you become that person? What will you say to others and to yourself? Your goal is to move into a "state of being" and *become* this ideal.

For instance, think back to those piano players who *mentally* rehearsed piano exercises without touching any keys, and how they achieved almost the same brain changes as people who *physically* played the same scales and chords for the same length of time. The "mental" players' daily rehearsal changed their brains to look like they had already had the experience of physically executing the activity. Their thoughts became their experience.

If you recall the finger-exercise experiment involving mental rehearsal, there were also significant physical changes demonstrated in the body, without the subjects' ever lifting a finger. In this step, your daily rehearsals will change your brain and your body to be ahead of time.

That's why it's so important to rehearse—to bring up again—how you will act as your new self. This is how you biologically change the brain and body to no longer live in the past but rather to chart a map to the future. If the body and brain are changed, then there is physical evidence that *you are changed.*

Becoming Very Familiar with the New You

This part of Step 7 is about making the leap to get to the "unconsciously skilled" level of expertise. When you are *unconsciously skilled* at something, that means you just do it without having to place a great deal of conscious thought or attention on the activity. It's like going from a novice driver to an experienced one. It's like being able to knit without having to consciously will each of the actions into motion. It's like the old Nike ad slogan: you are just doing it.

If you are getting bored around this point in the exercise, take that as a good sign. It means that your new mode of operation is beginning to become familiar, common, and automatic. You have to get to this juncture in order to hardwire and embody this information into long-term memory. You must make an effort to go beyond your boredom, because each time you engage in your new ideal, you manage to be more of the new you with less effort. You engrave your new model of *you* into a memory system that then becomes more subconscious and natural. If you keep practicing it, you won't have to think about *being* it. You will have *become* it. Bottom line, practice makes perfect. You are training yourself in this process, like any sport.

If you're doing rehearsal correctly, then each time you practice, it should be easier for you to accomplish. Why? Because you're primed; you already have those circuits firing in tandem in your brain, and it's already warmed up. You also manufactured the right chemistry, and it's circulating in your body, selecting a new genetic expression; your body is naturally in the right state. In addition, you have restrained and "quieted down" other brain regions connected to the old you. Consequently, the feelings that were associated with the old you are less likely to stimulate your body in the same inherent ways.

Bear in mind that most of the mental-rehearsal exercises that activate and grow new circuits in the brain involve learning knowledge, getting instruction, paying attention, and repeating the skill over and over. As you know, learning is making new connections; instruction is teaching the body "how to" in order to create a new experience; paying attention to what you are doing is absolutely necessary to rewire your brain, because it involves your being present to the stimuli . . . both physical and mental; and last, repetition fires and wires long-term relationships between nerve cells. These are all the ingredients that it takes to grow new circuits and make a new mind—and this is exactly what you're doing in your meditations. Repetition is what I want to emphasize here.

Cathy's story illustrates every facet of mental rehearsal. A massive stroke had damaged the language center in her brain's left hemisphere, leaving her unable to talk for months. Doctors told Cathy, a corporate trainer, that she would probably never speak again. Having read my book and completed one of my workshops, Cathy refused to accept this devastating prognosis.

Instead, based on knowledge she had learned and instruction she received, and applying focused attention and repetition, Cathy mentally rehearsed speaking in front of groups of people. Every day, she practiced this in her mind. Over a period of several months, she demonstrated physical changes in her brain and body, to the extent that she repaired the language center in her brain . . . and completely regained her ability to speak. Today Cathy once again addresses audiences fluently and flawlessly, with no hesitation.

In your own study of this material, you made some important synaptic connections as the precursor for you to have new experiences. Both of these elements—studying information and having experiences—evolve your brain. You are also being given the proper instruction in the unlearning and relearning process of change. You understand the importance of focus in attending to both mental and physical activity to mold your brain and change your body to reflect your efforts. And finally, it is your repeated efforts to rehearse your new ideal that will produce the same level of mind and body, over and over again. Repetition will seal long-lasting circuits and activate new genes for you to revisit the next day with greater ease. This step is for you to practice reproducing the same state of being so it gets simpler.

The keys for you to focus on are *frequency, intensity,* and *duration.* That is, the more you do it, the easier it gets. The better your focus and concentration are, the easier it is for you to tap into that particular mind the next time. The longer you can linger in the thoughts and emotions of your new ideal, without letting your mind wander to extraneous stimuli, the more you will memorize this new state of being. This step is all about getting into *becoming* your new ideal in your waking day.

Becoming a New Personality Produces a New Reality

Your goal in this step is to become a new personality, a new state of being. So if you are a new personality, you are being somebody else, right? Your old personality, based on how you thought, felt, and acted, has created the reality that you presently are experiencing. In short, how you are as a personality is how you are in your personal reality. Remember, also, that your personal reality is made up of how you think, feel, and act. By doing each of those in a new way, you are creating both a new self and a new reality.

Your new personality *should* produce a new reality. In other words, when you are being someone else, you naturally will have a different life. If you suddenly changed your identity, you would be another person, and therefore, you would certainly live as someone else. If the personality called John became the personality known as Steve, we could say that John's life will change because he is no longer being John but is now thinking, acting, and feeling like Steve.

Here is another example. One time while I was lecturing in California, a woman approached me in front of the audience with her hands on her hips, intensely focused, angrily exclaiming, "How come I'm not living in Santa Fe?!"

I calmly replied, "Because the person who was just talking to me is the personality who is living in Los Angeles. The personality who would be living, and is already, in Santa Fe looks nothing like that."

Thus, from a quantum perspective, this new personality is the perfect place to create from. The new identity is no longer emotionally anchored to known situations in your life that keep recycling the same circumstances; therefore, it is a perfect place from which to envision a new destiny. This is the place you want to be to call out a new life. The reason why your prayers were hardly ever answered in the past is that you were trying to hold a mindful intention while being lost in lower emotions such as guilt, shame, sadness, unworthiness, anger, or fear connected to the old self. It was those feelings that were governing your thoughts and attitude.

The 5 percent of your mind that is conscious was fighting against the 95 percent that is the subconscious body-mind. Thinking one way and feeling another cannot produce anything tangible. Energetically, that broadcasts a mixed signal to the invisible web that orchestrates reality. Thus, if you were "being" guilty because your body memorized the mind of guilt, then you probably received whatever you were being—situations in your life that evoked more reasons to feel guilty. Your conscious aim could not stand up against your *being* that memorized emotion.

As this new identity, however, you are thinking and feeling differently than the old identity. You are in a state of mind and body that now is sending a perfect signal free from your past memories. For the first time, the lens of your mind is now lifted above the present landscape to see a new horizon. You are looking to the future, not your past.

Simply said, you can't create a new personal reality while you are still being the old personality. You have to become someone else. Once you are in a new state of being, *now* is the time to create a new destiny.

Creating a New Destiny

This part of the step is where you, as this new state of being, this new personality, create a new personal reality. The energy that you released from the body earlier is now the raw ingredient to create a new future with.

So what do you want? Do you want healing in some area of your body or your life? Do you want a loving relationship, a more satisfying career, a new car, a paid-up mortgage? Do you want the solution to overcoming an obstacle in your life? Is your dream to write a book, to send your kids to college or go back to school yourself, to climb a mountain, to learn to fly, to be free from an addiction? In all of these examples, your brain automatically creates an image of what you want.

From an elevated state of mind and body; in love, joy, self-empowerment, and gratitude; in a greater, more coherent energy, here is where you see those images in your mind of what you want to create in your new life as this new personality. Craft the specific future events you want to experience, by observing them into physical reality. Let yourself go and begin to free-associate without analysis. The pictures you see in your mind are the vibrational blueprints of your new destiny. You, as the quantum observer, are commanding matter to conform to your intentions.

With clarity, you will hold the image of each manifestation in your mind for a few seconds, and then let it go into the quantum to be executed by a greater mind.

Just like the observer in quantum physics, who looks for an electron and it collapses from a wave of probabilities into an event called a particle—the physical manifestation of matter—you are doing the same on a much larger scale. But you are using your "free energy" to collapse waves of probability into an event called a new experience in your life. Your energy is now entangled with that future reality, and it belongs to you. Thus, *you* are entangled with it, and it is your destiny.

Finally, give up trying to figure out how or when or where or with whom. Leave those details to a mind that knows so much more than you do. And know that your creation will come in a way that you will least expect, that will surprise you and leave no doubt that it came from a higher order. Trust that the events in your life will be tailored to your conscious intentions.

Now you are developing a two-way communication with this invisible consciousness. It shows you that it noticed you emulating it as a creator; it speaks to you directly; it demonstrates that it is responding to you. How does it do all this? It creates and organizes unusual events in your life; these signify direct messages from the quantum mind. Now you have a relationship with a supreme, loving consciousness.

Overview: Guided Mental-Rehearsal Meditation

It's time to reinvent a new you, by moving into a new state of being that reflects your new expression of self. After you do so—by priming a new mind and body—then you rehearse that state of being again. Your efforts to re-create the same familiar state will biologically change your brain and body ahead of the new experience. Then once you are a new being in your meditation, a new being is a new personality, and a new personality creates a new personal reality. Here is where you, from an elevated energy, create the specific events in your life as the quantum observer of destiny. Although this Guided Mental-Rehearsal Meditation has three parts, when it is incorporated into your Week Four meditation (as the Guided Meditation in Appendix C), the parts blend seamlessly together.

Guided Mental-Rehearsal Meditation:
Creating the New You

Now close your eyes, eliminate the environment, and let yourself go by "creating" how you want to live your life.

Your job is to move into a new state of being. It's time to change your mind and think in new ways. When you do, you will emotionally recondition your body to a new mind by signaling new genes in new ways. Let the thought become the experience, and live that future reality now. Open your heart and give thanks ahead of the actual experience so much so that you convince your body to believe that future event is unfolding now.

Pick a potential in the quantum field, and live it completely. It is time to change your energy from living in the emotions of the past to living in the emotions of a new future. You cannot get up as the same person you were when you sat down.

Remind yourself who you will be when you open your eyes. Plan your actions with regard to how you will be in your new reality. Imagine the new you and how you will speak and what you will say to yourself. Think about what it will feel like to be this ideal. Conceive of yourself as a new person—doing certain things; thinking certain ways; and feeling the emotions of joy, inspiration, love, empowerment, gratitude, and power.

Become so attentive to your intention that your thoughts of a new ideal become the experience internally, and as you feel the emotion from that experience, you go from thinking to being. Remember who and what you really are in your new future.

Rehearsing the New You

Now, relax for a few seconds. Then "re-view," re-create, and rehearse what you just did; do it over again. Let go and see if you can do it repeatedly and consistently.

Can you initiate being that new ideal with greater ease than the last time? Can you bring it out of nothing one more time? You should naturally be able to recall who you are becoming so that you know how to call it up at will. Your repeated efforts will mean doing it so many times that you'll just "know how" to. When you move into this new state of being, "memorize the feeling." This is a great place to be.

Creating Your New Destiny

Now, it's time to command matter. From this elevated state of mind and body, what do you want in your future life?

As you unfold the new self, remember to move into that state of mind and body that feels invincible, powerful, absolute, inspired, and overjoyed. Let the pictures come; see them with certainty, with a knowingness that unifies you to those events or things. Bond with your future as if it is yours, without any concern other than expectancy and celebration. Let yourself go and begin to free-associate without concern. Become empowered by your new sense of self. With clarity, hold the image of each manifestation in your mind for a few seconds, and then let it go into the quantum to be executed by a greater mind . . . then go to the next one . . . keep going . . . this is your new destiny. Allow yourself to experience that future reality in the present moment until you convince your body to emotionally believe that the event is coming to pass now. Open your heart and experience the joy of your new life before it actually manifests. . . .

Know that where you place your attention is where you place your energy. The energy that you released from the body earlier has become the raw materials for you to use to create a new future. In a state of divinity, true greatness, and gratitude, create by blessing your life with your own energy, and be the quantum observer of your future. Become entangled to your new reality. As you see the images of what you want to experience in the energy of this new personality, know that those pictures will become the blueprints of your destiny. You are commanding matter to conform to your intentions. . . . When you finish, simply let go and know that your future will unfold in a way that is perfect for you.

**WEEK FOUR
GUIDE TO MEDITATION**

Now that you have read the text and journaled for Step 7, you are ready to practice your Week Four meditations. Every day, listen to (or do from memory) the full Week Four meditation.

A helpful hint: During the Guided Meditation, you may find yourself feeling so good that you naturally make statements like these to yourself or out loud: *I am wealthy, I am healthy, I am a genius*—because you *feel* like that in a very real way. That's great. It means mind and body are aligned. It's important for you not to analyze what you are dreaming. If you do, you will leave the fertile ground of the Alpha-wave patterns and return back to Beta-wave patterns, and separate yourself from your subconscious mind. Just create a new you without any judgment.

Guide to Continuing Your Meditation

You've just devoted the past several weeks to learning a meditation practice that can become a lifelong means to help you evolve and create the life you choose. You also used that new skill to start pruning away a particular aspect of the old you, and to begin creating a new self and a new destiny.

At this point, many people ask questions such as these:

- How can I continue to get better at the steps and skills of meditating?

- Once I have mastered this process, should I keep doing it the same way indefinitely?

- How long should I keep working on the same aspect of self that I've focused on up to now?

- How will I know when I'm ready to peel away another "layer of the onion"?

- As I keep using this process, how can I decide which part of my old self to change next?

- Can I use this process to work on more than one aspect of my personality at a time?

Make This Meditative Process Your Own

If you continue to do all the steps every day, what used to feel like seven steps will begin to feel simpler, with more of a flow from step to step. Like anything you have mastered in your life, you will only get better if you continue to meditate daily.

As for the Guided Meditation and induction techniques, you might think of them like training wheels on a bicycle. If using them helped you while you were learning this process, continue to listen to them for as long as they assist you to move ahead. But once you're so familiar with the process that you've made it your own, and you feel that listening to guided instructions is holding you back, then let them go.

Keep Peeling Away Those Layers

Making periodic adjustments to your meditations is natural and to be expected, because you aren't the same person you were when you began. If you keep up the daily sessions, your state of being will continue to evolve, and thus you will continue to recognize aspects of your old self that you want to change.

Only you can determine when and how quickly you are ready to move ahead. And as I'll talk about in the next chapter, your progress will depend not just on your meditations, but on making *change* an integral part of your daily life. But in general, working on one particular aspect of yourself in your sessions for four to six weeks will likely bring enough results that you feel an inner prompting to begin removing another layer of self.

So approximately every month, do some self-reflection. Look to your life for feedback on what you're creating, and how you're doing. You might revisit the questions in Part III and notice any that you would now answer differently. Reevaluate how you're feeling, who you've been "being" in your life, and whether you still have the attitude you were working on. If that attitude feels like it has diminished, have you noticed other unwanted emotions, states of mind, or habits that feel more prominent now?

If so, one approach might be to focus on that aspect of your personality and redo the entire process you just completed. Alternatively, you may want to keep working on one area while adding another.

Once you've mastered the basic template for how to meditate, you can combine the emotions you're working on in a more unified way, addressing several aspects of yourself at the same time. After a lot of practice, I now work on my whole self at once, taking what I think of as a holistic, nonlinear approach.

Of course, elements of the new destiny you want to create will surely change as well. When that new relationship or career change comes into your life, you won't want to stop there. And every so often, you may also opt to vary your meditation just to shake things up a bit. Trust your instincts.

Advance Your Understanding Even More

If you haven't already done so, I invite you to visit my website: **www.drjoedispenza.com**. Whenever you feel the need for new inspiration, here you will find an array of practical tools and techniques to reprogram your thoughts and remove self-destructive habits to empower you to change from the inside out. Your next steps might be to:

- Read my first book (and the companion to this one), *Evolve Your Brain: The Science of Changing Your Mind,* to deepen the knowledge that, as you now know, is the precursor to experience. This book will walk you through the structures of your brain, teach you how your thoughts and emotions become hardwired, and give you the understanding to not only change your life, but to change *you* into the person you've always wanted to be.

- Attend one, two, or all three of the workshops I personally conduct around the world on *Breaking the Habit of Being Yourself.*

- Participate in a series of live teleclasses, including Q & A sessions.

- Broaden the foundation of your knowledge through the DVDs and audio CDs described on my website.

CHAPTER FOURTEEN

DEMONSTRATING AND BEING TRANSPARENT: LIVING YOUR NEW REALITY

When you demonstrate change, you've memorized an internal order that is greater than any environmental cue. It's keeping your energy up, staying conscious in a new reality, independent of your body, independent of the environment, and independent of time. How are you going to be when you walk into your life? Remind yourself with your family, at your job, with your children, at lunch tomorrow. Can you maintain this modified state of being? If you can live your life in the same energy that you created with, then something different should show up in your world—that's the law. When your behaviors match your intentions, when your actions are equal to your thoughts, when you're being someone else, then you are ahead of your time. Your environment is no longer controlling how you think and feel; how you think and feel is controlling your environment. That's greatness, and it's always been within you. . . .

When how you appear is who you are, you are free from the enslavement of your past. And when all of that energy now is liberated, the side effect of that freedom is called joy.

Demonstrating: Living as the New You

When your internal neurochemical state is so orderly and coherent that no stimulus in your incoherent, external world can disrupt who you are "being," then your mind and body are now working in harmony. You are now a new *being*. And by memorizing that state of being—a new personality—your world and your personal reality will begin to reflect your internal changes. When your outward expression of self is equal to your inner self, you are headed to a new destiny.

Can you maintain the change in your life so that your body does not return to the same mind? Since emotions are stored in the subconscious memory system, it is your job to consciously keep your body aligned to your new mind so that nothing in your environment emotionally hooks you back to the old reality. You must memorize your new self and insist on being it, so that nothing in your present reality can move you from it.

Remember that when you get up from your meditation, if you did it properly, you will advance from thinking to being. Once you are in that state of being, you are more prone to do and think *equal to* who you are being.

To Demonstrate Is to "Be It" All Day Long

In a nutshell, demonstration is living as if your prayers have already been answered. It is rejoicing in your new life with a new level of expectation and excitement. It is reminding yourself that you must be in that same state of mind and body that you were in when you created your new ideal. You cannot create a new personality in your meditation and then live as the old self for the rest of the day. It would be like eating a really healthy meal in the morning and then spending the rest of the day snacking on junk food.

In order for a new experience in reality to happen to you, you have to match your behavior with your goal; you align your thoughts and your deeds. You must make choices that are consistent with your new state of being. When you demonstrate, you physically apply what you have mentally rehearsed, getting the body involved and making it do what the mind has learned.

Therefore, in order for you to see the signals unfolding in your life, you must live and be in the same energy that you created from. Simply put, if you want the universe to begin to talk back to you in new and unusual ways, the energy and the mind that you demonstrate in your life must be the same as the energy and mind of your meditation as that new ideal. This is when you are connected with or entangled to the energy you created in a dimension beyond space and time, and this is how you attract the new event into your life.

When both aspects of the self are aligned, the "you" living in the "now life" is the same being you constructed during your meditation. You are *being the future you* that existed as a potential in the quantum field. And when the new self that you created in your meditation is the exact same electromagnetic signature as the future you that you are being in your life, you are unified to that new destiny. When you are physically "being one with the future you in the now moment" that you dreamed about, you will experience the bounty of a new reality. There will be a response from a greater order.

Look Forward to Feedback

The feedback you experience in your life is the result of matching the state of being/energy of your creative process to the state of being/energy of your demonstrative process. It is "being" that being you invented in this particular plane of demonstration. You have to live in that line of time in present physical reality. Thus, if you maintain that modified state of mind and body the entire day, something different should show up in your life.

And what type of feedback should you begin to witness? Look forward to synchronicities, opportunities, coincidences, flow, effortless change, better health, insights, revelations, mystical experiences, and new relationships, to name a few. New feedback then will inspire you to keep doing what you have been doing.

When external feedback occurs as a result of your internal efforts, you will naturally correlate whatever you were doing inside of you with whatever happened outside of you. This is a novel moment in and of itself. It basically shows evidence that you are now living by the quantum law. You become astonished that the feedback that you are experiencing is the direct result of the internal workings of your mind and emotions.

When you correlate what you did in the implicit world with the explicit manifestation, you will pay attention and remember whatever you did earlier to produce that effect, and you will do it again. And when you can connect your inner world with the effects in the outer world, you are now "causing an effect" instead of living by cause and effect. You are creating reality.

Here is the test: Can you be the same person in your external environment that you were being in your internal one, while you were meditating? Can you be greater than your present environment, which is connected to your past personality, memories, and associations? Are you able to cease your routine reactions to the same situations? Have you conditioned your body and molded your mind to be ahead of the present reality in front of you?

This is the reason why we meditate. To become someone else in our lives.

Demonstrate the New-You Plan into the Equation of Your Life

Remind yourself that during the day, you will keep your energy up as the new you. Here you are to prompt yourself to stay conscious at different times in your waking hours. You can prime yourself to place little notes in consciousness on the canvas of your life.

For example:

I want to give thanks for different aspects of my life while I take my morning shower. I have to stay on track while I drive to work, so I'm going to be joyous during the whole trip. How will I be as this new ideal when I see my boss? Let me remind myself to take a moment at lunch and remember who I want to be. When I see my kids this evening, I will be elevated and have abundant energy, and we'll truly connect. I want to take a minute while I get ready for bed and remind myself who I am being.

End-of-the-Day Questions

These questions are a simple way to review your display of the new self when the day is over:

- How did I do today?
- When did I fall from grace, and why?
- Who was it I reacted to, and where?
- When did I "go unconscious"?
- How can I do better the next time that happens?

Before you go to bed, it might be a nice idea to contemplate where it was during your day that you lost your new ideal. Once you can see the obvious place in your life that stimulated you to fall into oblivion, ask yourself these simple questions: "If this situation happened again, how would I do it differently?" and "What piece of knowledge or philosophical understanding could I apply to this circumstance if it arose again?"

Once you can come up with a solid answer and attend to it with a bit of thoughtfulness, you will be mentally rehearsing a new element that rounds out another part of you. You will be putting the new neural network into your brain to prepare you for the event at some future time. This little move will assist you in upgrading and refining the model of the new-and-improved you. You then can add that into your morning or evening meditation.

Being Transparent: Going from the Inner to the Outer

When you are transparent, how you appear is who you are, and your internal thoughts and feelings are reflected in your external environment. Having achieved this state, your life and your mind are synonymous. It is your final relationship between *you* and all of your outward creations. This means that your life reflects your mind in all arenas. You are your life, and your life is a reflection of you. If, as quantum physics suggests, the environment is an extension of the mind, this is when your life reorganizes itself to reflect your *new* mind.

Transparency is a state of true empowerment, in which you have realized (made real) your dream of personal transformation. You have gained wisdom from experience, and are greater than the environment and your past reality.

The telltale sign of becoming transparent is that you do not have many overly analytical or critical thoughts. You wouldn't want to think that way. It would take you away from your present state. Since the side effect of transparency is true joy, more energy, and freedom of expression, any thought that is connected to an ego drive would lower the elevated feeling within you.

There Will Come a Moment . . .

When your life begins to unfold with new and wonderful events, there will come a moment that you will be in awe, wonder, and utter wakefulness when you realize it was your mind that created them. In your rapture, you will look back from this vantage point at your entire life, and you will not want to change anything. You will not regret any action or feel bad about whatever has happened to you, because in that moment of your manifestation, it will all make sense to you. You will see how your past got you to this great state.

As the result of your efforts, the consciousness of the greater mind has begun to be your conscious mind; its nature is becoming your nature. You naturally become more divine. This is who you really are. This is your natural state of being.

Equally, as the invisible giver of life begins to move through you, you will feel more like yourself than you have in a long time. Those traumas that produced emotional scars knocked your true personality from its center. You became more complicated, more polarized, more divided, more inconsistent, and more predictable. When you unmemorize those survival emotions that naturally lower the frequency of the mind and the body, you are lifted to a higher electromagnetic expression, and a greater frequency is now turning you on. And you free yourself by unlocking the doors to make room for a greater power to become you.

Finally, it is you and you are it. You are one. And you feel a coherent energy called love. It is the *within* that then manifests an unconditional state.

Once you connect to and drink from the well of consciousness, you might experience a real paradox. It is quite possible that there will come such a sense of personal wholeness that you will find it difficult to want anything. This dichotomy was a veritable realization for me.

Wants and desires come from lacking something, someone, someplace, or some time. In being truly connected to this consciousness, I have had moments that it was hard to think about anything else because I felt so great. I felt so complete that any thought that would take me away from it would not be worth my moving from this place.

So the irony is that once you arrive at this space to create from, you no longer *need* anything, because the lack and emptiness from which you desired those things has been eliminated, replaced by a feeling of wholeness. As a result, you just want to linger in the feeling of balance, love, and coherence.

This, I feel, is the beginning of true unconditional love. Feeling a sense of love and awe for life without needing anything from outside of us is freedom. It is no longer being attached to external elements. It is a feeling that is so coherent that to judge another or to emotionally react to life and change from this state is compromising self. This is when the greater consciousness that we are all connected to begins to move *out* of us, and we begin to express this *through* us. We move from human toward divine. We become more like it. We become more loving, more mindful, more powerful, more generous, more intentional, more kind, and healthier. That's its mind.

Something else amazing begins to occur as well. When you feel elevated and joyful, you will feel so wonderful that you will want to share the feeling of what you are experiencing with someone. And how do you share such great feelings? You give. You think, *I feel so superb and uplifted that I want you to feel the way I feel. So here is a gift.* And you will begin to give so that others can feel the gift that you're expressing from within. You are selfless. Imagine a world like that.

If, however, you can fashion a new reality from this internal order of wholeness, you must know that you will be creating from a state of being in consciousness that is no longer separate from whatever it is you desire. You are in absolute oneness with your creation. And if you can slip into it naturally, and forget about everything that is tied to the old you, you will feel such a sense of exuberance that you will begin to know that the creation you are focusing upon is yours. It will feel like hitting a tennis ball in the sweet spot or parallel parking without mirrors within inches of the curb. It just feels right. You somehow know.

⚫⚫⚫

This is how I end my daily meditation, and I offer it to you as a suggestion:

> *Now close your eyes. Become aware that there is an intelligence that is within you and all around you. Remember that it is real. Contemplate that this consciousness is noticing you and is aware of your intentions. Recall that it is a creator that exists beyond space and time.*

In your journey past the cravings of the body and the nuances of the ego mind, you have made it to this final step. So if in fact this consciousness is real and it exists, ask for a sign to let you know that you made contact with it. Say to the creator, "If I emulated you in any way as a creator today, send me a signal in the form of feedback in my world to let me know that you were noticing my efforts. And bring it in a way that I least expect, that wakes me up from this dream, and leaves no doubt that it has come from you, so that I am inspired to do this again tomorrow."

Let me remind you of what I stated in the chapter on the quantum. If the feedback comes to you in a way that you could have expected or predicted, then it is nothing new. Resist the temptation to ascribe novelty and unpredictability to what you know deep in your soul to be the familiar. In your new life, you must be startled and, in a sense, taken unaware—not by what came to you, but by how it came about.

When you experience surprise, you wake up from the dream, and the novelty of whatever is happening to you is now so thrilling that it captures all of your attention. You are lifted out of your normal feelings. To "leave no doubt" means it has to be so cool and fun that you know that what you are doing is actually working. You want to know that this unusual event is coming from this greater mind and that it can't be anything else.

The Ultimate Experiment

You now have a relationship with the higher consciousness, because it's talking back to you, and only you know that what you are doing *within* is affecting the "without." Once you know this, you should be inspired to do it again the next day. In essence, you can now use the emotion of the new experience as new energy with which to create your next outcome. You become like a scientist or an explorer, experimenting with your life and measuring the results of your efforts.

Our purpose in life is not to be good, to please God, to be beautiful, to be popular, or to be successful. Our purpose, rather, is to remove the masks and the façades that block the flow of this intelligence and to express this greater mind *through* us. To become empowered by our efforts of creativity and to ask greater questions that will inevitably lead us to a more enriched destiny. To expect the miraculous instead of the worst-case scenario and to live as if this power is in favor of us. To ponder the uncommon, to contemplate our achievements in utilizing this unseen power, and to open our minds to more expanded possibilities challenges us to evolve our being, to let more of this mind come through us.

For instance, by your truly healing yourself of some type of malady, then it should naturally lead to more evolved questions like: "Can I heal someone else with a touch? And if I accomplish that feat, is it possible to heal a loved one from a distance?" And once you master that possibility because you changed the physical matter in that person, you might ask, "Can I create something out of nothing?"

How much further can we go? There is no end to this adventure. We are only limited by the questions we ask, the knowledge we embrace, and our ability to keep an open mind and heart.

AFTERWORD

Inhabit Self

One of the biggest lies we have come to believe about ourselves and our true nature is that we are nothing more than physical beings defined by a material reality, devoid of dimension and vital energy, and separate from God—which I trust you know by now is within us and all around us. To keep the truth about our real identity from us is not only enslaving, but it asserts that we are finite beings living a linear life that lacks real meaning.

The dictum that there are no realms and no life beyond our physical world and that we have no control over our destiny is not a "truth" that you and I should ever believe in. It is my desire that you have become empowered by a bit of knowledge in this work to help you see who you really are.

You are a multidimensional being who creates your reality. Helping you accept this idea as your law and new belief has been my labor in this book. *Breaking the Habit of Being Yourself* means that you are going to have to lose your mind and create a new one.

But when we fully lay down the old, familiar life or mind and start creating the new, there is a moment between the two worlds that is bereft of anything we know, and most rush back from this void to the familiar. That place of uncertainty—the unknown—is what the maverick, the mystic, and the saint know to be fertile ground.

To live in the realm of the unpredictable is to be all potentials at once. Can you become comfortable in this empty space? If you can, you are at the nexus of a great creative power, the "I am."

To biologically, energetically, physically, emotionally, chemically, neurologically, and genetically change ourselves and to stop living by the unconscious affirmation that competition, strife, success, fame, physical beauty, sexuality, possessions, and power are the be-all and end-all in life is when we break from the chains of the mundane. I fear that this so-called recipe for ultimate success in life has kept us looking outside of ourselves for answers and true happiness, when the real answers and true joy have always been within.

So where and how do we find our true self? Do we create a persona that is shaped by associations with the outer environment, which perpetrates the lie? Or do we identify with something within us that is as real as everything outside us, and create a unique identity, which has awareness and a mind that we can emulate?

That's right—it is that infinite resource of information and intelligence, personal and universal, that is intrinsic to all human beings. It is an energetic consciousness that is filled with such coherence that when it moves through us, we can only call it love. When the door opens, its frequency carries such vital information that it changes who we are from within. This is an experience that I have humbly learned to live for.

It is my hope that you know that you always have access to it, if you choose. But if you live life as a materialist, then you will struggle with its existence. Why? Well, realists will use their senses to define reality; and if they can't see it, taste it, smell it, touch it, or hear it, then it doesn't exist, right? This duality is a perfect scheme for keeping people lost in the illusion. Just keep their attention on an outer reality that is ultimately so sensually pleasurable or chaotic, and going within will seem too difficult.

Your attention is where your energy is. Put all of your attention on the external, material world, and that becomes your investment in reality. On the contrary, command your mindfulness to unfold a deeper aspect of yourself, and your energy will expand that reality. You, as a human being, have the freedom to place your awareness on anything. To develop your ability to manage and properly use this abundance of power is the gift. Wherever you put your thoughts and your awareness becomes your reality.

If you stop believing that thought is real, you will fall back into materialism and stop doing the work. You'll simply choose some emotional addiction or habit for immediate gratification and then talk yourself out of possibility.

Herein lies the dilemma: The future reality we create in our minds does not yet provide any sensory feedback, and by the quantum model, our senses should be the last to experience what we create. For this reason, many of us make materialism our law once again, and we go unconscious.

I want to remind you that all things material come from the invisible field of the immaterial, beyond space and time. Simply said, by planting seeds in this world, you see that in time they bear fruit. If you can experience a dream so completely in mind and emotion within the inner world of potentials, then it has already happened. So just surrender; it has to sprout into your outer life. It is the law.

But here is the hardest part of this whole process: *making or taking the time for your precious self to actually do it.*

That's it. We are divine creators. It is what we do when we are inspired and pressed to know more. But you and I are also creatures of habit. We develop habits for everything. We possess three brains that allow us to evolve from *knowledge* to *experience* to *wisdom.* To make whatever we learn implicit through the repetition of experience, we can teach the body to become the mind—that is our definition of a habit.

The problem is that we have developed habits that limit our true greatness. The survival emotions, which are so addictive, cause us to live with limitation, feeling separate from the Source, and forget we are creators. In fact, the corresponding states of mind that correlate with stress truly are the reasons why we are controlled by our emotions, live by a lower denominator of energy, and are enslaved by a set of beliefs rooted in fear. These so-called normal psychological states have been accepted by most as ordinary and common. They are the real "altered states" of consciousness.

Hence, I want to emphasize that anxiety, depression, frustration, anger, guilt, pain, worry, and sadness—the emotions regularly expressed by billions of people—are why the masses live life knocked out of balance and altered from the true self. And maybe the supposed altered states of consciousness achieved in meditation during true mystical moments are actually "natural" human states of consciousness that we should strive to live by on a regular basis. I accept that contention as my truth.

It's time to wake up and to be the living example of the truth. It's not enough to espouse these understandings; it's time to live them, demonstrate them, and be "at cause" in all areas of our lives. When you and I "in-body" such ideals as truth, and make them a habit, then they innately become part of us.

Since we are wired to create habits, why not make true greatness, compassion, genius, ingenuity, empowerment, love, awareness, generosity, healing, quantum manifestation, and divinity our new habits? To remove the layers of personal emotions we decided to memorize as our identity; to shed our selfish limitations that we have given such power to; to abandon false beliefs and perceptions about the nature of reality and self; to overcome our neural habituations of destructive traits that repeatedly undermine our evolution; and to relinquish the attitudes that have kept us from knowing who we really are . . . are all part of finding the true self.

There is an aspect of the self that is a benevolent being who waits behind all of those veils. This is who we are when we are not feeling threatened; fearing loss; trying to please everyone; racing to succeed and scrambling to get to the top at any cost; regretting the past; or feeling inferior, hopeless, desperate, or greedy, just to name a few. When we overcome, and remove whatever stands in the way of our infinite power and self, we are demonstrating a noble deed, not only for ourselves but for all of humanity.

So the greatest habit you will ever break is the habit of being yourself, and the greatest habit you will ever create is the habit of expressing the divine through you. That is when you inhabit your true nature and identity. It is to *inhabit self.*

BODY-PART INDUCTION

(Week One)

Now, can you become aware of the space that your lips occupy in space, and can you sense the volume of space that your lips are in . . . in space. . . .[1]

And now can you sense the space that your jaw occupies in space . . . can you notice the volume of space that your entire jaw is in . . . in space. . . .

And now can you feel the space that your cheeks occupy in space . . . and the density of space that your cheeks take up . . . in space. . . .

And now notice the space that your nose occupies in space. Can you sense the volume of space that your entire nose is in . . . in space. . . .

And now, can you sense the space that your eyes occupy in space, and can you feel the volume of space that your eyes are in . . . in space. . . .

And now can you pay attention to the space that your entire forehead occupies in space, all the way to your temples. . . . Can you sense the volume of space that your entire forehead is in . . . in space. . . .

And now can you notice the space that your entire face occupies in space. Can you sense the density of space that your entire face is in . . . in space. . . .

And now can you notice the space that your ears occupy in space. Can you sense the volume of space that your ears are in . . . in space. . . .

And now can you feel the space that your entire head occupies in space. Can you sense the volume of space that your entire head is in . . . in space. . . .

And now can you notice the volume of space that the column of your neck occupies in space. And can you sense the density of space that your entire neck is in . . . in space. . . .

And now can you notice the space that your entire upper torso occupies in space; the density of space taken up by your chest, your ribs, your heart and lungs, all the way to your back and shoulder blades to your shoulders. . . . Can you sense the volume of space that your entire upper torso is in . . . in space. . . .

And now can you become conscious of the space that your entire upper limbs occupy in space, and the weight of space that your upper extremities are in . . . in space . . . your shoulders, your arms, to your elbows and forearms; the density of your wrists and hands. Can you notice the weight of space that your entire limbs are in . . . in space. . . .

And now can you sense the volume of space that your entire lower torso occupies in space . . . your abdomen, your flanks, to your ribs, all the way to your lower spine and back. . . . Can you sense the volume of space that your entire lower torso is in . . . in space. . . .

And now can you feel the density of space that your entire lower extremities occupy in space . . . to your buttocks, to your groin, to your thighs, the density of space of your knees, the weight of your shins and your calves. Can you notice the volume of space that your ankles and feet down to your toes—your entire lower limbs—occupy . . . in space. . . .

And now can you notice the space that your entire body occupies in space. . . . Can you sense the density of space that your entire body is in . . . in space. . . .

And now can you sense the space around your body in space, and can you notice the volume of space that the space around your body takes up in space, and can you sense the space that that space is in . . . in space. . . .

And now can you sense the space that this entire room occupies in space. And can you sense the volume of space that this room takes up, in all of space. . . .

And now can you sense the space that all of space takes up in space, and the volume of space that that space is in . . . in space. . . .

WATER-RISING INDUCTION

(Week One)

Your job in this induction is to completely surrender into your body, let the warm water relax your tissues, and allow yourself to feel consumed by this liquid. I recommend that you sit up in a chair with your feet flat on the floor, hands resting on your knees.

Imagine warm water beginning to rise in the room . . . first, as it covers your feet and ankles, feel the warmth of your feet as they're immersed in the water. . . .

And allow the water to move higher now, up past your calves and shins, to right below your knees; and feel the weight of your legs from your feet to your calves, underwater. . . .

Let yourself relax as the water reaches your knees and rises over your thighs. . . . As it surrounds your thighs, feel your hands immersed in this warm water . . . feel the warmth consume your wrists and forearms. . . .

Now become aware of the soothing water as it encircles your buttocks, your groin, and your inner thighs. . . .

And as the water rises all the way up to your waist, feel it submerge your forearms and elbows. . . .

As the warm water continues to climb to your solar plexus, notice it as it moves halfway up your arms. . . .

Now, sense the weight of your body, immersed up to your rib cage under the warm liquid, and feel it consuming your arms. . . .

And now allow the water to encircle your chest and move across your shoulder blades. . . .

As the water rises all the way up to your neck, allow it to cover your shoulders . . . and from your neck down, feel the weight and density of your body, immersed under this warm liquid. . . .

Now, as the water moves up past your neck, feel the column of your neck, up to your chin, immersed underwater. . . .

And allow the soothing water to move up over your lips and around the circumference of the back of your head . . . as it rises over your upper lip and over your nose, relax and let it consume you, so that the warmth of the water is now right below your eyes. . . .

Allow the water to rise above your eyes, and feel everything from your eyes down immersed in this warm liquid. Feel it move up around your forehead, above the crown of your head; and as the circumference gets smaller and smaller, allow it to move above your head. . . .

And now surrender into this warm, relaxing water and allow yourself to feel your body in its weightlessness, embraced by this water. Allow your body to feel the density of itself, immersed in this liquid. . . .

Feel the volume of the water around your body and the space that your body is in, underwater. Let your awareness take in the entire room, submerged underwater. Sense the space that is filled by the room, consumed by warm water . . . and for a few moments, just feel your body floating in that space. . . .

※◉※

GUIDED MEDITATION: PUTTING IT ALL TOGETHER

(Weeks Two Through Four)

You may wish to lead off this meditation with the Body-Part Induction in Appendix A, the Water-Rising Induction in Appendix B, or any other method you have used in the past or devised on your own.

Close your eyes and take a few deep, slow breaths to relax your mind and body. Breathe in through your nose and out through your mouth. Make your breaths long, slow, and steady. Rhythmically inhale and exhale until you move into the present. When you are in the moment, you are entering a world of possibility. . . .

Now, there is a powerful intelligence within you that is giving you life, which loves you so much. When your will matches its will, when your mind matches its mind, when your love for life matches its love for you, it always responds. It will move in you and all around you, and you will see evidence in your life as a result of your efforts. To be greater than your environment, to be greater than the conditions in your life, to be greater than the feelings that are memorized in the body, to think greater than the body, to be greater than time . . . means that you are tugging on the garment of the divine. Your destiny, then, is a reflection of, a co-creation with, a greater mind. Love yourself enough to do this. . . .

Week Two

Recognizing. *Now, you cannot create a new future while holding on to the emotions of the past. What was the emotion that you wanted to unmemorize? Remember what that emotion feels like in your body. . . . And recognize the familiar state of mind that is driven by that emotion. . . .*

Admitting. *It's time to turn to the power within you, introduce yourself to it, and tell it what you want to change about yourself. Begin to admit to it who you have been, and what you have been hiding. In your mind, talk to it. Remember that it is real. It already knows you. It doesn't judge you. It only loves. . . .*

Say to it, "Universal consciousness within me and all around me, I have been _____, and I truly want to change from this limited state of being. . . ."

Declaring. *It's time to free the body from the mind, to close the gap between how you appear and who you are, to liberate your energy. Release your body from the familiar emotional bonds, which keep you connected to every thing, every place, and everyone in your past and present reality. It is the moment to free up your energy. I want you to say the emotion you want to change, out loud, and liberate it from your body as well as your environment. Say it now. . . .*

Surrendering. *And now it's time to surrender this state of being to a greater mind and to ask it to resolve this in a way that is right for you. Can you relinquish control to a greater authority that already has the answers? Surrender to this infinite mind and understand that this intelligence is absolutely real. It only waits in admiration and in willingness. It only responds when you ask for help. Surrender your limitation to an all-knowing intelligence. Simply open the door, give it up, and let go completely. Let it take your limitation from you. "Infinite mind, I give you my _____. Take it from me and resolve this emotion into a greater sense of wisdom. Free me from the chains of my past." Now, just feel how you would feel if you knew this mind was taking this memorized emotion from you. . . .*

Week Three

Observing and Reminding. *Now let's make sure that no thought, no behavior, no habit that causes you to return back to the old self goes unnoticed by you. To make sure, let's become conscious of those unconscious states of mind and body—how did you used to think when you felt that way? What did you say to yourself? What voice did you believe that you no longer want to accept as your reality? Observe those thoughts. . . .*

Begin to separate yourself from the program. How did you once behave? How did you speak? Become conscious of those unconscious states to such an extent that they would never go unnoticed by you again. . . .

To begin to objectify the subjective mind, to begin to observe the program, means you are no longer the program. Awareness is your goal. Remind yourself who you no longer want to be, how you no longer want to think, how you no longer want to behave, and how you no longer want to feel. Become familiar with all aspects of the old personality, and just observe. With firm intention, make a choice to no longer be that person, and let the energy of your decision become a memorable experience. . . .

Redirecting. *Now it's time to play the "Change Game." I want you to imagine three scenarios in your life where you could start to feel like the old self again, and when you do, I want you to say "Change!" out loud. First, imagine that it is morning and you are in the shower, and as you are getting ready for your day, all of a sudden you notice that familiar feeling just starting to come up. And the moment you notice it, you say "Change!"—that's right, you change it. Because living by that emotion is not loving to you. And it is no use signaling the same genes in the same way. And nerve cells that no longer fire together, no longer wire together. You control that. . . .*

Next, I want you to see yourself in the middle of the day. You are driving down the road, and suddenly, that familiar feeling that drives those familiar thoughts starts to come up, and what do you do? You say, "Change!" That's right, you change. Because the rewards of being healthy and happy are so much more important than returning back to the old self. And by the way, living by that emotion has never been loving to you. And every time you change your state, you know that nerve cells that no longer fire together, no longer wire together, and you no longer turn on the same genes in the same ways. . . .

Now I want you to play the Change Game one more time. I want you to see yourself getting ready for bed, and you are pulling the covers back, and as you start to get into bed, you notice that familiar feeling coming up, which is tempting you to behave as the old personality, and what do you do? You say, "Change!" That's right. Because nerve cells that no longer fire together, no longer wire together. Signaling that gene in that way is not loving to you, and nobody and nothing is worth it. You control that. . . .

Week Four

Creating. *Now, what is the greatest expression of yourself that you can be? How would a great person think and act? How would such an individual live? How would he or she love? What does greatness feel like? . . .*

I want you to move into a state of being. It is time to change your energy and broadcast a whole new electromagnetic signature. When you change your energy, you change your life. Let the thought become the experience, and let that experience produce an elevated emotion so that your body begins to emotionally believe that the future you is already living now. . . .

Allow yourself to turn on new genes in new ways; signal the body emotionally ahead of the actual event; allow yourself to fall in love with the new ideal; open your heart and begin to recondition your body to a new mind. . . .

Let the inward experience become a mood, then a temperament, and finally a new personality. . . .

Move into a new state of being. . . How would you feel if you were this person? You can't get up as the same person who sat down. You have to feel so much gratitude that your body begins to change ahead of the actual event, and accept that the new ideal already is you. . . .

Become it. . . .

To be empowered—to be free, to be unlimited, to be creative, to be genius, to be divine—that is who you are. . . .

Once you feel this way, <u>memorize this feeling</u>; remember this feeling. This is who you really are. . . .

Now let go and release it into the field for a moment; just let go. . . .

Rehearsing. *Now, like those piano players who changed their brains and the finger exercisers who changed their bodies, let's do it again. Can you create your new self out of nothing one more time? . . .*

Let's fire and wire a new mind and recondition the body to a new emotion. Become familiar with a new state of mind and body. What is the greatest expression of your <u>self</u>? Allow yourself to begin to think like this ideal again. . . .

What would you say to yourself, how would you walk, how would you breathe, how would you move, how would you live, what would you feel? Allow yourself to emotionally feel like this new self, so much so that you begin to move into a new state of being. . . .

It is time to change your energy again and remember what it feels like to be this person. Expand your heart. . . .

Who do you want to be when you open your eyes? You are signaling new genes in new ways. Feel empowered once again. Move into a new state of being; a new state of being is a new personality; a new personality creates a new personal reality. . . .

This is where you create a new destiny. From this elevated state of mind and body, it is time to command matter as a quantum observer of your new reality. Feel invincible, powerful, inspired, and overjoyed. . . .

From this new state of being, form a picture of some event you want to experience and let the image become the blueprint of your future. Observe that reality and allow the particles, as waves of probability, to collapse into an event called an experience in your life. See it, command it, hold it, and then move to the next picture. . . .

Let your energy now become entangled to that destiny. That future event has to find you because you created it with your own energy. Let yourself go and create the future you want in certainty, trust, and knowingness. . . .

Do not analyze; do not try to figure out how it is going to happen. It is not your job to control the outcome. It is your task to create, and leave the details to a greater mind. As you see your future as the observer, simply bless your life with your own energy. . . .

From a state of gratitude, be one with your destiny from a new state of mind and body. Give thanks for a new life. . . .

Feel how you will feel when these things manifest in your life, because living in a state of gratitude is living in a state of receivership. Feel like your prayers are already answered. . . .

Finally, it is time to turn to that power within you and ask it for a sign in your life: if today you emulated this greater mind as a creator who is observing all of life into form, and you made contact with it, and it has been observing your efforts and intentions, then it should show cause in your life. Know that it is real, that it exists, and that you now have a two-way communication with it. Ask that this sign from the quantum field come in a way that you would least expect, that surprises you and leaves no doubt that this new experience has come from universal mind, so that you are inspired to do it again. I want you now to ask for a sign. . . .

And now move your awareness back to a new body in a new environment and in a whole new line of time. And when you are ready, bring your awareness back up to Beta. Then you can open your eyes.

ENDNOTES

Introduction

1. Bohr, Niels, "On the constitution of atoms and molecules." *Philosophical Magazine,* 26: 1–24 (1913). If you really want to split the hairs of the subatomic world, the volume of an atom (roughly 1 angstrom, or 10^{-10} meters in diameter) is about 15 orders of magnitude larger than the volume of the nucleus (roughly 1 femtometer, or 10^{-15} meters in diameter)—meaning the atom is roughly 99.9999999999999 percent empty space. Although the electron cloud around the nucleus accounts for most of the atom's area, this cloud is mostly empty space, and the electrons within it are minuscule to begin with. The highly dense nucleus contains most of the mass of the atom. The relative size of an electron in reference to the nucleus would be like the volume of a pea compared to an SUV, and the perimeter of the electron cloud relative to the SUV would be about the size of Washington State.

Chapter 1

1. For example, see Amit Goswami, Ph.D., *The Self-Aware Universe* (New York: Jeremy P. Tarcher, 1993). Also, the "Copenhagen interpretation" of quantum theory developed by Niels Bohr, Werner Heisenberg, Wolfgang Pauli, and others says, among other things, that "reality is identical with the totality of observed phenomena (which means reality does not exist in the absence of observation)." See: Will Keepin, "David Bohm," available at: **http://www.vision.net.au/~apaterson/science/david_bohm.htm**.

2. Leibovici, Leonard, M.D., "Effects of remote, retroactive intercessory prayer on outcomes in patients with bloodstream infection: randomised controlled trial." *BMJ (British Medical Journal),* vol. 323: 1450–1451 (22 December 2001).

3. McCraty, Rollin, Mike Atkinson, and Dana Tomasino, "Modulation of DNA conformation by heart-focused intention." HeartMath Research Center, Institute of HeartMath, Boulder Creek, CA, publication no. 03-008 (2003).

4. *Christ Returns—Speaks His Truth* (Bloomington, IN: AuthorHouse, 2007).

Chapter 2

1. Hebb, D. O., *The Organization of Behavior: A Neuropsychological Theory* (Mahwah, NJ: Lawrence Erlbaum Associates, Inc., 2002).

2. Pascual-Leone, A., et al., "Modulation of muscle responses evoked by transcranial magnetic stimulation during the acquisition of new fine motor skills." *Journal of Neurophysiology,* vol. 74(3): 1037–1045 (1995).

Chapter 3

1. Szegedy-Maszak, Marianne, "Mysteries of the Mind: Your unconscious is making your everyday decisions." *U.S. News & World Report* (28 February 2005). Also see: John G. Kappas, *Professional Hypnotism Manual* (Knoxville, TN: Panorama Publishing Company, 1999). My first exposure to this concept was in 1981 when I studied hypnosis with John Kappas at the Hypnosis Motivation Institute. Back then, he stated the subconscious was 90 percent of the mind. Recently, scientists are estimating that it's about 95 percent. Either way, it is still a lot.

2. Sapolsky, Robert M., *Why Zebras Don't Get Ulcers* (New York: Henry Holt and Company, 2004). Sapolsky is a leading expert on stress and its effects on the brain and body. Also see: Joe Dispenza, *Evolve Your Brain: The Science of Changing Your Mind* (Deerfield Beach, FL: Health Communications, Inc., 2007). In addition, emotional addiction is a concept taught at Ramtha's School of Enlightenment; see JZK Publishing, a division of JZK, Inc., the publishing house for RSE, at: **http://jzkpublishing.com** or **http://www.ramtha.com**.

3. Church, Dawson, Ph.D., *The Genie in Your Genes: Epigenetic Medicine and the New Biology of Intention* (Santa Rosa, CA: Elite Books, 2007).

4. Lipton, Bruce, Ph.D., *The Biology of Belief* (Carlsbad, CA: Hay House, 2009).

5. Rabinoff, Michael, *Ending the Tobacco Holocaust* (Santa Rosa, CA: Elite Books, 2007).

6. Church, Dawson, Ph.D., *The Genie in Your Genes: Epigenetic Medicine and the New Biology of Intention* (Santa Rosa, CA: Elite Books, 2007).

7. Murakami, Kazuo, Ph.D., *The Divine Code of Life: Awaken Your Genes and Discover Hidden Talents* (Hillsboro, OR: Beyond Words Publishing, 2006).

8. Yue, G., and K. J. Cole, "Strength increases from the motor program: comparison of training with maximal voluntary and imagined muscle contractions." *Journal of Neurophysiology,* vol. 67(5): 1114–1123 (1992).

9. Cohen, Philip, "Mental gymnastics increase bicep strength." *New Scientist* (21 November 2001).

Chapter 4

1. Dispenza, Joe, *Evolve Your Brain: The Science of Changing Your Mind* (Deerfield Beach, FL: Health Communications, Inc., 2007).

2. Goleman, Daniel, *Emotional Intelligence* (New York: Bantam Books, 1995). See also: Daniel Goleman and the Dalai Lama, *Destructive Emotions: How Can We Overcome Them?* (New York: Bantam Books, 2004).

Chapter 5

1. Bentov, Itzhak, *Stalking the Wild Pendulum: On the Mechanics of Consciousness* (Rochester, VT: Destiny Books, 1988). See also: Ramtha, *A Beginner's Guide to Creating Reality* (Yelm, WA: JZK Publishing, 2005). The quantum model of reality states that every "thing" or "no thing" is waves of information vibrating at different frequencies. It makes sense, then, that the slower the vibration, the more dense matter is, and vice versa. The emotions of stress lower our vibrations to be more matter and less energy.

2. Wallace, B. Alan, Ph.D., *The Attention Revolution: Unlocking the Power of the Focused Mind* (Boston: Wisdom Publications, Inc., 2006).

3. Robertson, Ian, Ph.D., *Mind Sculpture: Unlocking Your Brain's Untapped Potential* (New York: Bantam Books, 2000). See also: Andrew Newberg, Eugene D'Aquili, and Vince Rause, *Why God Won't Go Away: Brain Science and the Biology of Belief* (New York: Ballantine Books, 2001).

4. From a conversation with Rolin McCraty, Ph.D., Director of Research, Heart-Math Research Center, Boulder Creek, California, in October 2008 about his research relating to the movement of energy from the body to the brain through the heart during coherence. See: Rollin McCraty, et al., "The coherent heart: heart-brain interactions, psychophysiological coherence, and the emergence of system-wide order." *Integral Review,* vol. 5(2) (December 2009).

Chapter 6

1. Dispenza, Joe, *Evolve Your Brain: The Science of Changing Your Mind* (Deerfield Beach, FL: Health Communications, Inc., 2007).

Chapter 8

1. Laibow, Rima, "Medical Applications of NeuroFeedback," in *Introduction to Quantitative EEG and Neurofeedback,* by James Evans and Andrew Abarbane (San Diego: Academic Press, 1999). See also: Bruce Lipton, Ph.D., *The Biology of Belief* (Carlsbad, CA: Hay House, 2009).

2. Fehmi, Les, Ph.D., and Jim Robbins, *The Open-Focus Brain: Harnessing the Power of Attention to Heal Mind and Body* (Boston: Trumpeter Books, 2007).

3. Kappas, John G., Ph.D., *Professional Hypnotism Manual* (Knoxville, TN: Panorama Publishing Company, 1999).

4. Murphy, Michael, and Steven Donovan, *The Physical and Psychological Effects of Meditation: A Review of Contemporary Research with a Comprehensive Bibliography, 1931–1996, 2nd edition* (Petaluma, CA: Institute of Noetic Sciences, 1997).

5. Lutz, Antoine, et al., "Long-term meditators self-induce high-amplitude gamma synchrony during mental practice." *PNAS (Proceedings of the National Academy of Sciences)*, vol. 101(46): 16369–16373 (16 November 2004). Also, I had a wonderful conversation with Richard Davidson in April 2008 at the Mayo Clinic during the "Mind and Life" conference in Rochester, Minnesota.

Chapter 10

1. Fehmi, Les, Ph.D., and Jim Robbins, *The Open-Focus Brain: Harnessing the Power of Attention to Heal Mind and Body* (Boston: Trumpeter Books, 2007).

Appendix A

1. In the Body-Part Induction, there is a reason why I say the words *in space* repeatedly: According to EEG monitoring that took place while subjects were led through guided meditation, the subjects transitioned into the Alpha brain-wave state when they were guided to become aware of the space that their bodies occupy in space and the volume that that space takes up in space. That wording and those instructions produced functional differences in subjects' brain-wave patterns that were immediately noticeable. See: Fehmi, Les, Ph.D., and Jim Robbins, *The Open-Focus Brain: Harnessing the Power of Attention to Heal Mind and Body* (Boston: Trumpeter Books, 2007).

INDEX

Note: Page numbers in *italics* denote illustrations.

Self. *See* Identity
Self-awareness, 111–112, 177, 179, 184, 199,
   233, 245–248, 265. *See also* Observation, of
   self
Senses
   going beyond, 47, 49, 245
   memories and, 43, 71
   mind/thoughts and, *201*
   overcoming, 34
   quantum field and, 31–32
   reality and, 102, 106
   time and, 33
Serotonin, 206
Sexual gland, *56*
Spontaneous remissions, xv
Stress. *See also* Fight-or-flight response
   affecting future, 91, 93, 100, 101
   anticipating, 93, 101, 208
   Beta waves and, 192–194, 197
   genes and, 77, 81, 100
   health and, 75, 78, 107
   hormones and, 102, 116
   response, 98–101, 104, 106, 117, 193
   in survival mode, 97
Subconscious mind
   aspects of, *203*
   associative memories in, 267
   automatic programs in, 65, 124
   autonomic nervous system and, 86–87
   Beta waves and, 199
   body and, 62, 85, 88, 233
   cerebellum and, *126*
   in children, 185, 186, 199–*200*, *202*
   emotions and, 290
   meditation and, *204*
   past and, 86, 88
Survival mode
   affecting identity, 101–105
   Beta waves and, 192, 193, 195, 235
   body in, 97, 101, *119*
   emotions and, 102–*103*, 105, 240–243
   energy in, 267
   environment and, 97, 101
   mind/thoughts in, *119*
   stress and, 97, 101
   of time, 97
Sympathetic nervous system, 98, 208
Synchronicity, 31, 210, 292. *See also* Mind/
   thoughts, coherent

Temperament, 89, *90*, 107, 152, 243
Theta waves
   in adults, 189, *190*
   in children, 185, *187*
   conscious mind and, 189
   during meditation, 205–206, *207*, 227, 231
   qualities of, 184, 185
Thoughts. *See* Mind/thoughts
Thymus gland, *56*
Thyroid gland, *56*
Time. *See also* Future; Past; Present moment
   Beta waves and, 196, *197*
   consciousness and, 32
   electromagnetic field and, *21*
   going beyond, 16–17, 32–33, 85, 94–95,
      106, 110, *157*
   gratitude and, 25–26
   during meditation, 206–207, 227–228
   prayer experiment and, 17–18
   present moment overcoming, 85
   quantum entanglement and, 16–17
   quantum field and, 33
   senses and, 33
   universal intelligence and, 28
Transcendent moments, 94
Transparency, *167*, 171, 294

Universal intelligence, 26–28
   alignment with, 29
   consciousness and, 28–29, 30
   manifesting and, 35–37
   quantum field and, 26–28, 210
   relationship with, 245–247
   time and, 28

Wallace, William, 47
Water-Rising Induction, 235, 307–308
Wisdom, 136, 138, 159, 164, 294, 301

ACKNOWLEDGMENTS

What makes our dreams become a reality (aside from the topics I've discussed in this book) are the people we surround ourselves with who share in our vision, who subscribe to a similar purpose, who support us in the simplest ways, who demonstrate accountability, and who are truly selfless. I have been fortunate during this creative process to have wonderful and competent people in my life. I would like to introduce you to those individuals and show tribute to them.

First, I want to acknowledge the folks at Hay House who have supported me in innumerable ways. Many kind thanks to Reid Tracy, Stacey Smith, Shannon Littrell, and Christy Salinas. I appreciate your trust and confidence in me.

Next, I want to express my sincere gratitude to Alex Freemon, my Hay House project editor, for your honest feedback, your encouragement, and your expertise. Thank you for being so kind and thoughtful. To Gary Brozek and Ellen Fontana, for contributing to my work in your own ways.

I also want to thank Sara J. Steinberg, my personal editor, for taking the journey with me again. We've grown together once more. Bless your soul for being so caring, gentle, and committed. You are a gift to me.

I want to acknowledge John Dispenza for effortlessly creating the cover design. You always make it look so simple. To the talented Laura Schuman, for creating such beautiful graphics and art for the interior of the book. Thanks to Bob Stewart, for also contributing to the cover art with such patience, skill, and selflessness.

Thank you, Paula Meyer, my amazing personal assistant, who has the ability to juggle a thousand elephants while always staying completely present. I appreciate your attention to detail. Also, heartfelt thanks go to the rest of the Encephalon team. To Chris Richard for such tender support; to Beth and Steve Wolfson, I appreciate the way you both have aligned with my work; to Cristina Azpilicueta, for your meticulous and refined production skills; and to Scott Ercoliani, for always keeping a high standard of excellence.

I also want to acknowledge the staff at my clinic. I am so honored to work with Dana Reichel, my office manager, who has a heart as big as the moon and has grown with me in so many ways. And among the rest of my team, a big thanks to Dr. Marvin Kunikiyo, Elaina Clauson, Danielle Hall, Jenny Perez, Amy Schefer, Bruce Armstrong, and Ermma Lehman.

I also am very inspired by the people around the world who have embraced these ideas, from whatever source, and applied them to their life. Thank you for repeatedly putting your mind into possibility.

In addition, I want to extend a warm and genuine thank-you to Dr. Daniel Amen for his earnest contribution in the Foreword to the book.

I want to also mention my mother, Fran Dispenza, who has taught me to be strong, clearheaded, loving, and filled with determination. Thanks, Mom.

And to my children, I can't express how you have taught me unconditional love by allowing me the time and space to write another book while also lecturing around the world. You have given me such consistent support in so many selfless ways. Thank you for showing me such virtue.

Finally, this book has been dedicated to my love, Roberta Brittingham. You still remain the most amazing person I have ever met. Thank you for being such light. You are grace, nobility, and love packaged into one beautiful woman.

ABOUT THE AUTHOR

Joe Dispenza, DC, studied biochemistry at Rutgers University. He also holds a Bachelor of Science degree with an emphasis in neuroscience, and received his Doctor of Chiropractic degree from Life University in Atlanta, Georgia, graduating *magna cum laude.*

Dr Joe's postgraduate training has been in neurology, neuroscience, brain function and chemistry, cellular biology, memory formation, and aging and longevity. He is an honorary member of the National Board of Chiropractic Examiners, the recipient of a Clinical Proficiency Citation for clinical excellence in doctor-patient relationships from Life University, and a member of Pi Tau Delta, the international chiropractic honor society.

Over the last 12 years, Dr Joe has lectured in more than 24 countries on six continents, educating thousands about the role and function of the human brain and how to reprogramme their thinking through scientifically proven neurophysiological principles. As a result, many individuals have learned to reach their specific goals and visions by eliminating self-destructive habits. His simple yet powerful teaching approach creates a bridge between true human potential and the latest scientific theories of neuroplasticity. Dr Joe explains how thinking in new ways, as well as changing beliefs, can literally rewire one's brain. His work is founded in his total conviction that within every person on this planet is the latent potential of greatness and unlimited abilities.

Dr Joe's first book, *Evolve Your Brain: The Science of Changing Your Mind,* connects the subjects of thought and consciousness with the brain, mind and body. It explores 'the biology of change'. In other words, when we truly change our minds, there is physical evidence of change in the brain.

As an author of several scientific articles on the close relationship between the brain and the body, Dr Joe explains the roles played by brain chemistry and neurophysiology in physical health and disease. His latest DVD release of *Evolve Your Brain: The Science of Changing Your Mind* looks at the ways in which the human brain can be harnessed to affect reality through the mastery of thought, and he has created an educational and inspiring CD series in which he answers some of the questions he is most commonly asked. In his research into spontaneous remissions, Dr Joe has found similarities among people who have experienced so-called miraculous healings, showing that they have actually changed their minds, which then changed their health.

One of the scientists, researchers, and teachers featured in the award-winning film *What the BLEEP Do We Know!?*, Dr Joe has made additional guest appearances in the theatrical director's cut as well as the extended Quantum Edition DVD set, *What the BLEEP!? Down the Rabbit Hole*, along with the new docudrama *The People vs. The State of Illusion*. He also serves as an editorial advisor of *Explore!* magazine.

When not travelling and writing, Dr Joe is busy seeing patients at his chiropractic clinic near Olympia, Washington.

www.drjoedispenza.com

NOTES

NOTES

NOTES

NOTES

NOTES

NOTES

NOTES

NOTES

Hay House Titles of Related Interest

YOU CAN HEAL YOUR LIFE, the movie, starring Louise L. Hay &
Friends (available as a 1-DVD program and an expanded 2-DVD set)
Watch the trailer at: **www.LouiseHayMovie.com**

THE SHIFT, the movie, starring Dr Wayne W. Dyer
(available as a 1-DVD program and an expanded 2-DVD set)
Watch the trailer at: **www.DyerMovie.com**

❊

*THE BIOLOGY OF BELIEF: Unleashing the Power of Consciousness,
Matter & Miracles,* by Bruce H. Lipton, PhD

THE DIVINE MATRIX: Bridging Time, Space, Miracles and Belief,
by Gregg Braden

*THE END OF SUFFERING AND THE DISCOVERY OF HAPPINESS:
The Path of Tibetan Buddhism,* by His Holiness the Dalai Lama
(available May 2012)

EVERYTHING YOU NEED TO KNOW TO FEEL GO(O)D,
by Candace B. Pert, PhD, with Nancy Marriott

POWER UP YOUR BRAIN: The Neuroscience of Enlightenment,
by David Perlmutter, MD, FACN, and Alberto Villoldo, PhD

POWER vs. FORCE: The Hidden Determinants of Human Behavior,
by David R. Hawkins, MD, PhD

SOUL-CENTERED: Transform Your Life in 8 Weeks with Meditation,
by Sarah McLean (available May 2012)

WISHES FULFILLED: Mastering the Art of Manifesting,
by Dr Wayne W. Dyer

All of the above are available at your local bookstore,
or may be ordered by contacting Hay House (see next page).

We hope you enjoyed this Hay House book. If you'd like to receive our online catalog featuring additional information on Hay House books and products, or if you'd like to find out more about the Hay Foundation, please contact:

Hay House UK, Ltd.
292B Kensal Rd., London W10 5BE
Phone: 44-20-8962-1230 • *Fax:* 44-20-8962-1239
www.hayhouse.com® • **www.hayfoundation.org**

❋❋❋

Published and distributed in the United States by: Hay House, Inc., P.O. Box 5100, Carlsbad, CA 92018-5100 *Phone:* (760) 431-7695 or (800) 654-5126 *Fax:* (760) 431-6948 or (800) 650-5115 • www.hayhouse.com

Published and distributed in Australia by: Hay House Australia Pty. Ltd., 18/36 Ralph St., Alexandria NSW 2015 *Phone:* 612-9669-4299 *Fax:* 612-9669-4144 • www.hayhouse.com.au

Published and distributed in the Republic of South Africa by: Hay House SA (Pty), Ltd., P.O. Box 990, Witkoppen 2068 *Phone/Fax:* 27-11-467-8904 • www.hayhouse.co.za

Published in India by: Hay House Publishers India, Muskaan Complex, Plot No. 3, B-2, Vasant Kunj, New Delhi 110 070 • *Phone:* 91-11-4176-1620 *Fax:* 91-11-4176-1630 • www.hayhouse.co.in

Distributed in Canada by: Raincoast, 9050 Shaughnessy St., Vancouver, B.C. V6P 6E5 • *Phone:* (604) 323-7100 • *Fax:* (604) 323-2600 www.raincoast.com

❋❋❋

Take Your Soul on a Vacation

Visit **www.HealYourLife.com®** to regroup, recharge, and reconnect with your own magnificence.Featuring blogs, mind-body-spirit news, and life-changing wisdom from Louise Hay and friends.

Visit **www.HealYourLife.com** today!